WHAT IS EDUCATION FOR?

The views of the great thinkers and their relevance today

Nicholas Tate

First Published 2015

by John Catt Educational Ltd,
12 Deben Mill Business Centre, Old Maltings Approach,
Melton, Woodbridge IP12 1BL
Tel: +44 (0) 1394 389850 Fax: +44 (0) 1394 386893
Email: enquiries@johncatt.com
Website: www.johncatt.com

ISBN: 978 1 909717 40 4

Set and designed by Theoria Design Limited
www.theoriadesign.com

Printed and bound in Great Britain
by Ashford Colour Press

CONTENTS

About the author

DR NICHOLAS Tate has had a long and eminent career in many aspects of education, both in the United Kingdom and internationally.

After state schools in the north of England he attended the universities of Oxford (Balliol College), Bristol (Department of Education), and Liverpool (Institute of Latin American Studies). He has a Doctorate in history.

Following a career as a teacher, teacher trainer and chief examiner in England and Scotland and with the Open University, he joined England's National Curriculum Council in 1989, becoming chief executive of the School Curriculum and Assessment Authority (SCAA) from 1994 to 1997 and then chief executive of the new Qualifications and Curriculum Authority (QCA) from 1997 to 2000, advising both Conservative and Labour Secretaries of State for Education. He subsequently became Headmaster of Winchester College (2000-2003), and director general of the International School of Geneva, the world's oldest and largest international school, from 2003 to 2011. From 2000 to 2005 he was a member of the Haut Conseil de l'évaluation de l'école, an advisory body to the French minister of education.

Among many other posts he has been governor of four English schools; trustee of The National Trust; chairman for ten years of the Oxford Conference in Education; and, as director general in Geneva, member of the G20 group of head teachers of leading schools from around the world.

He gave the International Baccalaureate's Peterson Lecture in 2004 and has frequently spoken on educational issues at conferences both in the UK and other parts of the world. From 2009-15 he was a member of the IB board of governors and for most of this period chair of the board's education committee. He speaks and writes both French and Spanish, having spent nine years living in France and Switzerland and one year living in Spain.

He was appointed Commander of the British Empire (CBE) in 2001.

Introduction

THE 20TH century political theorist Hannah Arendt felt that in the modern world there had been a break in the Western philosophic tradition that was now forcing us to 'discover the past for ourselves, that is, read its authors as though nobody had ever read them before', rather than seeing them within a framework inherited from previous generations.[1] She quoted her friend and fellow writer Walter Benjamin, who had argued that this needed a new kind of thinking:

> (which), fed by the present, works with the 'thought fragments' it can wrest from the past and gather about itself. Like a pearl diver who descends to the bottom of the sea, not to excavate the bottom and bring it to light but to pry loose the rich and the strange, the pearls and the coral in the depths ... and to bring them up into the world of the living ... as something 'rich and strange'...[2]

It is these 'thought fragments', these 'pearls' that are the subject of this book.

The aims and nature of education have been a concern of the Western philosophical tradition from Plato onwards and the writings of our major philosophers are a source of educational ideas that remain fresh and relevant today. One of the themes emerging from these ideas is that schools are central to cultural transmission, the passing on, in Matthew Arnold's words, of 'the best that has been thought and said', as a basis for helping new generations to face better their current world.[3] It is in this spirit that I have also written this book.

I do not set out to provide a history of the philosophy of education or an in-depth philosophical analysis of the various authors, though I do summarise their key educational ideas, link them to their philosophy, and draw in each case on the relevant scholarly literature. Instead my aim is to show how engaging with interesting past minds can both help put current issues in a new perspective and suggest additional ones to be addressed. In all cases I have given priority to going back to the original writings and seeing, like Walter Benjamin's pearl diver, what interesting 'thought fragments' I can bring back to the surface.

Most of the great texts referred to in the book have been interpreted in very different ways over the centuries. As Peter Burke has said, 'All ... classics are reinterpreted afresh by every generation; if this did not happen, they cease to be classics.' Texts develop posthumously with 'latent meanings gradually becoming manifest' with some writers, in Burke's view, being 'particularly myriad-minded, multi-faceted, or polyvalent', and thus continuing 'to appeal to a succession of very different posterities'. This, he feels, is perhaps the secret of a 'past master'.[4]

While doing my best not to interpret these philosophers as sharing my own particular quirks and enthusiasms, or to turn them into honorary 21st century citizens, I have felt free at times to apply their ideas to new contexts or even to speculate what they might have thought about our contemporary world, on the grounds that this, rather than treating them as museum pieces, was the best way of keeping them alive. As Antoine Compagnon wrote, in the context of commenting on multiple interpretations of Montaigne's *Essays*:

> A great text survives through the diversity of its readings. People have read everything into the *Essays* and that's fine; it shows the continuing power of the text. If we stopped arguing about its meanings it would mean that we had become indifferent to it. You won't therefore hear me complaining about how one uses and abuses texts, even when they are taken out of context. I would be more worried if one ceased to interpret them in radically different ways, as this would mean that they had stopped speaking to us. The best defence of (these texts) is to make them one's own, not to treat them with deference as if they were some kind of frozen monument. [5]

The choice of the ten thinkers is partly personal and partly because of the importance of the impact they have had on Western educational thought and practice. It would have been difficult not to begin with Plato and Aristotle given their influence on European and Western thought over nearly two-and-a-half millennia. Similarly it would have been impossible to exclude both Rousseau and Dewey given how, between them, for more than a half century, they have shaped the dominant 'progressive' thinking about education, at least in the English-speaking world.

Aquinas had relatively little to say about education, but I felt it essential to include a major representative of Christian thought, given how this has shaped the West, Western education and the education I myself received. As for Nietzsche I have been reading him for many years and was keen to include a discussion of the relatively little known educational writings of someone who, more perhaps than any other philosopher, has helped to shape modern (and my own) thought.

There were many other 19th and 20th century candidates I would have liked to write about, including Matthew Arnold, John Stuart Mill and George Steiner, as well as the Spaniards José Ortega y Gasset and Miguel de Unamuno, whom I first read when teaching in Spain many years ago, but space precluded their inclusion.

Plato, Aristotle, Rousseau and Dewey apart, the list therefore reflects little more than my own interests. I have deliberately only included thinkers for whom education was a part, and sometimes only a small part, of their wider thought, but whose educational views in most cases (Locke being a possible exception) were nonetheless profoundly influenced by the rest of their work. Given that education can never be understood except in connection with its wider cultural, philosophical and political context, and that this context is often ignored in contemporary educational debates, I wanted to focus on thinkers who had thought deeply about these issues as well. Many of the well-known 'educational thinkers' not included in this book cannot be said to fall into this category.

My choice of thinkers is unashamedly Western and illustrates the huge diversity to be found within Western traditions: Rousseau, for example, had little time for Locke, Hannah Arendt was in profound disagreement with Dewey, and Nietzsche can be found pouring vitriol on almost all of his predecessors, sometimes simultaneously.

This is not to suggest that there are not interesting educational thinkers outside Europe and North America. The *Analects* of Confucius, given their huge influence on Chinese educational practice over more than two millennia, would be an extremely interesting study, as would aspects of Judaic and Islamic educational traditions, and Dewey's Indian contemporaries Gandhi and Rabindranath Tagore, both of whom had strong views on education.

There are three reasons for the absence of non-Western thinkers. The first is lack of space. The second is that I would not feel competent to do justice to thinkers emerging from cultural contexts and philosophical and religious traditions with which I am completely unfamiliar. I would also find it unacceptable to pretend otherwise just so that I could offer a selection of thinkers that ticks the right diversity criteria boxes.[6] The third is the more ideological one that I have always felt driven, first and foremost, to try and understand the historical and cultural context in which I find myself – which is English, British and European – and then only secondly to move beyond this.

Given that one can spend a lifetime studying just one of the thinkers in this volume – and a fair number of scholars have done this – it seems more sensible, if one is trying to improve one's mind alongside work and family, not to spread oneself too thinly so that one ends up understanding superficially a large number of things but nothing profoundly and, above all, nothing profoundly about the things that affect one the most.

Depth versus breadth is a key issue when choosing curriculum content in schools and will be discussed later in the book. Giving priority to the study of a society's majority culture is not a case of Western ethnocentrism. The dangers of failing to do this are indeed even greater in non-Western societies given the cultural pressures on those societies from the global dominance of the English language and US popular culture. Contrary to widespread belief the preservation of diversity *requires* this degree of specific focus, not its reverse.

It was many years ago that I first started reading some of these thinkers, alongside a succession of busy educational jobs. They were never my main reading and were initially an attempt to convince myself that I was at least doing something worthwhile in terms of 'ongoing professional development', PD or CPD (C for 'Continuing'), as it is called within the jargon-laden educational world.

The alternative forms of 'ongoing professional development' never had great attractions for me. Education conferences seemed to be focused overwhelmingly on the *how* of teaching, rarely on the *why*, and never on the *what* of the subjects to be taught. It was assumed that teachers, if they had been certified, knew all about the *what*. This was both patently untrue, given that mastering a discipline (or a range of disciplines in the case of primary school teachers) ought to be a lifelong process, and highly dangerous as signalling the low level of priority that needed to be given to this.

I also came to dislike how, in education conferences, I was constantly being asked during speeches to turn to my neighbour and share instant, banal and un-reflected comments on topics I knew nothing about, as a way of keeping the audience engaged and in accordance with the theory of 'active learning'. The low point in this regard was when one speaker at a conference in the USA asked us to turn to our neighbours and tell him or her "you're doing a great job". As the conference theme was 'respect for other cultures' my plea that the request was culturally impossible for an Englishman guaranteed me a safe exit from an embarrassing situation.

Reading contemporary books on education, with few exceptions (such as Howard Gardner on types of minds or Alan Ryan on liberal education), also rarely tempted me. The ones I tried tended to be clumsily written, excessively present-centred or full of inflated optimism about how new approaches were going to transform the world. What was also missing, and what one gets by contrast from most of the ten thinkers in this book, was the sense that what is at stake in education are deep issues about the nature of humanity and that one is in contact with original minds who are wrestling with these issues and challenging and surprising one to think again.

The contemporary educational world is marked by a striking uniformity, with exclusion zones around those who fail to emit the right noises of approbation and disapproval. A recent English Secretary of State for Education, Michael Gove, referred to this world, with which he felt he was fighting a losing battle, as 'the Blob'. It could be more elegantly described, in a French phrase that has no exact English equivalent, as a *pensée unique*, a single way of looking at things that brooks no opposition and that is so pervasive that it goes un-recognised by those encased within it. One benefit of continually diving into the past in search of 'thought fragments' and 'pearls', even when one ends up disliking what one has brought up, is that it helps one stand back from the claustrophobic certainties of the present.

As someone used to pouring over obscure historical journals I also tried my luck with some of the numerous educational research journals. These were even more off-putting. For every article that caught my eye there were at least a dozen titles that sounded impossibly narrow, ludicrously puffed up, or just plain weird. It was obvious at a glance that, as one of the 'social sciences', education was doing its bit to erect barriers between these 'sciences' and the everyday world of common sense and common language.

It was the time when French structuralism was all the rage and the temptation to use its arcane vocabulary to make one sound serious, special and difficult was proving irresistible. A recent foray back into this world suggests that little has changed, with the following titles popping up at my first casual search of one journal alone: *The Impact of Ignoring a Level of Nesting Structure in Multilevel Mixture Model. A Monte Carlo Study* (it is not clear whether this is about teaching children or the habits of migrating birds on the Côte d'Azur); *Invitational Rhetoric and the Case for Service Learning*; *Universal Design for Learning Principles in a Hybrid Course*; and (my favourite) *Consuming My Way Gay. An Auto-ethnographic Account of Coming Out as Consumptive Pedagogy.*

Reading major philosophers on education was also a welcome respite from the official documents one had to attend to as part of one's job, even in schools that were supposedly private. At Winchester College, where I was Headmaster, I knew I would never have the time to retire of an evening to the library to translate Ovid or Tacitus as some of my 55 predecessors, going back to the 14th century, would have done (not that my feeble Latin would have been up to it anyway), but at least in reading Montaigne and Rousseau on education I had found an intellectual stimulus directly related to my job.

In Geneva, where, as Head, I had to write a 700-word article twice a term for each of three separate campuses, I even found a practical use for my reading by illustrating my discussion of current educational issues with links to one of my current authors. As I rarely got to the end of the Head's letters that came home from my own children's schools, I doubt if what I wrote was widely read, though when one parent towards the end of my time there told me that she had kept a file of my articles and sometimes re-read them I felt for a moment as if I had been awarded the Nobel Prize.

The book is therefore designed for anyone interested in education, whether teachers, parents or the general public, who wishes to be made to think about what most of the writers in this book felt to be one of humanity's most important tasks (and in quite a few cases *the* most important task) and to do so in the context of the long Western tradition of reflection on these issues. No prior knowledge of education, or of any national education system, is assumed.

The reading I have done in preparation for this book has made me realise how much contemporary educational discussions have turned their backs on the two-and-a-half millennia of educational thinking that has preceded us. There is a peculiar arrogance about the modern world that can lead it both to dismiss out of hand 'old-fashioned practice' and to think that all the good ideas are its own invention.

Parts of the 'educational establishment' in some Western countries have long defined themselves as engaged in a crusade (though the word itself would never now be used) against the forces of didacticism, memorisation and knowledge transmission which were felt to have been dominant in schools until relatively recent times. Such a mind-set fails to acknowledge the diversity of past schooling or its many achievements, some of which are strikingly illustrated in the careers of the thinkers discussed in this book.

It is also based on the illusion that the principles underlying what we would see today as a liberal and 'child-centred' (in the positive sense of that term) education are the product largely of our own enlightened and emancipated times. Again and again in reading the thinkers in this book I have been struck by how most of the basic modern ideas about learning and teaching are not new at all and have often been expressed with greater clarity and subtlety by people thinking and writing hundreds and thousands of years ago.

The arrogance of late modernity also shows itself in the offence it can take when past writers, either in their writings or their lives, say or do things that are felt to be unacceptable and in particular when they infringe taboos on race, gender and sexuality. When organising a Rousseau exhibition at my school in Geneva, to commemorate in 2012 the 300th anniversary of his birth, I was taken aback by the suggestion from some of my colleagues that I should not be doing this on behalf of someone who, quite shamefully, had put all five of his own children into an orphanage.

My riposte was, first, that people's ideas should be kept separate from their actions and treated on their intrinsic merits and demerits, and, second, that it would be ludicrous if we only paid attention to writers and thinkers whose ideas we could wholly approve. The ideas about women of many of the thinkers in this book, with Rousseau and Nietzsche in the lead, can be shocking. Plato, Aristotle and Nietzsche defended slavery, and Nietzsche put up a defence for cruelty. Aquinas does not endear us to his world picture when he says that the saved in heaven will rejoice that God's justice has been done in condemning the damned to hell. Kant's racial views, unacceptable to us today, were also those of his time. None of this should deter us from paying the closest attention to what these thinkers have to say on other matters, and even on some of the disputed matters, examining these on their merits rather than resorting to the blanket kneejerk rejection of the offence-taker. In a liberal post-Enlightenment society no one should have the right not to be offended (and this includes the students' union of that former pinnacle of liberal learning University College London which in June 2014 took the extraordinary decision to ban the university's Nietzsche Club, fearing for the 'safety' of its members.[7])

The educational issues raised by the ten thinkers I have chosen are highly diverse. There is a lot of discussion about the fundamental question 'what is education for?': how this depends on one's aims for individuals, societies, states and humanity in general; which qualities and virtues are most valued; what this means in terms of preparation for leisure (and how leisure should be used); the extent to which education should train the heart as well as the head; whether utilitarian, including economic, objectives are legitimate.

The extent to which education should be conservative and centred on the transmission of humanity's past achievements is also a recurring theme. Some thinkers are very exercised by the question of who should provide education and make decisions about its contents, whether it should be exclusively provided by the state or (in some cases) whether the state should be discouraged from getting its hands on it. They have different views about the stages of education, the structure of the curriculum and the relative importance of subjects. The roles of teacher and pupil also come under scrutiny and, underlying this one finds different notions about the nature of childhood, child-adult relations and the meaning of authority.

Each chapter summarises the views of the thinker in question on issues such as these, illustrates them with short extracts from his or her writings, and tries to tease out some of the implications of these views for contemporary educational debates. The starting point is the author rather than our current concerns. My commentaries have not been framed to form a coherent set of recommendations or theory of education. They are personal reflections designed to encourage others to have their own reflections on issues that affect us all.

For each thinker I try to outline their own educational experiences, both as student and, where appropriate, as teacher. This often helps to explain their interest in educational issues and can be a starting point for their reflections, though rarely determines the particular stance they have taken. I will therefore conclude this introduction by providing a similarly brief *cv* for myself.

My primary and secondary education, beginning in a Staffordshire infant school with classes of 40+ and ending in Yorkshire grammar schools, was wholly state-provided, as Aristotle would have wished. I then, like Locke, went to Oxford, though happily to Balliol rather than Christ Church, reading history and learning, mostly informally, what it was to aspire to become an educated person. Unlike any of the thinkers in this book I then underwent formal training as a teacher at the University of Bristol, in the days when the history and philosophy of education were still part of the initial postgraduate teacher education course, and worked for six years as a history teacher in a north of England Roman Catholic boys' grammar school with some of whose practices Aquinas would have felt at home. There followed a long period in teacher training, first in Birmingham and then in Edinburgh where I became familiar with a very different national education system in which I played a number of roles outside my main job. Simultaneously I completed a doctorate (like Kant, Nietzsche, Dewey and Arendt, though in history), alongside a full-time job, lecturing part-time for the Open University, acting as chief examiner for an English examining board, and helping to bring up three children (unlike Plato, Aquinas, Locke, Kant, Nietzsche and Arendt who had none, though Dewey compensated by having seven and I have already mentioned what Rousseau did with his).

When England's first national curriculum was introduced in 1989 I returned to England and worked throughout the 1990s for a succession of national curriculum, assessment and qualifications bodies, ending up as chief executive of both the School Curriculum and Assessment Authority and the Qualifications and Curriculum Authority and adviser to both Conservative and Labour Secretaries of State for Education.

Since 2000 I have been back in schools, as Headmaster of Winchester College, Director-General of The International School of Geneva, and executive chairman of a group of small private schools in England, South Africa, Hungary and the USA, while, for part of this time, also serving on an advisory body to French ministers of education, as a governor of the International Baccalaureate, and as a trustee of a university with joint UK-US accreditation. As with many other contemporary personal trajectories a small-town mono-cultural beginning has belatedly, and unexpectedly, merged into something global, driving me, not without many reservations, towards the kind of 'cosmopolitan' educational perspective advocated by Kant.

The experience of being educated, educating myself, watching my own children's education, teaching children, young adults and, in the Open University, some very mature adults (including prisoners serving life sentences), writing school textbooks, running parts of a national education system, and being a head and governor of schools, has left me with few certainties, no over-arching theories, and a great distrust of educational evangelists of all kinds (and they are legion). Like Matthew Arnold, writing about state-funded education, 'I have no pet scheme to press, no crotchet to gratify, no fanatical zeal for giving this or that shape to the public establishment'.[8] My experience instead has left me with an urge, borrowing a phrase from T S Eliot, to 'purify the (jargon-ridden) dialect of the (educational) tribe'.[9] I can think of no better way to do this than to encourage those interested in education today to go back to some of the original sources of the West's reflection on these matters. That is the modest intention of this book.

References

1. Arendt, H, *The Crisis in Culture*, in *Between Past and Future*, p. 204, 1961, Viking, New York.

2. Arendt, H, *Men in Dark Times*, pp. 205-6, 1970, Jonathan Cape, London.

3. Arnold, M, *Culture and Anarchy*, preface to 1869 edition, p. 6, 1932, Cambridge University Press, Cambridge. Matthew Arnold's phrase is frequently misquoted both as 'the best that has been known and said' and as arguing for a rather passive kind of cultural transmission. The full text is as follows:

   The whole scope of this essay is to recommend culture as the great help out for our present difficulties; culture being a pursuit of our total perfection by means of getting to know, on all the matters which most concern us, the best which has been thought and said in the world, and, through this knowledge, turning a stream of fresh and free thought upon our stock notions and habits...

   This view of transmission brings Arnold much closer to those of Dewey and Arendt on this question than the truncated quotation might suggest.

4. Burke, P, *Montaigne*, p. 73, 1981, Oxford University Press, Oxford.

5. Compagnon, A, *Montaigne Aujourd'hui, in Magazine Littéraire*, no. 464, mai 2007, p. 29 (author's translation).

6. Hannah Arendt is not included as a token woman, in an overwhelmingly male Western tradition, but because her works make me stop and think radically about the world in a way few others do.

7. *The Independent*, 13 June 2014; O'Neill, B, *Students of dogma, The Spectator*, 22 November 2014.

8. Arnold, M, *A French Eton; or, Middle Class Education and the State*, p. 66, 1864, Macmillan, London and Cambridge.

9. The quotation is an adaptation of a line from T S Eliot's poem *Little Gidding in his*

Four Quartets. Eliot also wrote very interestingly about education in the following: *The Aims of Education*, lectures given at the University of Chicago in 1950-1, and *The Classics and the Man of Letters*, an address to the Classical Association in 1942, in Eliot, T S, *To Criticize the Critic and other writings*, 1965, Farrar, Strauss and Giroux, New York; *Notes towards the definition of culture*, 1962, Faber and Faber, London; and *Modern Education and the Classics*, in *Essays Ancient and Modern*, 1936, Faber and Faber, London. See also Bantock, G H, *T S Eliot and Education*, 1970, Faber and Faber, London.

Chapter 1

The unexamined life is not worth living: Socrates and Plato

FEW THINKERS have had a greater and more long-term impact than Socrates, especially given that he left no writings of his own and given the difficulty of distinguishing between views attributed to him by Plato and Plato's own views. Even fewer thinkers have had such an impact on educational thought and practice.

Socrates was born in 469 BC in Athens where he spent the whole of his life. His mother was a midwife and his father a stonemason. He was an active Athenian citizen, serving as an infantryman in a number of military campaigns, though never holding any office or command. Most of his time is said to have been given over to thinking and talking. His trial for impiety and for corrupting the minds of the young, condemnation and subsequent death by poison in 399 BC give us one of the founding stories of Western culture and a constant theme for artists throughout the ages.

At the heart of Socrates's thinking was the idea that human life is one long effort to move closer to truth and to goodness, an effort that continues up to the moment of death. One of his friends asked the oracle at Delphi whether anyone was wiser than Socrates and received the answer 'No'. Socrates interpreted this as meaning that his wisdom arose from the fact that he alone fully understood his own ignorance. What the oracle was telling him to do was to show others how they were similarly ignorant and thus help them take the first steps towards knowledge and goodness.

This is what Plato shows him as doing throughout the many dialogues he wrote in which Socrates is the main character. Socrates sometimes said that he was like his midwife mother in that all he was doing was helping others bring their thoughts to birth. It is this Socratic technique that influences educational practice to the present day.

Plato (c.429-347 BC) was Socrates's disciple and the source of most of our knowledge of his life and thought. His background, as a member of an aristocratic Athenian family, was different from that of Socrates. Plato's own thought ranged widely and has indelibly shaped the course of Western thought, in metaphysics, epistemology, ethics, politics and aesthetics. It also had a huge impact on the later development of Christianity and in many ways also on Judaism and Islam.

Of all the great thinkers discussed in this book, it is probably Socrates, as relayed to the world by his disciple Plato, whose name most frequently crops up in modern educational discourse, even among those who may never have read any of Plato's Socratic dialogues. This is partly because of Plato's founding and central role in Western philosophy. It is also because the Socratic idea that individuals need to come to knowledge though their own efforts rather than through teaching has been at the core of modern educational thought in the West from Rousseau in the 18th century onwards, and is very much the orthodoxy of current western education. Behind all those speakers at educational conferences who tell us, in matey but imperious fashion, that 'the sage on the stage' must now be replaced by 'the guide on the side' (or the equivalent – there are variants) lurks the shade of Plato.[1] Behind Plato lurks the shade of Socrates.

Calling up Socrates in aid of modern enquiry-based learning is not wide of the mark. He was most certainly an 'educator' and a 'facilitator', to use the two words that many people in education feel most comfortable with at the present time, though 'teacher' – a noble word mistakenly thought to have didactic overtones and thus somewhat out of fashion – does just as well. What he most certainly was not was an 'instructor'.[2]

Plato's educational philosophy grew out of this Socratic approach, but was far more than just an educational method. Thoughts and prescriptions about education permeate Plato's writings and are at the heart of both *The Republic*, in which he outlines his plans for an ideal state, and his late work the *Laws* in which he lays down in detail what a second best state might look like. As with all the thinkers in this volume, but unlike much current educational policy and practice, Plato's starting point was always the question 'what is education for?'

★★★★★

> Moreover, when a community has once made a good start, its growth proceeds in a sort of cycle. If a sound system of nurture and education is maintained, it produces men of a good disposition; and those in their turn, taking advantage of such education, develop into better men than their forebears, and their breeding qualities improve among the rest, as may be seen in animals.
>
> Plato, *The Republic*, trans. Cornford, IV, 424

> ...Any training which has as its end wealth, or perhaps bodily strength, or some other accomplishment unattended by intelligence and righteousness, (one) counts vulgar, illiberal, and wholly unworthy to be called education.
>
> Plato, *Laws*, I.644, in *The Collected Dialogues of Plato*, p. 1243

> *Crito*: When I glance at any one of those who profess to educate people, I am horrified; each one I look at seems to me to be quite unsuitable, to tell you the truth, so I don't see how I am to direct (my son) to philosophy.
> *Socrates*: My dear Crito, don't you know that in every line of life the stupid are many and worthless, the serious are few and worth everything?
>
> Plato, *Euthydemus*, 306d/3071,
> in *The Collected Dialogues of Plato*, pp. 419-20

> ...the style of teaching was Socratic in nature; ideas and theories were elucidated through the leaders asking and answering questions.
>
> Nelson Mandela, *Long Walk to Freedom*, 1994
> (writing about the education that prisoners gave each other on Robben Island)

What is education for?

In the dialogues *Protagoras* and *Gorgias* Plato shows Socrates in dispute about the purposes of education with the sophists, after two of whom these dialogues are named. Sophists were professional paid teachers who trained young men of good family in the skills needed to be successful both in private life and public affairs. They placed great emphasis on rhetoric, debating and public speaking. Their view of education was essentially utilitarian. Knowledge was not important in itself but because of its practical value as a means to whatever ends the individual had set for himself.

The sophists were neutral about what their pupils did with the skills and qualities they were encouraging them to develop. Their job was to help individuals to win an argument, however false it might be, to get on in life, however damaging their personal success might be to others, or to run a state in whatever way, as a ruler, appealed to them even if this might not be in the interests of the community for which they were responsible. Socrates and Plato were very critical of this emphasis on the art of persuasion and firmly opposed to the ethical relativism implicit in the sophists' position.

By contrast Socrates and Plato saw the purpose of education as enabling individuals to distinguish between good and evil and between truth and error and to search after wisdom and goodness in their own lives and in the life of their community. If they did this, they would be less likely to be tempted, like the pupils of the sophists, by the attractions of wealth, power and the pursuit of mere pleasure. As Socrates is supposed to have said when on trial for his life:

> I tried to persuade each one of you not to think more of practical advantages than of his mental and moral well-being, or in general to think more of advantage than of well-being in the case of the state or of anything else.[3]

If wealth and power ceased to be their objectives they would be more likely to live in well-ordered societies in which the activities of rulers and citizens were directed towards the common, rather than the individual, good. Plato's *The Republic* has as its central thesis that states should be ruled by those who have learned that the purpose of life is to see behind the appearances of things, to acquire wisdom and to understand the nature of the good.

The unexamined life is not worth living

But if the sophists' tricks of the trade are rejected, what does Socrates put in their place? His starting point, arising from his sense of the aims of human life and thus of education, is his notion, articulated again towards the end of his trial, that 'the unexamined life is not worth living'. The key element in education is therefore self-examination, an enquiry into oneself, one's beliefs and actions that is lifelong and ends only with death.

One Plato scholar has described this as 'a radical openness to constant re-examination'.[4] In the dialogue *Meno* Plato shows Socrates constantly pushing Meno to interrogate his own thoughts and repeatedly refusing Meno's request that Socrates tell him the answers. The pupil in a Socratic dialogue is forced to articulate his or her own opinions, clarify them, probe the reasons for them, accept that one may be wrong, strive for the truth but accept that this may not be easily achieved.

It may not be a comfortable process, and indeed may be painful. What is genuinely radical about this approach is the rejection of any authority other than that of goodness and reason. One's beliefs must be right in themselves and not right simply because they are the ones held by the majority, or the wealthy, or the powerful, or because they have been handed down by tradition.

At its higher levels the Socratic self-examination, and with it the aspirations for a good life, may also not be for everyone. Ideally Socrates and Plato want everyone not just to have the right moral opinions and to act morally but to do so because they understand why they must do so. For some and perhaps most people, however, they recognised that habituation into a moral life, without knowing why it is the best life, may be the most one is able to hope for.

Plato's *The Republic*

In his greatest work, *The Republic,* Plato turns to how states might be organised. His main objective is to outline the characteristics of an ideal state, one run by philosophers who have a deep understanding of the nature and purpose of the world and of the Good. The rulers of this ideal state must be motivated solely by the wish to promote the good life and uninfluenced by any desires for wealth, prestige or power.

Plato recognised that such a utopia might never be realised and accepted that it should perhaps be seen instead 'as a pattern in heaven, where those who wish can see it and found it in their own hearts'.[5] *The Republic* also includes (Books VIII and IX) an analysis of the failings of different kinds of state: democracy, oligarchy, timocracy (a state where the love of honour usurps the rule of reason), and despotism.

Plato himself had personal experience of the difficulties of trying to turn rulers into philosopher kings. He made three visits to the Greek state of Syracuse in Sicily, ruled in succession by the tyrants Dionysius I and Dionysius II, and ended up outmanoeuvred, in danger of his life, and having been completely unsuccessful in all his efforts to persuade the two rulers to govern in a more philosophic manner.

It is in *The Republic* that Plato most conflicts with the contemporary assumptions of the democratic West and where he has been most criticised, often very controversially, for being, in the eyes of the philosopher Karl Popper, the enemy of liberal democracy and of 'an open society'.[6] Popper, writing during the Second World War, accused Plato of distorting the legacy of Socrates by showing him in *The Republic* as a supporter of an ideal state which had some of the characteristics – censorship, indoctrination, interference in private life, severity towards dissidents, rule by 'those who know best' – of the totalitarian regimes against which the Allies had been fighting. One of the reviewers of Popper's *The Open Society and its Enemies*, the English philosopher Gilbert Ryle, even went so far as to describe Plato as 'Socrates's Judas'.[7]

The education of the Guardians

The Republic provides us with the most detailed account of the kind of education that Plato envisaged for those called to rule states. His starting point was that most people would not be capable of accessing the higher levels of knowledge and moral understanding needed to be a fully educated human being. He also does not appear to have challenged a society in which a large section of the population, being slaves, had no citizenship rights.

In a world which kept women firmly in the home Plato did, however, have the revolutionary idea that girls and boys, within his ruling elite, should receive the same education, and that girls should be equally eligible for the higher posts. Plato argued that 'there is ... no function in society which is peculiar to woman as woman or man as man' and that 'it is natural (therefore) for women to share all occupations with men'.

Women of all ages were to take part in athletics training alongside men and, like men, to do so naked, without fear of disrespect or ridicule. They should also undergo the same military training. The fact that Plato also saw women as 'the weaker partners' in these activities should not lead us to under-estimate the radical nature of his proposals. No philosopher can ever step right outside the constraints of his time, but Plato tried harder than most.[8]

Plato's ideal state required a group of people who would be set apart and would receive an education suitable for their future roles. These were the Guardians who would own no property of their own and who would even share wives and children. Their education in childhood and adolescence would not be that different in its main components from the one already offered to Athenian boys in Plato's own day: reading and writing, learning and reciting poetry, playing music and choral singing, arithmetic and geometry, and athletic exercises.

Plato on the arts in education

Where Plato's plans were distinctive, however, is in his insistence on censoring the literature used in the education of future Guardians, and in the state as a whole, so that they are only exposed to representations of moral behaviour. Plato is fundamentally distrustful of poetry and drama as not being primarily concerned with truth and virtue, as appealing to the inferior emotional parts of the soul, and as being focused on the world of shifting appearances rather than on that of the underlying and unchanging nature of reality.

Even the great Greek poets, Hesiod and Homer, and myths of the gods, were not spared. It is not good, Plato feels, for children or indeed anyone to hear in *The Iliad* that Achilles, son of a goddess, wailed in grief at the death of Patroclus, poured ashes on his own head, and slaughtered Trojan captives to put them on his friend's funeral pyre. Only those myths and stories that encourage virtue – hymns to the gods and eulogies to good people – are worth the telling.[9]

Plato's views hardened, becoming more ascetic and authoritarian in the course of his life. Already in Book X of *The Republic* he is concluding that 'all tragic poetry, epic or dramatic ... has no serious value' and that this applies to the visual arts as well.[10] By the end of his life when he wrote the *Laws* he seems more sceptical still about the value of the arts and concerned above all to legislate to ensure that exposure to the arts was only to forms productive of virtue, observing that 'the youthful mind will be persuaded of anything, if one will take the trouble to persuade it', a remark that illustrates both his recognition of the power of the wrong kind of art and his readiness to resort to extremes to counter it.[11]

The art form about which Plato was most positive was music, which included playing an instrument, singing and dancing. This was because of music's potentially beneficial impact on the mind, and in particular its ability to express and to encourage 'courage and moderation in good fortune or in bad' and thus to shape character. This, not the giving of pleasure, was to be the function of music. Careful control was to be exercised over the choice of music to be taught and performed and over the types of instrument to be used (lyres, citharas and pipes, but not flutes and harps) and the modes in which the music could be composed (Dorian and Phrygian but definitely not Ionian and Lydian, which were associated with drinking songs).[12]

Philosopher kings

At the age of 15 those felt to be suitable for the Guardian's role continue in education for another three years and then spend two years in military training. At that point there is a further selection and the few who look as if they might develop into the real rulers of the state – the philosopher kings – embark on a long programme designed to equip them for this role from age 50 onwards. From 20 to 30 they focus on mathematics (geometry, arithmetic, solid geometry and astronomy) and on harmonics, subjects designed to take them behind the world of ephemeral appearances to the underlying unchanging truths about the world.

From 30 to 35 they are trained in dialectic, the method of philosophic enquiry that will enable them to see the links between their different studies (an early version perhaps of Howard Gardner's Synthesizing Mind) and to move closer to a deep understanding of the nature of truth, beauty and goodness.[13] From 35 to 50 they will begin to gain practical experience of life through public service in a variety of subordinate roles. At 50 the best will be ready to start governing the state, while still spending part of their time in study.

One should not necessarily see Plato's educational prescriptions as a practical blueprint, but more as a way of illustrating the main elements of a fully developed human mind. He did, however, practice some of what he preached, establishing in Athens his own Academy, a kind of university that drew students from all over Greece. The many dialogues that Plato wrote, with Socrates as the main character, were its textbooks. The Academy, which lasted for over 300 years and kept alive Plato's methods of philosophic enquiry, was not the least of his legacies.

*****

How Socrates and Plato can help us think about education today

Education is not just about enabling us 'to make and sell more stuff'

Plato was the first of many great thinkers to emphasise the non-utilitarian aims of education and to go back, endlessly, to the question 'what is education for?' He is an antidote to our modern sophists for whom the pursuit of knowledge is largely for the sake of the so-called 'knowledge economy', in other words the pursuit of material gain.

'Making and selling more stuff', as the novelist Jeanette Winterson once put it, is not to be ignored, but it cannot be the main purpose of an education that is preparing people to make the best of their short and infinitely precious lives. With the decline in the West both of traditional religious meta-narratives and of secular ideas of progress, we have ceased to see continuous ethical and intellectual self-improvement as the main aim of our existence.

The impoverishment which results from this not only damages individuals, it makes societies function less well and damages economies too. The best way to prepare people for the 'knowledge economy' may indeed be to make sure that we do *not* focus on this as the main aim.

How we can underestimate what children have already in their minds

One of Socrates's and Plato's most fundamental assumptions was about how much can be drawn out of what individuals already have inside them. Teaching is not so much a question of filling empty receptacles but of helping people to examine themselves. Plato believed that human beings had immortal souls and that they came into this world endowed with innate truths that could be teased out by a process of recollection.

We do not need to share this belief to feel that there is an important insight here. Anyone who has witnessed well-conducted primary school philosophy lessons, based on the Socratic technique, will have been struck by the extraordinary ability of even young children to reason and make distinctions. One of my most embarrassing memories is being invited to talk to a school's philosophy club, following press coverage of a speech I had given on ethics and education, and tying myself up in knots in response to some unbelievingly penetrating Socratic-type questions from an 11 year-old. I have been much more cautious ever since about pronouncing on such topics.

This does not mean that prescribed curricula, including lists of things that need to be learned, are wrong. That would be to swing the pendulum too far the other way. It is just that they must leave space for in-depth exploration of issues, and more space than is sometimes left by over-anxious modern ministers of education keen to make their mark.

Teaching is about the relationship between one individual and another

Another of Socrates's and Plato's insights was the importance of the one-to-one teacher-pupil relationship. Education at its best requires transmission – if only of values and attitudes – from an experienced individual to one who is less experienced. It thrives when there is a role model and an atmosphere of mutual respect and admiration. Aids to learning, from the early teaching machines through to Massive Open Online Courses (MOOCs) and beyond, can and will play a major role, but are not a substitute for the core relationship between one individual and another.

All is not fun

Socrates and Plato believed that education was hard work, a matter of sustained application over long periods of time. Not only was it not a matter of fun, but the absence of fun and the experience of failure and of delayed gratification were key elements in enabling us to make progress. This is a tough message in a world in which advertising surrounds us with constant images of happy smiling people having fun and in which all the children in prospectuses are always brimming over with joy at the marvellous experiences offered by their school.

How, given that we live in this world, do we allow for failure and learning from failure, and get across the message that much of learning, and of life, is a hard slog and an intrinsically rather dull means to an end, without undermining the will to keep going? This is the core of the teacher's task.

Censorship in education: ancient and modern

We may recoil in liberal horror at Plato's plans for censorship and indoctrination in his ideal state, especially when it is older children and adults we are talking about. We may indeed begin to feel that Popper was right in comparing this state with a modern totalitarian regime. Is it so different, however, to live in a world that inserts into films and soap operas the correct social, ethnic, gender, disability and sexual preference diversity ratios (with the very best of intentions, *ie* to make us good, à la Plato), re-writes *Huckleberry Finn* and *Tom Sawyer*, restricts the ways in which people are allowed to criticise each other's religious beliefs, recoils in abject and shameful terror from ever again performing Voltaire's *Mahomet*, spawns vigilante groups like the ominously named Parents Against Bad Books In Schools (PABBIS) in the USA, and, through its non-stop global publicity machine, pushes in front of us, at every moment of the day, the images of a consumerist idyll based not on Plato's use of reason but on distortion, hyperbole, lies and appeals to our baser instincts?

Instead of feeling superior to the benighted thinkers of the past – a common attitude within our contemporary world – it would be interesting instead to reflect on what we and Plato have in common, what drives us both in a similar direction, the dangers of taking this path, and how these can be avoided while still enabling us to promote what we want to be our society's core values.

Although Plato sometimes criticised the arts *per se*, his attacks were more often than not directed at specific forms of art the negative moral effects of which he feared. Underlying these fears was a sharp sense of the factors shaping the culture and ethos of a society. A tightly controlled education would be ineffective, he rightly felt, if the wider ethos continually pulled individuals in an altogether different direction.

It was not just access to the arts in education therefore that had to be regulated, but the arts in the state as a whole. Tragedy and comedy in Athens could be performed before crowds of 14,000; one recital of Homer attracted 20,000. As the classicist M F Burnyeat has put it: Plato's 'subject is the words and music you hear at social gatherings, large and small. Think pubs and cafés, karaoke, football matches, the last night of the Proms. Think ... Elton John singing to the nation from Westminster Abbey'.[14] It was because education was so important, but only part of a wider cultural transmission, that Plato, for the sake of the young and the future of the state, felt the need for the whole of culture to be purged.

We reject Plato's illiberal solution but ignore at our peril the problem it was trying to tackle. It is a problem writ large in our own world where all-pervasive and highly debased mass media stand poised to swamp the independent cultural transmission that may be taking place in home and school. Addressing Plato's *bien pensant* critics, Burnyeat minces no words: 'Either grasp the nettle of devising democratic alternatives to Plato's authoritarianism, or stop bleating'.[15]

An 'intelligent heart'

We may not share Plato's distrust of poetry and the theatre as ways of manipulating our feelings and distracting us from the search for truth but nonetheless still be able to see his views as the basis for a reflection on the relationship between reason and emotion in our lives and in the education that we provide for young people. In a world in which our senses and emotions are constantly stimulated and manipulated through the mass media, where there is less and less silence and less and less space in which to stand back and reflect, and which is swept by occasional outbursts of mass hysteria in the streets and on social media, have educators got the balance right?

King Solomon in the Bible asked God to give him 'an intelligent heart'. How should our teaching ensure that this is an aim for everyone? The study of philosophy, thinking skills, the analysis of mass media, the way school communities resolve their daily problems – all these may have a role to play.

The educational needs of current politicians

Few of us would wish to live in Plato's ideal state or feel that one could entrust oneself to rule by a philosopher king. Utopias have an unvarying habit of ending up as unspeakable tyrannies when people try to apply them in the real world. But we can take the features of this ideal state as so many pointers to how things might be in less utopian situations. Some of us, for example, would not mind being ruled, in a democracy, by politicians who had spent rather more time studying higher things, who had experience of governing and managing outside political parties and partisan think tanks, and who only came to power when they had attained maturity and acquired a few grey hairs.

In 2009 the French President, Nicolas Sarkozy, publicly mocked the country's Ecole nationale d'administration (ENA) – the breeding ground of many French ministers, public servants and business leaders – for continuing to require applicants to read the 17th century novel *La princesse de Clèves.* There was an immediate run on copies in bookshops and the country's intellectual elite, or at least those members of it committed to the transmission of France's literary canon, responded by sporting heart-shaped badges proclaiming *J'aime la princesse de Clèves.*

Plato may have had reservations about most works of imaginative literature, but one likes to think that he might have made an exception for a work that celebrates sobriety and self-control in the face of passion, qualities in which M Sarkozy was sometimes notably lacking, and needed by all rulers, not just philosopher kings.

How to ensure good educational leadership in a state

Modern states could also learn from Plato's plans in the *Laws* for the appointment of the 'supervisor' or 'minister' of education. This, by 'far the most important of the highest posts' in Plato's state, should be given to the man 'who is in all points best of all the citizens'. He was to be chosen from among existing 'curators of laws', to be 'not less than 50 years, and the father of a legitimate family, preferably of both sexes'.

Voting was to be by secret ballot which would take place appropriately in the temple of Apollo, god of harmony, order and reason, and the electorate would consist of all officials, including it seems, school superintendents. Members of the state's governing council and its committees would not have a vote and would have to accept the electorate's verdict. Once elected the post-holder would serve for five years.[16]

Compare this with the years 2000-2005 in which I served on the French Minister of Education's Haut Conseil de l'évaluation de l'école. There were five different ministers of education during this five-year period. I began to set off for meetings wondering whether by the time I arrived in Paris the current one would still be in post.

Things have not got better: in 2014 three French ministers of education held the post within the year. This is part of the wider problem within modern democracies of governments constantly changing policies and personnel in response to the ephemeral pressures of public and media opinion. France is far from being the only country around the world crying out for a dose of Platonic stability in the leadership of its national education system.

Is there a case for educational segregation?

Plato's hierarchical view of society, and belief in the inequality of people's intellectual and moral endowment, is radically unacceptable to us. We tend on the whole to have a healthy belief in the deep potential that lies within all people, including those falling behind, and a sense of obligation not to give up on them, not to label or stereotype them, and to find new ways of helping them to achieve.

Our commitment to equality of opportunity can lead us, however, to drift into situations in which what we are seeking begins to include equality of outcome, or at least a diminishing of inequalities of outcome, in ways that infringe other principles of justice, through positive discrimination or through access policies that reduce the curriculum demands on the highest achievers in order to ensure that more of the lower achievers succeed.

Democratic societies are faced with major issues in deciding to what extent and at what point the education of their future elites – and all complex societies have and need an elite, however open and fluid – should take place separately from that of the rest of the population, and the implications of this for their education systems as a whole.

T S Eliot, who shared Plato's wish to give primacy to the education of the few, raised these issues in the wake of England's 1944 Education Act, suggesting that for 'most of the time, when we talk of "equality of opportunity", we either do not know what we mean, or do not mean what we say, or else are driven to conclusions from which most people would shrink'. Even more fundamentally, he felt, we continually evade the question that should underlie all such discussion which is 'opportunity for what?'[17]

In England one hears few criticisms of a university system that admits students of different levels of prior attainment to a hierarchy of institutions, just concerns that the system of selection discriminates against those who have been disadvantaged by family background or previous educational experience. The idea, that one might have a similar selective system before the age of 18 – a return to the old grammar schools, with selection at age 11 – is generally opposed.

We privilege the communal coherence that comes from being educated together up to the age of 18 (or 16). We have a sense that this is both more egalitarian and more just. Plato, in the wider interests of the state, would have privileged keeping the future elite together and apart so that they could grow up and be educated in an environment more likely to be steeped in the intellectual interests appropriate to those who are going to occupy leading positions in society.

Would that be wholly wrong? It must at least be a matter for discussion, as this is what many private schools practice with their policies of selection, at least in the UK and the USA, and as this kind of segregation happens well before university level among many of the countries of continental Europe.

It is an issue on which I continue to be pulled in different directions, as someone who benefitted from the stimulus of being educated in the fast stream of a grammar school and who saw the intellectual elite of Winchester College (the Scholars) flourish in their separate boarding house (College), but who was also responsible for developing national curricula designed for the whole ability range and ran a large international school with a wholly open intake in which future Oxford and Harvard entrants rubbed shoulders with children with Down's Syndrome to the benefit of all. Reading the Socratic dialogues reassures one that dilemmas like this are part of life.

*****

Socrates speaks

Socrates shows how much people can learn by drawing things out of themselves when prodded to do so

Those who frequent my company at first appear, some of them, quite unintelligent, but, as we go further with our discussions, all who are favoured by heaven make progress at a rate that seems surprising to others as well as to themselves, although it is clear that they have never learned anything from me. The many admirable truths they bring to birth have been discovered by themselves from within.

Plato, *Theaetetus*, 150d, in *The Collected Dialogues of Plato*

Socrates lays down rules for the use of stories in education

Socrates: Then shall we simply allow our children to listen to any stories that anyone happens to make up, and so receive into their minds ideas often the very opposite of those we shall think they ought to have when they are grown up?

Adeimantus: No, certainly not

Socrates: It seems, then, our first business will be to supervise the making of fables and legends, rejecting all which are unsatisfactory; and we shall induce nurses and mothers to tell their children only those which we have approved, and to think more of moulding their souls with these stories than they now do of rubbing their limbs to make them strong and shapely. Most of the stories now in use must be discarded...

Adeimantus: Which kind are you thinking of, and what fault do you find in them?

Socrates: The worst of all faults, especially if the story is ugly and immoral as well as false – misrepresenting the nature of gods and heroes, like an artist whose picture is utterly unlike the object he sets out to draw.

Plato, *The Republic*, trans. Cornford, II.376, p. 67

Socrates describes the role of philosopher kings

Socrates: ...when they are 50, those who have come safely through and proved the best at all points in action and in study must be brought at last to the goal. They must lift up the eye of the soul to gaze on that which sheds light on all things; and when they have seen the Good itself, take it as a pattern for the right ordering of the state and of the individual, themselves included. For the rest of their lives, most of their time will be spent in study; but they will all take their turn at the troublesome duties of public life and act as Rulers for their country's sake, not regarding it as a distinction, but as an unavoidable task. And so, when each generation has educated others like themselves to take their place as Guardians of the commonwealth, they will depart to dwell in the Islands of the Blest...
Glaucon: That is a fine portrait of our Rulers, Socrates.
Socrates: Yes, Glaucon, and you must not forget that some of them will be women. All I have been saying applies just as much to any women who are found to have the necessary gifts.
Glaucon: Quite right, if they are to share equally with the men in everything, as we said.

Plato, *The Republic,* trans. Cornford, VII.540, p.256

Socrates addresses the Athenian jury that has just condemned him to death

For my own part I bear no grudge at all against those who condemned me and accused me, although it was not with this kind intention (*ie* to release him from the distractions of his worldly existence) that they did so, but because they thought they were hurting me; and this is culpable of them. However, I ask them to grant me one favour. When my sons grow up, gentlemen, if you think that they are putting money or anything else before goodness, take your revenge by plaguing them as I plagued you; and if they fancy themselves for no reason, you must scold them just as I scolded you, for neglecting the important things and thinking that they are good for something when they are good for nothing. If you do this, I shall have had justice at your hands, both I myself and my children.

Plato, *The Apology*, 41-42, in Plato, *The Last Days of Socrates*, p. 76

Socrates argues the case for education as essential for the sake of our immortal souls and their existence in the next life

If death were a release from everything, it would be a boon for the wicked, because by dying they would be released not only from the body but also from their own wickedness together with the soul; but as it is, since the soul is clearly immortal, it can have no escape or security from evil except by becoming as good and wise as it possibly can. For it takes nothing with it to the next world except its education and training; and these, we are told, are of supreme importance in helping or harming the newly dead at the very beginning of his journey there.

Plato, *Phaedo* in Plato, *The Last Days of Socrates*, p.170

References

1. King, A, *From Sage on the Stage to Guide on the Side, College Teaching* Vol. 41, No. 1 (Winter, 1993), pp. 30-35.

2. The contemporary insistence, endlessly repeated, that to 'educate' comes from Latin 'educere', to draw out, and is therefore not about instruction, does not appear to hold water. The *Complete Oxford English Dictionary* gives its root as Latin 'educare', to raise or to bring up (from childhood), although it points to the link between the two verbs.

3. Plato, *The Apology, in Plato, The Last Days of Socrates*, p. 70, 1966, Penguin, Harmondsworth.

4. Scolnicov, S, *Plato's Metaphysics of Education*, p. 17, 1988, Routledge, London and New York.

5. Plato, *The Republic*, trans. Lee, H D P, p. 369, 1959, Penguin, Harmondsworth.

6. Popper, K R, *The Open Society and its Enemies*, Volume 1, The Spell of Plato, 1962, Routledge & Kegan Paul, London.

7. Ryle, G, "Popper, K.R. - *The Open Society and its Enemies*", Mind, 40: 167–172. See also Faas, E, *The Genealogy of Aesthetics*, pp. 28-30 and 40, 2002, Cambridge University Press, Cambridge. Faas compares the views of Plato's Socrates with the much less puritanical and authoritarian attitudes attributed to him in the contemporary writings of Xenophon.

8. Plato, *The Republic*, trans. Lee, V.452, 455 and 457, p. 209. See also Laws, VII, 813e, p. 1384 in *The Collected Dialogues of Plato*, ed. Hamilton, E, and Cairns, H, Bollingen Series LXXI, 1961, Princeton University Press, Princeton.

9. Books II, III and X of *The Republic* and Books II and VII of *Laws* contain Plato's most extended discussions of art and beauty in education. See also Iris Murdoch's *The Fire and the Sun: Why Plato Banished the Artists*, 1978, Oxford University Press, Oxford, and Nehamas, A, *Plato and the Mass Media*, in Denham, A E (ed.), *Plato on Art and Beauty*, 2012, Palgrave Macmillan, Basingstoke.

10. Plato, *The Republic*, trans. Lee, X.602, p. 379.

11. Faas, E, *The Genealogy of Aesthetics, op.cit.*, pp. 15-27; Moss, J, *Art and Ethical Perspective: Notes on the* Kalon *in Plato's Laws*, in Denham, A E (ed.), *Plato on Art and Beauty*.

12. Plato, *The Republic*, trans. Lee, III.398-399, pp. 139-140. See also *Laws*, II.655.

13. Gardner, H, *Five Minds for the Future*, 2007, Harvard Business School Press, Cambridge, MA.

14. Burnyeat, M F, *Art and Mimesis in Plato's Republic*, pp. 54-5, in Denham, A E (ed.), *Plato on Art and Beauty*.

15. *ibid.*, p. 55.

16. Plato, *Laws*, VI.766, p. 1344 in *The Collected Dialogues of Plato*.

17. *The Aims of Education*, p.102 and pp. 119-120, in Eliot, T S, *To Criticize the Critic*, 1965, Farrar, Strauss and Giroux, New York.

Chapter 2

Education for leisure: Aristotle

THERE ARE few more telling examples of the power of teachers to shape the world than the line of succession that goes from Socrates to Plato and then to Aristotle. In the same way that Plato was steeped in the thought and educational practices of Socrates, while developing them further, so too was Aristotle shaped by the influence of Plato even on those occasions when he decided, after reflection, to take another path.

Aristotle was born in 384 BC, 15 years after the death of Socrates. In 367 BC, he moved to Athens where he became a member of Plato's Academy, remaining there for the next 20 years until Plato's death in 347 BC. There followed the first of Aristotle's two periods of exile from Athens, both of which can be probably explained by his family's links with Philip of Macedon whose expansionist ambitions were unpopular with many Greeks and most Athenians.

It was at this point that Philip invited Aristotle to Macedon to be the tutor of his heir, the young prince Alexander. In taking on this role Aristotle joined the long line of thinkers and teachers, initiated by Plato, whose efforts to put into practice their educational theories have met with stunningly less success than they might have wished. Alexander the Great (coming to the throne in 336 BC) proved to be the opposite of the kind of prudent and virtuous ruler that Aristotle was to commend in his *Politics*, the book that will be the main theme of this chapter.

Aristotle returned to Athens in 335 BC and began teaching in the Lyceum, an informal university-style centre of education, research and debate, where he gathered around him, as Plato had done, a group of young men interested in science and philosophy. His Macedonian links continued to plague him and once again in 322 BC he was driven into exile. This time he was not to return, dying later the same year.

Aristotle was massively influenced by Plato's concern for logic, epistemology and ontology (the branch of metaphysics concerned with the nature of being) and by Plato's wish to develop a unified theory of human knowledge. But he did not share all of Plato's beliefs, including in education.

Aristotle was a polymath, much more so than Plato. Only a fifth of his works have survived but even these have been estimated as encompassing up to 50 volumes of print. His writings (many of them lecture notes) are of huge scope and immense variety, embracing logic, language, the arts, ethics, politics, law, constitutional history, the history of ideas, psychology, physiology, zoology, biology, botany, chemistry, astronomy, mechanics, mathematics, the philosophy of science, and metaphysics.

He was the founder of the science of biology and of a new science of logic whose influence continued right up to the end of the 19th century. Rejecting Plato's idea of the Forms, he helped to establish the idea that empirical research precedes theory and that science should be based on observation.

Aristotle's philosophical ideas were influential throughout the period of the Roman empire and again central to philosophical debates in medieval Christendom, and in the Renaissance, following the rediscovery of manuscripts of his writings that had been preserved in Byzantium, in Western monasteries and in the Islamic world.[1] Christianity, Judaism and Islam were all marked by his influence to varying extents and at different times. Aristotle continues to figure prominently in contemporary philosophical debates.

★★★★★

> All would agree that the legislator should make the education of the young his chief and foremost concern. There are two reasons for taking this view. In the first place, the constitution of a state will suffer if education is neglected... In the second place, every capacity, and every form of art, requires as a condition of its exercise some measure of previous training and some amount of preliminary habituation. Men must therefore be trained and habituated before they can do acts of goodness, as members of a state should do.
>
> Aristotle, *Politics*, Book VIII, Chapter 1

> Life as a whole is also divided into its different parts – action and leisure, war and peace; and in the sphere of action we may further distinguish acts which are merely necessary, or merely and simply useful, from acts which are good in themselves... It is true that the citizens of our state must be able to lead a life of action and war; but they must be even more able to lead a life of leisure and peace. It is true, again, that they must be able to do necessary or useful acts; but they must be even more able to do good acts. These are the general aims which ought to be followed in the education of childhood and of the stages of adolescence which still require education.
>
> Aristotle, *Politics*, Book VII, Chapter 14

> It is pretty definitely settled, among men competent to form a judgment, that Aristotle was the best educated man that ever walked on the surface of this earth. He is still, as he was in Dante's time, the 'master of those that know'. It is, therefore, not without reason that we look to him, not only as the best exponent of ancient education, but as

one of the worthiest guides and examples in education generally.

Thomas Davidson,
Aristotle and Ancient Educational Ideals, 1892, p. 154

Education and the state

Aristotle's lengthiest discussion of education is in Books VII and VIII of his *Politics*. This is a work which both sketches the features of an ideal state and analyses the variety of states with which Aristotle was familiar in the ancient Greek world. The relationship between education and the state is fundamental to Aristotle's views about education's purposes. He is clear that the type of education to be provided will vary according to the nature of the state that an education is designed to serve – a fundamental principle that those who in the contemporary world enthusiastically promote borrowings from 'educationally successful' states sometimes ignore. In the *Politics*, however, he is concerned to outline what education should be like in an ideal state.

To Aristotle the purposes of the state and the purposes of individuals are the same, and these are that human beings should flourish and have lives that are successful, happy and virtuous. The word he uses to describe the highest human good is *eudaimonia* which is usually translated as 'happiness'.

As with Plato, one has to be very careful with the words that one uses to translate the terms found in Aristotle's writings. 'Goodness', the 'good life', 'virtue' and 'happiness' do not necessarily have the same connotations as the Greek words from which they are translated. There is no doubt, however, that Aristotle believed that people should live their lives in such a way that they engaged in satisfying and self-improving activities, showed good judgment, and were courageous, generous and wise.

The range of characteristics that to Aristotle made up 'the good life' was wide but ethically discriminating. A state or an individual would not have met the ends that were laid down for them by Aristotle if the main purpose of life for such a state or such an individual was the accumulation of money or the pursuit of 'vulgar' pleasures that did nothing to improve one's mind or soul.

The multiple purposes of education

In thinking about education, Aristotle was keen to identify the various aspects of an individual's life, and of the life of the state, for which it needed to prepare. He was critical of many Greek city states for not framing their constitutions (by which he meant all aspects of their political arrangements) with the highest ideals in mind, and for focusing simply on what was felt to be useful.

He was critical of Sparta for its past preoccupation with the qualities needed to prepare the state for war and conquest, a preoccupation driven by an obsession with material prosperity at the expense of other goods. States needed to prepare for war, in order to defend themselves from attack, and Aristotle was keen to maintain a period of military training for all young men, but a balance was required.

States and their education systems should prepare citizens for all aspects of human life: useful activities, leisure, peace and war. Similarly education should maintain a balance between the different elements that make up a human being: his body, his appetites and desires, his habits, and his capacity for reasoning.

Aristotle drew a particular distinction between education that is designed to habituate individuals to certain attitudes, emotions and patterns of behaviour and education that is designed to make them think. He saw the core purpose of education, and of the state, as being to produce individuals capable of the highest levels of thought:

> The exercise of rational principle and thought is the ultimate end of man's nature. It is therefore with a view to the exercise of these faculties that we should regulate, from the first, the birth and the training in habits of our citizens.[2]

All aspects of education, even when concerned largely with habituation, must therefore bear this ultimate end in mind and contribute towards it. Aristotle's view was that, chronologically, one started with the training of the body, then moved on to regulation of appetites such as desire, anger and self-will (the irrational part of the soul), and concluded with the training of minds (the rational and superior part of the soul). The first part of the process existed to prepare for the second and the second for the third.

Aristotle was not dismissive, however, of education that consisted mostly of habituation. He indeed saw habituation, not direct teaching, as the main route to moral virtue. We become virtuous by being helped to practise good actions, not just by learning in the abstract about virtue. Through habituating people to the practice of virtue and by taming and regulating their passions such an education allowed them to live successful lives and contributed to the smooth functioning of successful states.

He was also clear that reason, in the form of what he called 'practical wisdom', played an important role in helping one to make the right moral choices in life. He accepted, however, that for some people the higher rational parts of the soul, the exercise of which he saw as the ultimate end of human existence, might never be achieved.

Aristotle made a distinction between education that enabled people to learn how to be ruled and that which enabled them to rule. Aristotle's ideal state, unlike Plato's, was one in which all the citizens took part – he had no time for Guardians or philosopher kings – and therefore one in which an individual needed both the wisdom and good judgment to enable him to rule and the self-discipline required in situations where his role was to obey the law, accept the decisions of the properly constituted authorities, and perform the duties allocated to him.

Aristotle's ideal state, though a democracy, did not include slaves, women and non-citizens. Like Plato he did not challenge the prevailing assumptions of his day in relation to these matters. This in no way invalidates his views when these are applied to what is needed to enable citizens to perform all aspects of their functions within a more inclusive democracy.

The role of leisure

Education for leisure played a central role in Aristotle's plans for education. He distinguished between 'leisure' and 'occupation'. Education needs to prepare people for both these states of existence. 'Occupation' is a matter of utility and necessity whereas 'leisure' is the state of existence in which one pursues activities for their own sake. 'Leisure' should not be confused with 'play', which is the corollary of 'occupation', *ie* how we seek relief from work and exertion.

'Leisure', by contrast, involves what Aristotle considers to be the highest form of human activity: the pursuit of intellectual excellence and of the noble and the beautiful as ends in themselves and not as means to an end. As the ends of the state are the same as the ends of human beings the best form of state is therefore the one that makes 'leisure' possible and that educates men to take advantage of it. This education involves both that of the young, which is what Aristotle writes about in the *Politics*, and that of mature persons.

Aristotle's idea of a leisured citizenry or class of cultured 'gentlemen' who had their 'occupations' and performed their civic duties but whose main interest and activity in life was the disinterested cultivation of their minds was to be an influential one. It shaped for centuries how ruling elites saw themselves and was at the root of much of the learning and practice of those arts that have constituted the 'high culture' of the Western tradition.

One finds it again in the 18th-century English philosopher Bishop Berkeley who, referring explicitly to Aristotle, commented that 'whatever the world may say, he who hath not much meditated upon God, the human mind, and the *summum bonum*, may possibly make a thriving earthworm, but will most indubitably make a sorry patriot and a sorry statesman'.[3] One of its last echoes can be found in an essay by the German Catholic writer Josef Pieper (*Leisure: The Basis of Culture*), translated and published in the UK in 1952 with an introduction by the poet T S Eliot.[4] Eliot was explicit, elsewhere in his writings, that this small intellectual and leisured elite (in the Aristotelian sense of the word 'leisured') was the audience for which he wrote his poetry. Modern democracy, modern capitalism and massive socio-economic change have rendered such ideas largely unthinkable.

The different stages of education

Aristotle identified three stages in a person's education: from age seven to puberty; from puberty to age 21; and after age 21. Each of the first two stages should be seen, not in itself, but as a step towards the final stage. This is a difference in perspective from the contemporary assumption that primary education should not be seen just as a preparation for secondary education, and secondary education not just seen as a preparation for higher education and work, but as also enabling children to live more satisfying lives *while they are still children*.

The implications for educational practice of this difference in perspective may not be major, but it is a shift that reflects a focus on education more inclined to start with the child than with the ends of education as seen in the abstract. More fundamentally it reflects a shift in perspective in the modern world concerning the relationship between childhood and adulthood, and in particular a downplaying of the traditional notion of the superiority of adulthood.

During the first phase of education, from age seven to puberty, Aristotle placed great emphasis on gymnastics and the training of the body, in order to develop its strength and health, but also on learning the rudiments of letters and of other subjects. Education at this stage was driven by the need to establish good habits in the child and to learn that which would be useful in later life.

From puberty to age 21 there would be an important shift in focus. The emphasis, however, would still be on habituating young men to a life of virtue and noble enjoyment, rather than on the training of more philosophic minds. This phase would involve practice in the exercise of reason, but with a stress on its more practical rather than speculative aspects.

The main element in education at this phase would be music in its broader Greek sense which includes the works of all the Muses, and in particular poetry, drama and drawing, as well as all the different aspects of music itself. In addition gymnastics would continue and would be supplemented, over a four year period, by military training.

After the age of 21 those who had developed the right habits, as a result of their earlier education, would be poised to shape their minds in the use of speculative reason, through the study of philosophy and the theoretical sciences and the continuing study of the works of the Muses. It is this which would prepare them for the good use of their leisure, and for the use of the products of their leisure, in terms of their deeper understanding, wisdom and moral character, in the service of their state.

This is one area where, at least in the *Politics*, Aristotle's thoughts have not survived and so, unlike in Plato's *Republic*, we lack a detailed prescription for this lifelong learning. Other works by Aristotle, and in particular his *Nicomachean Ethics*, make clear the virtues and qualities that an educated man was expected to show.

State versus private education

Education in ancient Greek city states was largely a matter of private provision and the responsibility of the family. For Aristotle it was much too important to be left to the whim of individuals and he was therefore insistent that it should be the responsibility of the state. This is not just the state exercising its responsibility in relation to those – *ie* children – who are unable to make autonomous decisions and require protection other than that provided by their families. It is much more fundamental than that. In Aristotle's view:

> We must not regard a citizen as belonging just to himself: we must regard every citizen as belonging to the state.[5]

This active role for the state has many contemporary echoes. Western democracies are increasingly keen to prod their citizens from all sides into being healthy, happy and good, with ever escalating levels of intervention into people's lives through regulation and exhortation.

A more passive non-Aristotelian view of the state is, however, far from dead, with John Rawls as one of its most eloquent modern spokesmen.[6] From this point of view the state's role is to create a space in which individuals have the rights, means and guarantees that will enable them to flourish in whatever ways they see fit but, if they wish to over-eat, smoke, drink, and not develop their higher skills, then to do that instead.

For Aristotle the role of the state is to enable people to flourish, to live satisfying and fulfilled lives, in ways that are in accordance with the ends that are intrinsic to human beings and to states as they ought to be constituted. For this reason the state must have a say in how its citizens are educated. Aristotle was much less negative about the family than Plato had been. He accepted its role in education, but saw this as subordinate to that of the state.

Despite his exclusion of women and slaves from citizenship, and despite his acceptance that some citizens might never stretch themselves into the realm of speculative reason, Aristotle was also insistent that all the citizens of a state should not just have a state education but have the same education, 'that education ... must be one and the same for all'. As an Aristotelian scholar has put it: 'Education (for Aristotle) must be one for the sake of the unity of the city; and education must be public for the sake of the unity of education'.[7]

This is a view at variance with contemporary practice in many democratic states in which greater educational freedom is allowed, out of a concern for individual rights (a notion absent in Aristotle) and because of what are felt to be the desirable educational, social and political effects of giving parents more choice in the education of their children.

Music and the arts in education

More than half of Book VIII of the *Politics* concerns education in music, and mostly music in the modern, and more limited, sense of the word. To Aristotle music was important not mainly for the pleasure that comes from listening or participating or from the exercise of aesthetic judgment, important though these might be, but above all because music can help to form the character and educate the soul.

It is because it is felt that music can contribute so much to this central aim of an Aristotelian education that Aristotle spends so much time discussing exactly what form a musical education should take, and in particular whether it should involve learning an instrument, and if so which instrument, and which are the various modes or scales that are best suited to the objectives of a musical education.

Aristotle envisages that music will play a key part in the way the educated adults of his state spend their leisure time. They will appreciate it for its own sake and by doing so will continue to refine their minds, for example through their appreciation of musical forms and structure.[8]

In music, and also in epic poetry and dramatic tragedy, Aristotle also rated highly the educational role played by catharsis in purging, through pity and fear, the excesses of the passions and thus disposing individuals to a life of principled and intelligent moral action. The discussion of this in the *Politics* that is promised is missing but it is a theme in Aristotle's *Poetics*. Aristotle saw the arts as activities concerned with engaging our moral sympathy or antipathy and, although in imitating reality they might point us in the direction of generalisations about human nature and life, their purpose was not to establish truth.

Aristotle was generally more positive than Plato about the effects of exposure to the arts and valued the role of the arts in education. Like Plato, however, he saw them as inferior to activities such as the study of philosophy, theology, logic, mathematics, and physics whose core purpose was the pursuit of truth. As one Aristotelian scholar has put it, 'Aristotle's hierarchy of values ... puts literature and music in the kitchen, logic and mathematics in the dining-room, and philosophy and theology in the drawing-room'. Even if we might disagree with this hierarchy it is a useful antidote to the contemporary hyperbole one sometimes hears from arts lobbyists – and those who work in this area constitute a major vested interest – about the centrality of the arts in the school curriculum.[9]

*****

How Aristotle can help us think about education today

Starting from first principles and admitting that one has doubts

Part of the freshness of the *Politics* comes from how Aristotle does not hide his doubts and hesitations.

> At present opinion is divided', he writes, 'about the subjects of education. All do not take the same view about what should be learned by the young... If we look at actual practice, the result is sadly confusing; it throws no light on the problem whether the proper studies to be followed are those which are useful in life, or those which make for goodness, or those which advance the bounds of knowledge. Each sort of study receives some votes in its favour; none of them has a clear case.

It is a refreshing contrast to all those politicians and educational reformers for whom there are no doubts as to what needs to be done. When Aristotle comes to make recommendations about specific aspects of pedagogy – whether children should learn to play musical instruments, and which they should play, for example – these are always based on first principles, on his answers to the question 'what is education for?'

As an example, do we always ask this question when we put on yet again the school fashion show or decide to stage *High School Musical* or *Grease*, rather than *The Crucible* or *A Midsummer Night's Dream*, as the end of year school production? Having encountered at least three performances of *High School Musical*, and avoided even more fashion shows, at schools for which I was responsible, I finally put this question directly to a group of Heads in a talk I gave them on 'intellectual leadership in schools'. I illustrated it, making no comment, with a photograph of International School of Geneva students performing Sophocles back in the 1950s. In discussion I came to see that there might be a defence of *High School Musical*, but was unable to admit to any Aristotelian doubts when it came to fashion shows.

Education for duty, obedience and restraint

Aristotle stresses the importance of preparing future citizens both to rule and to be ruled, to exercise their leadership and to do their duty to obey decisions that they may have opposed and do not like. The latter involves self-discipline, self-abnegation, modesty and restraint, qualities also at the core of the Judaeo-Christian tradition but less prominent in a world which emphasises individualism, people's rights, consumer choice and an unlimited entitlement to 'respect'.

Schools are often in the lead in struggling to maintain a balance in this area and would not survive without an emphasis on obedience to rules. It is the wider society that frequently fails to give them the words and the narrative with which to explain what they are doing.

The uses and abuses of leisure

Aristotle's emphasis on leisure as the means to a life in which one cultivates one's sensibility through study, thought and the arts – all for its own sake – has echoed down the ages. Its traces can be found in medieval justifications for the contemplative life.

It has shaped the self-image and way of life both of aristocracies and, in more recent centuries, of the middle class. It has also shaped how writers, artists and philosophers have seen themselves. 'I have never bothered or asked', wrote Goethe in 1830, 'in what way I was useful to society as a whole; I contented myself with expressing what I recognized as good and true'.[10]

For Aristotle self-cultivation for its own sake was an aim for all citizens, not just for a small minority of Guardians or philosopher kings. In the 20th century this ambition re-emerged with the spread of democracy, and of communism. The Italian communist Gramsci, an immensely learned man, as his letters from prison to his two young sons testify, wished everyone to have access to a culture previously reserved for a few.[11] The Scottish communist poet Hugh MacDiarmid even fantasised, albeit tongue in cheek, about a future world in which the urban proletariat, freed from what he saw to be the mindlessness of football and mass entertainment, queued up to attend literary debates and bought like hot cakes abstruse poems sold on Glasgow street corners.[12]

In England the post-1945 Labour government had similar dreams. The Minister of Education, Ellen Wilkinson, presiding over the creation by the BBC of a new 'Third Programme' (the precursor of the current Radio 3) devoted to all aspects of 'high culture', spoke optimistically about the fostering in Britain of a 'Third Programme nation'.

These Aristotelian aspirations have not been realised. The old aristocracy and the *haute bourgeoisie* have been replaced by a new elite of pop stars, footballers and celebrities who are unlikely to listen to Radio 3, dip into Gramsci's favourite classics or attend literary debates. Politicians who had retired to bed at night to read Gibbon (Churchill), Trollope (Macmillan) and Voltaire (Mitterand) have also been replaced by a new generation more inclined to spend their leisure playing the Fruit Ninja iPad game (Cameron), lounging on expensive yachts (Sarkozy), or taking part in bunga bunga parties (Berlusconi).

In the former Communist bloc, following the fall of the Berlin Wall and the spread of capitalism, the bookshops that had previously stocked Lessing and Hölderlin quickly filled up with video cassettes and the novels of Jackie Collins.[13] In France, according to one of its leading intellectuals, the current elite has lost all sense of real connection with the country's cultural past.[14]

None of this probably has much to do with changes in education. It can be explained by the spread of the mass media, the evolution of global capitalism, and the collapse of traditional social and cultural hierarchies within democratic societies. It raises major questions about what *ought to be* the focus of education, for the sake of the individual and the community, and particularly about education's role in cultural transmission and as preparation for leisure.

There are many features of the modern world that diminish our leisure – its complexity, its bureaucracy, its clutter, its gadgets – but most of us can look forward to large chunks of it during both our working lives and the long years of our retirement. Increasing numbers of us can also expect to spend long periods of our lives living alone. How education can help us fulfil Aristotle's aspirations for human beings and their communities remains an important question 2300 years after it was first posed.

How far should freedom of choice in education extend?

Aristotle's idea that the education of the young should be the sole responsibility of the state deserves more discussion than in has received in recent decades. At one time there were those on the far left in England who argued for the abolition of the private schools in which a small minority of the population, and a large part of the country's elite, were educated. It is a long time since this demand commanded much attention. Western democracies universally permit parents to educate their children outside the state education system, and may even allow them to educate them at home. States also sometimes offer a choice of types of school within publicly funded provision, including schools run by faith groups and those set up by groups of parents and teachers.

Capitalist economies based on consumer choice do not sit easily with restrictions on parental freedom of the kind envisaged by Aristotle and as practised in some authoritarian and totalitarian states. Nor do they sit easily with societies that emphasise individualism at the expense of communities and rights at the expense of duties.

In Western democracies, however, Aristotle's fundamental principle with regard to state control has been generally maintained in that the state, in most countries, retains a considerable degree of control over alternative educational provision, including when it is not publicly funded. The state has a duty, it is felt, to look after the interests of those who are not autonomous decision-makers, in this case children.

The fact that there may be few pressures to upset the current balance of compulsion and choice does not mean that we have necessarily got this right. There are some areas in which the interests of the state and of civic society may be overlooked in attempts to maximise consumer choice. Some western democracies have a tradition of state subsidies for schools run by faith groups; others do not. England has long had state-funded Anglican, Roman Catholic and Jewish schools.

Recent efforts to allow even greater choice, through Free Schools which are outside government control and have greater curricular freedom, are leading to a new proliferation of state-funded faith schools (Christian, Anglican, Roman Catholic, Greek Orthodox, Jewish, Islamic and Sikh). One does not have to be a member of the British Humanist Association to share that body's concern that such a policy, and indeed any subsidy given to faith-based schools, might not be in the best interests of the wider functioning of the state.

States obviously come in different shapes and sizes. Those that are most stable and most successful tend to be those where the centrifugal forces outweigh the centripetal ones. States in which loyalties to subordinate communities are stronger than those to the nation as a whole, *ie* 'multicultural states' drifting towards what Amartya Sen has called 'plural monoculturalism', often have less happy histories.[15] Multiple identities are possible and generally desirable, but educational policies that look as if they might encourage ghettoization require more thought than they seem to be getting. France has many educational and social problems, and in some areas has been less successful in coping with increased diversity than its island neighbour, but its Aristotelian notion of schools as lay places, in which people of different backgrounds leave these firmly behind once they enter precincts whose role is to equip them to be citizens of the same republic, has a lot of life in it left.

*****

Aristotle writes

Aristotle explains why the state should control education

> The whole of a state has one common End. Evidently, therefore, the system of education in a state must also be one and the same for all, and the provision of this system must be a matter of public action. It cannot be left, as it is at present, to private enterprise, with each parent making provision privately for his own children, and having them privately instructed as he himself think fit. Training for an end which is common should also itself be common.
>
> Aristotle, *Politics*, Book VIII, Chapter I

Aristotle on learning, effort and pain

> It is clear that amusement is not the object with a view to which the

young should be educated. Learning is not a matter of amusement. It is attended by effort and pain.

Aristotle, *Politics*, Book VIII, Chapter V

Aristotle on the reasons for studying music

...music should not be pursued for any single benefit which it can give, but for the sake of several. There are three benefits which it can give. One is education; a second is release of emotion (the sense of the term will be explained more clearly in our lectures on poetics...); a third is the benefit of cultivation, with which may be linked that of recreation and relaxation of strain. It is clear from the view we have stated that all the modes (or scales) should be used, but not in the same sort of way. When education is the object in view, the modes which ought to be used are those which express character best: when it is a question of listening to the performance of others, we may also admit the modes which stimulate men to action or provide them with inspiration.

Aristotle, *Politics*, Book VIII, Chapter VII

Aristotle on the proper use of leisure

Our very nature has a tendency... to seek of itself for ways and means which will enable us to use leisure rightly, as well as to find some right occupation; indeed it is the power to use leisure rightly, as we would once more repeat, which is the basis of all our life. It is true that both occupation and leisure are necessary; but it is also true that leisure is higher than occupation, and is the end to which occupation is directed. Our problem, therefore, is to find modes of activity which will fill our leisure. We can hardly fill our leisure with play. To do so would be to make play the be-all and end-all of life. That is an impossibility.

Aristotle, *Politics*, Book VIII, Chapter III

A modern philosopher on Aristotle's idea of leisure

...it is essential to begin by reckoning with the fact that one of the foundations of Western culture is leisure. That much, at least, can be learnt from the first chapter of Aristotle's *Metaphysics*. And even the history of the word attests the fact: for leisure in Greek is *skole*, and in Latin *scola*, the English 'school'. The word used to designate the place where we educate and teach is derived from a word which means 'leisure'. 'School' does not, properly speaking, mean school, but leisure.

Pieper, J, *Leisure: The Basis of Culture*, p.21, Collins, London, 1965

References

1. Gougenheim, S, *Aristote au Mont Saint-Michel. Les racines grecques de l'Europe chrétienne*, 2008, Éditions du Seuil, Paris.
2. Aristotle, *Politics*, Book VII, Chapter 15, 1334 b 8, trans. Barker B, 1948, Oxford University Press, Oxford.

3. Quoted in Barnes, J, introduction to The *Ethics of Aristotle*, 1976, Penguin Books, London.

4. Pieper, J, *Leisure: The Basis of Culture*, 1965, Collins, London.

5. Aristotle, *Politics*, Book VIII, Chapter 1, 1337 a 11, trans. Barker B, 1948, Oxford University Press, Oxford.

6. Kraut, R, *Aristotle and Rawls on the common good*, in Deslauriers, M, and Destrée, P, *The Cambridge Companion to Aristotle's* Politics, pp. 350-74, 2013, Cambridge University Press, Cambridge.

7. Lord, C.R., *Education and Culture in the Political Thought of Aristotle*, p. 49, 1982, Cornell University Press, Ithaca and London.

8. Destrée, P, *Education, leisure and politics*, in Deslauriers, M, and Destrée, P, *The Cambridge Companion to Aristotle's* Politics, pp. 316-19.

9. Lord, C.R., *Education and Culture in the Political Thought of Aristotle*, pp. 105-150; Gulley, N, op.cit., p. 176; Nehamas, A, *Plato and the Mass Media*, p. 38, in Denham, A E, *Plato on Art and Beauty*, 2012, Palgrave Macmillan, Basingstoke.

10. Quoted in Pieper, J, *Leisure: The Basis of Culture*, p. 39, 1965, Collins, London.

11. Gramsci, A, *Prison Letters*, 1996, Pluto Press, London.

12. MacDiarmid, H, 'Glasgow, 1960' in *Collected Poems of Hugh MacDiarmid*, p. 430, 1962, Oliver & Boyd, Edinburgh and London

13. Steiner, G, *Errata: An Examined Life*, p. 132, 1997, Yale University Press, Yale.

14. Finkielkraut, A, *L'identité malheureuse*, pp. 151-3, 2013, Éditions Stock, Paris.

15. Sen, A, *Identity and Violence*, 2006, W. W. Norton, New York.

Chapter 3

Education for eternity: Thomas Aquinas

THOMAS AQUINAS (1225-1274) was a university teacher throughout his adult life, at a time when many boys (only boys went to university at that time) started their studies at university at the age of 14 or 15. His voluminous writings were also one long attempt to explain and to teach. He wrote little directly about education, though what he did write is interesting.

He is included in this volume for two reasons: first, because of his importance and influence as a philosopher, and, second, because a study of what great thinkers thought about education would be incomplete, as far as the Western tradition is concerned, without the presence of a thinker whose thought is steeped, as Aquinas's was, in Christianity.

We know relatively little about Aquinas's personal life, as opposed to his ideas, and although his writings reveal an incredibly intelligent, subtle, powerful, self-critical and inquisitive mind, they are completely free of what one would describe as personal feeling. Reading Aquinas one senses a mind that gains a deep, but quiet, satisfaction from its power to analyse, make distinctions, identify connections, find patterns, and impose order on chaos – qualities crucial for all higher order thought. Some might call him 'dry'; others might welcome the refreshing absence of ego by comparison with some popular 'philosophers' of our own days, with their TV appearances, personal websites and addiction to tweets.

Thomas was born in about 1225, the younger son of a noble Italian family, in a castle not far from the great Benedictine monastery of Monte Cassino, founded in the early sixth century (and destroyed in modern times in a major battle between the Germans and Allies in 1944). His uncle was the abbot and from the age of five to 13 Thomas was educated there, destined like many younger sons for a life in the Church. He went on to study at the university in Naples, where he came into touch with the newly-founded Order of Dominican friars, which he joined in 1244.

For the remaining 30 years of his life, apart from a spell with the papal court, he moved between the universities of Paris, Cologne and Naples, studying, writing, teaching and preaching. We know little of his life during these years. It cannot have been uneventful, as both the Dominican order and Thomas himself continually attracted controversy.

The 13th century was the great age of university expansion in western Europe, with schools in major cities turning into properly organised universities for the study of law, the arts and theology. The students and teachers of these universities, most of them priests, monks and novices, formed a group whose identity, like that of the Church itself, transcended the kingdoms, duchies and city states into which Europe at that time was divided. They followed similar studies, used the same (laboriously copied) text books, moved from one place to another despite the many limitations on travel, and wrote and spoke in the same language (Latin).

The 13th century was also a period of intellectual ferment, in part because of the gradual re-discovery of the writings of Aristotle, first those relating to logic, then his more philosophical works, and finally his treatises on ethics, politics and aesthetics. Knowledge of Plato had never faded in the intervening millennium, though his views about the immortality of the soul and the world of 'the Forms' had been re-interpreted in ways that made them fit more easily with Christianity. Aristotle, by contrast, with his this-world point of view, had fallen out of sight. His re-discovery compelled many Christian thinkers like Aquinas to start looking at key issues in a new light.

It was also not just a question of re-discovering a great Greek philosopher. Some of Aristotle's views reached Aquinas and other Christian scholars indirectly through the writings of the Arabian philosophers Avicenna and Averroës and the Jewish writer Maimonides. Arabian and Jewish influences were thus also brought into play as part of this process of transmission.

Aquinas wrote in Latin, like most Western philosophers from the time of the Roman Empire up to the 16th and 17th centuries (and indeed beyond). His two great works are his *Summa contra Gentiles* (A Summary against the Gentiles) and the *Summa theologica* (A Summary of Theology). He also wrote commentaries on Aristotle and on the Scriptures, and many writings – *Quaestiones disputatae* (Disputed Questions) – on topics such as *De veritate* (On Truth), one of whose 29 questions concerned the role of the teacher and formed the basis of the text *de magistro (On Teaching)*. Aquinas died, at the age of 49, in 1274, while travelling to Lyons in France to take part in a Council at the invitation of the Pope.

Aquinas's influence on the development of Christian thought, and Western philosophy more generally, has been massive, though his approach has been frequently contested both within and outside the Catholic Church. His philosophical followers, known as Thomists, have had a major influence on modern Catholicism and on Catholic education (as shown by the way Thomas keeps on popping up in the writings of James Joyce). Aquinas's moral philosophy and philosophy of mind also continue to be of great interest to some contemporary secular philosophers. Many hundreds of educational institutions – schools and universities – all over the world are currently named after St Thomas Aquinas.

*****

...the student's ideas are the primary foundation on which is built all the knowledge gained through teaching. The student's own lights are the immediate builder, while the teacher's are the middle builder.

Aquinas, *De magistro (On Teaching)*,
in *Quaestiones Disputatae de Veritate*
(Disputed Questions of Truth), q.11, a.1

The appropriate course of education will be as follows: the induction of the young in logical topics to begin with, for logic teaches method for all scientific inquiry; then a training in mathematics, which neither need experiment nor lie beyond the range of the imagination; thirdly, in physics, where much experimentation is demanded though sensation is not surpassed; fourthly, in moral science, which requires experience and a mind free from passion; finally, in wisdom or theology, which transcends imagination and demands robust understanding.

Aquinas, *Commentary, VI Ethics*, lect.7

Lynch made a grimace at the raw grey sky and said:
If I am to listen to your esthetic philosophy give me at least another cigarette. I don't care about it... I want a job of five hundred a year. You can't get me one. Stephen handed him the packet of cigarettes.
Lynch took the last one that remained, saying simply:
Proceed!
Aquinas, said Stephen, says that is beautiful the apprehension of which pleases.
Lynch nodded.
I remember that, he said, *Pulcra sunt quae visa placent*.

James Joyce, *A Portrait of the Artist as a Young Man*,
1916, p.217 Penguin edition 1963

Aquinas as philosopher and theologian

Aquinas was both a philosopher and a Christian theologian. The two ways of looking at the world are to be found throughout his writings. On the one hand, as a theologian, he is concerned with interrogating Christian revelation, as recounted in Scriptures which he believed to be divinely inspired, and working out both what revelation means and what its implications are for our lives in this world and beyond.

On the other hand, as a philosopher, he is interested in putting aside revelation for a moment and seeing what a human being, un-aided by revelation, is able to understand about the world through empirical observation based on our senses and through the use of reason in reflecting on the fundamental characteristics of being (*ie* through *metaphysical* reflection).

What was novel about Aquinas was the extent to which he emphasised the separation of philosophy from theology. In his philosophy he was fiercely intellectual, analysing words and concepts, searching out all the objections to a particular point of view, examining them rigorously in turn, and firmly rejecting all statements for which he did not have evidence or supporting arguments derived from the use of human reason unsupported by revelation.

He stressed, for example, that nothing arising solely out of human reflection could lead one to assert that the world at some point came into existence as opposed to having existed eternally, or to claim that the existence of God was self-evident.

Aquinas did not see empirical observation and metaphysical thought as incompatible with Christianity. In many ways, for example through his attempts to show how our knowledge of the world points to the existence of God, he was convinced that empirical observation and metaphysical speculation supported it. Ultimate truth in many of the things that mattered, however, only came through an understanding of revelation and through the operation of divine grace.

It was this separation between two kinds of reflection – the theological and the philosophical – that made Aquinas controversial with some of his contemporaries, in particular because his work as a philosopher relied so heavily on Aristotle, regarded by some in the Church as a pagan who might have some useful things to teach a Christian society, for example in the realm of logic, but whose world view was fundamentally antipathetic.

Aquinas was not, however, a slavish follower of Aristotle and integrated elements of other philosophies into his thought, and above all Platonism whose views on the immortality of the soul were closer to Christianity than those of Aristotle and whose classification of the four 'cardinal virtues' (prudence, justice, temperance and courage) Aquinas absorbed into his *Summa*. One writer sees Aquinas as bringing these two streams of philosophical thought – Platonism and Aristotelianism – together:

> Indeed, Aquinas makes so much use of ways of thought that are ultimately Platonic that it may almost be said of him that he achieves that fusion of the Academy and Lyceum that so many of his predecessors and contemporaries were attempting.[1]

Beatitudo: Aquinas's view of happiness and the ends of human life

Aquinas shared Aristotle's view that the end of human existence is the pursuit of happiness and satisfaction in ways that actualise the potentialities of human beings. He used the term *beatitudo* to describe this. The term has a sense which extends far beyond the modern word 'happiness', as did Aristotle's word *eudaimonia* in Greek which resonates in similar ways.

Aquinas, like Aristotle, was clear that the ends of human existence were not reached unless 'goodness' also entered into the equation, in other words that happiness and satisfaction depend on human beings developing themselves and acting in ways that are morally good rather than morally bad. It was also clear to Aquinas that having these ends and making these moral distinctions was quite possible for human beings without the benefits of Christian revelation.

The first stage therefore towards defining the good life, and thus enabling one to judge whether one was moving in the direction of achieving this, was open to non-Christians. To go beyond this transcended the natural powers of human beings, required an understanding of the final ends of man that could only come from revelation, and was dependent on supernatural grace. Aquinas was convinced that without revelation we would only have a partial and imperfect conception of the purpose of human life and of what constituted the supreme good for human beings. The ultimate end for a human being, for Aquinas, was a vision of God in His plenitude.

This would only be achieved when one's immortal soul was united with Him in the next world, or more specifically when, in accordance with Christian belief, the human personality was transfigured in its completeness following the Last Judgment and the Resurrection of the bodies of the Just. At that point we would be able to attain the 'beatitude' or state of 'blissfulness' also implied in the word *beatitudo.*

It is because of this vision of the world that Aquinas begins his short piece *de magistro* (On Teaching) by putting forward for examination, using the question-response dialectical approach so common in his writings, the view, taken from St Matthew's Gospel, that 'only God can teach or be called teacher'. This had been the theme of an influential text of the same name *(de magistro)* by his fourth-century Platonist predecessor St Augustine. Aquinas, as an Aristotelian, takes great pains to qualify the statement by showing how the student can learn things through his own observation of the world and the use of his own reason and how his teachers are crucial in helping him to do so.[2] He sees the passage in the Gospel as only warning teachers never to forget that whatever the importance of their role there is a 'supreme teacher' above them, stressing that:

> ...we should not place unlimited trust in human wisdom, but only in the divine truth which speaks in us through an impression in us of its likeness and by which we can judge all things.[3]

As well as having a distinctively Christian view of man's final ends, not to be found in Aristotle, Aquinas also had his own views about the virtues in relation to which we should be educated. In addition to the four Platonic cardinal virtues, which he saw as dispositions to behave in certain ways perceived as good in themselves, he also stressed the importance of the three 'theological virtues' of faith, hope and charity that dispose Christians to live in a relationship with God.

Faith is striving towards God as the ultimate good, believing in Him and bearing witness to this belief. Hope keeps man from discouragement, enables him to persevere to the end, and offers the prospect of eternal life. Charity is love of God above all things, and for His own sake, of one's neighbour as oneself, and (Aquinas stressed) also of oneself and of one's body. The three virtues are all closely related but charity is fundamental and the foundation of the other two. The theological virtues are implanted in man's mind by God but it is man's duty to develop and use them.

Inventio (discovery) and *disciplina* (teaching)

In *de magistro* Aquinas makes, with great brevity, an interesting point about the frequently discussed distinction between what students learn through discovery (*inventio*), 'when the mind moves by its own natural power to an understanding of things previously unknown to it', and what they learn as a result of the intervention of an 'outside power' or 'teacher' (*disciplina*). He does this through an analogy with medicine. In the same way as a doctor intervenes to help a patient by applying methods based on a knowledge of how the human body, unaided, might begin to return to health, so too a teacher practises his art by drawing on his knowledge of how a mind 'moves by its own natural power to an understanding of things previously unknown to it'.

There can have been few more succinct statements down the ages of the importance of, first, the active role of the learner, second, the need to achieve a balance between self-discovery and enquiry on the one hand and formal teaching on the other, and, third, the way teaching needs to be based on a deep understanding, akin to the doctors' knowledge of the human body, of how the mind, on its own, learns.

As with 'lifelong learning', to be discussed below, the idea of 'discovery' or 'enquiry' learning did not just emerge for the first time in the enlightened late 20th century, as some of its proponents would sometimes have us believe. Great minds had got there in the 13th century even if they had not yet teased out some of its implications.

*****

How Aquinas can help us think about education today

The starting point of education should be reflection on our fundamental purposes and aspirations

Aquinas follows on from Plato and Aristotle in seeing the aims of education as transcending the utilitarian. Although, as a pupil of Aristotle and a man of great common sense, he valued the acquisition of the skills needed in everyday life and of knowledge about the material world, he was also clear that education serves the end for which human beings have been created, which is the development of their souls.

The notion of an individual's education as a commodity contributing to the construction of 'the knowledge economy', or the idea that the pupil-teacher or parent-teacher relationship should be one of customer and provider, or the notion that the success of an education might be judged largely on the basis of quantitative attainment data – things that many western governments take for granted – would have been fundamentally at odds with everything he believed.

Like Plato and Socrates, Aquinas makes us think first about our fundamental purposes and aspirations for a life that is worthy and fulfilling and then deduces the nature of education from these first principles. Education must not ignore the demands of the everyday world, but that is neither its end nor the starting point of our reflections about it.

Education for virtue then and now

The four cardinal virtues – prudence, justice, temperance and courage (or fortitude) – and the three theological virtues – faith, hope and charity – emphasised by Aquinas and still prominent in the official catechism of the Catholic Church, have a clarity and simplicity that make them memorable. They, and their opposites the vices (hatred, envy, sloth, cowardice, intemperance), also analysed by Aquinas, have provided objectives for teaching for 2000 years. The four cardinal virtues are even older than that, expounded originally by Plato and adapted for Christian use by some of the early Christian Fathers.

In their clarity and simplicity these seven virtues have injected a sense of purpose and direction into many people's lives, giving them the idea that learning and self-development continue throughout one's life and setting standards in the light of which people have been able to examine their own conduct and judge themselves.

Following Aristotle, Aquinas also talked about intellectual virtues, by which he meant the ability to reason, both in an abstract and speculative way and also practically in relation to how one might act in particular situations. Possessing these intellectual virtues did not necessarily enable one to act morally but, allied to a disposition towards the various moral virtues, and in particular towards prudence, was an important component of a life well led. Aquinas called 'conscience' this process of reasoning by which one judges if an action is good or not. Like 'virtue' this is a word that has dropped out of our modern educational vocabulary.[4]

Aquinas also used the term 'natural law' to describe what reason tells us to do or not to do, independently of revelation, in order to function well as people. This 'natural law', though part of God's plan for the world, is accessible to all, including non-Christians. For Christians it is supplemented by revelation. It also needs the support of 'human law' as prescribed in particular societies to promote people's well-being.

Although human law involves penalties for wrongdoing people are expected to follow the natural law for its own sake, not through fear of penalties. Aquinas drew a distinction between the Old Law of the Old Testament, a written law obeyed out of fear or desire for reward, and the New Law of the New Testament, by which 'those who are possessed of virtue are inclined to do virtuous deeds through love of virtue, not on account of some extrinsic punishment or reward'.[5]

The main purpose behind looking at educational ideas and practices from other ages is not necessarily to revive things that are long dead – like the use of the seven virtues as an educational tool – but to put these ideas and practices alongside those of the present day the better to understand what it is we are doing and whether we are in fact doing what we think or say we are doing.

A glance at the websites of schools and colleges in the UK, USA and Canada shows a huge variety of contemporary 'moral codes'. The seven traditional virtues are nowhere to be found, even in Catholic schools, some of whose websites, including that of a school named after St Thomas Aquinas, have even dropped all references to God. In the place of the virtues, one finds a new type of moral code, based on acronyms on the dubious assumption that in an age of reduced attention spans these will make it more memorable. These new codes go hand in hand with obligatory mission and vision statements and the occasional motto. The latter are my particular *bête noire* and are almost invariably embarrassing or at the very least trite, one Texas school named after Aquinas urging its pupils to 'Discover. Grow. Soar'. At least when these things were in Latin most people were spared the full shock of their banality.

The number seven, however, is still alive and well, through the frequent use of the word RESPECT, often as an acronym for a bewilderingly different set of characteristics: **R** for Relationships or (at another school) for Recognition, rewards and sanctions (this one can't sustain the alliteration); **E** for Equality and Everywhere or for Environment; **S** for Standards and Staying Safe or for Self-discipline; **P** for a Positive attitude or for Partnership; **E** for Enthusiasm or Expectations; **C** for the right Choices we make or for Consistency; **T** for Together or for Treat others as you would be treated.

Some schools prefer a SMART moral code, as in **S**afety (such as 'No running on the woodchips in the structure area outside'), **M**anners ('in the cafeteria ... say Excuse Me when you burp or belch'), **A**ccepting ('Enjoy each other's differences'), **R**especting ('Wait your turn') and **T**eamwork ('Be a team player'). One SMART primary school has a SMART song, which goes 'Our school is happy, Our school is bright, And Fuzzy Bear says "It's just Right!"'

Two things strike one about the contrast between the list of the seven cardinal and theological virtues and the new moral codes. First, uniformity has been replaced by diversity. No one school's list of rules and exhortations is the same as that of any other. Where school codes are developed in consultation with pupils this can make them understand these better. One is more likely to follow rules that one has helped to draw up and whose purpose one has come to see.

But this has the disadvantage that the rules are not reinforced in the wider society and do not follow one through life. Once one leaves school one never hears again about 'equality and everywhere' or about 'standards and staying safe', let alone about 'Fuzzy Bear'. The school codes are replaced, if at all, by rather different workplace mission statements and codes of conduct or, for the most important parts of one's life, by nothing.

Second, the seven virtues (or the four cardinal virtues alone if one wishes to drop anything that is distinctively Christian) challenge one much more profoundly than the modern moral codes. They define qualities that require deep thought. They try to sum up the essence of what a person ought to be and present one with the demand that, throughout one's life, one should aim to form this essence. They carry the patina of time and of inherited wisdom. They convey a sense that one's life is immensely meaningful and that one has a purpose, which is to better oneself, and that the struggle to achieve this purpose continues until death.

Whatever one thinks about the virtues in question (post-1968, temperance may have been knocked off its perch and fortitude may also be less central to people's consciousness than it used to be) they are potentially a more powerful educational tool than the ones we currently use. By being offset against their corresponding vices they also make clear that 'respect' has its limits, sending the much-needed anti-relativistic message that there is much about humankind, and probably about oneself, that one ought not to respect.

And if anyone is thinking that Aquinas's view of the world sounds too 'holier than thou', he also had this to say:

> It is against reason to be burdensome to others, showing no amusement and acting as a wet blanket. Those without a sense of fun, who never say anything ridiculous, and are cantankerous with those who do, these are vicious, and are called grumpy and rude.[6]

Aquinas's 13th-century analysis of what is needed to enable us to live a virtuous life is intelligent, wise and nuanced. I can imagine many far worse starting points for the development of a contemporary school's policy on moral education.

Education with and without God

One reason for including Aquinas in this volume was to show a thinker for whom the ultimate ends of education and of human life lie beyond this world. Most of the other thinkers, by comparison with Aquinas, are largely or exclusively this-worldly in their concerns, but, despite his relative isolation in this company, there is nothing eccentric about Aquinas.

He is in fact much more representative of Western traditions than the others, reflecting as he does two millennia of Christianity during most of which the prevailing belief was in the immortality of the soul and in life after death. If one's ultimate goal is eternal life and union with God after death, and if one's hope of achieving this is related to how one lives one's life here on earth, the fundamental purposes of education must be, and often have been, very different.

One of the ironies about the late 20th century enthusiasm for 'lifelong learning' – one of those buzz phrases that sweeps the modern educational world from time to time, and is rarely critically examined by those who take it up – was the assumption of many of its historically ignorant proponents that it was something new. As we have seen, it was already central to Plato and Aristotle's ideas about education. With St Augustine, Aquinas and other Christian thinkers it acquired the new dimension of preparing human beings for eternal life. Indeed, how one fulfilled one's God-given potential, how one's thoughts and actions reflected the cardinal and theological virtues, and the extent to which one's soul was lit up with the love of God and of Jesus Christ, would determine one's fate in the next world.

In the contemporary Western world, even among those who say they believe in God or call themselves Christian, there is often little left of Aquinas's powerful meta-narrative. Even among those schools that still carry his name one can find mission statements, warm and encouraging though they may be, that are indistinguishable from those of any other non-faith school of their time:

> It is our aim here at ... and St Thomas Aquinas to foster a caring and loving environment by the encouragement of all members of the school community.
>
> We aim to ensure a welcoming friendly approach where parents and visitors feel comfortable and are positively encouraged to participate in the life of the school.
>
> For each child entrusted to our care, we seek to provide a haven of security and safety that will enable and encourage confidence and happiness to flourish in a community founded on love and respect.

There is little sign here of the influence of the *Summa*. This UK school's Thomist counterpart in Texas similarly nowhere explains on its website that when pupils are asked to 'soar' this might refer to anything other than success hereunder.

None of this is to criticize or to suggest that things can or should be different. Where beliefs wane, if one is an agnostic or unbeliever oneself, discretion is the prudent option. All that one *might* do is reflect on what *might* be said to have been lost (or, of course, gained) in education, as a result of the 'melancholy, long, withdrawing roar' of the 'Sea of Faith' which, in the words of Matthew Arnold, school inspector and poet,

> was once, too, at the full, and round earth's shore
> Lay like the folds of a bright girdle furled.[7]

But even that is a question probably best left to the individual, given the variety of perspectives that there are on the issue, though the disappearance from an individual's education of that sense of having a part to play in a much wider and supremely important story, and the drama and wonder attached to this, can perhaps be noted in conclusion as the current writer's occasional sense of loss.

*****

Aquinas writes

Aquinas on God as the supreme teacher

> Can humans teach each other? There are several different reasons to think that only God teaches and should be called teacher.
>
> In the Gospel of Matthew it says, 'There is one who is your teacher... Do not allow anyone to call you teacher.' The Gloss on this passage says, 'Do not let this divine honour be attributed to you or any human, or else you will be usurping what belongs only to God.' Therefore, only God can teach or be called teacher... My responses ... are as follows ... we should say that God's command to his disciples not to let themselves be called teacher is not an absolute

prohibition. We are prohibited to call someone a teacher as if he were the supreme teacher. The point is that we should not place unlimited trust in human wisdom, but only in the divine truth which speaks in us through an impression in us of its likeness and by which we can judge all things.

De magistro (On Teaching)

Aquinas on teaching as fertilising the seeds within us

...before virtuous qualities are fully actual in us they pre-exist in our natural inclinations, which are the seeds of virtue. Through practice they are brought to their proper completion.

The same sort of thing should be said about learning and teaching. The seeds of knowledge pre-exist in us. These are the elementary ideas (both simple and complex) which we understand immediately by the light of our own minds. From these common principles all other principles of knowledge grow, like a plant grows from a seed. Therefore, when from these common notions a mind moves into an actual state of knowing some more specific things (which before it knew only potentially and at a very general level), then someone can be said to have acquired knowledge.

De magistro (On Teaching)

Aquinas on the balance between teaching and discovery

Therefore, just as someone can be healed in two ways – first by the action of nature only, second by the collaboration of nature and medicine – so also there are two ways of acquiring knowledge. First, when the mind moves by its own natural power to an understanding of things previously unknown to it. This is called discovery (*inventio*). Second, when the mind is helped by an outside power of reason. This is called teaching (*disciplina*).

Now in those things that come about by nature and art, art works in the same way and uses the same sorts of tools as nature. For just as nature uses warmth to heal someone suffering from a cold, so also does a doctor. This is why art is said to imitate nature. Similarly, in the acquisition of knowledge, the teacher leads the student to the knowledge of things the student previously did not know in the same way that someone leads himself to discover what he previously did not know.

De magistro (On Teaching)

Aquinas on the two sources of wisdom

Wisdom by its very name implies an eminent abundance of knowledge, which enables a man to judge of all things, for everyone can judge well what he fully knows. Some have this abundance of knowledge as a result of learning and study, added to a native quickness of intelligence; and this is the wisdom which Aristotle counts among the intellectual virtues. But others have wisdom as a result of the kinship which they have with the things of God; it is of such that the Apostle says: 'The spiritual man judges all things'. The

Gift of Wisdom gives a man this eminent knowledge as a result of his union with God, and this union can only be by love, for 'he who cleaveth to God is of one spirit with Him'. And therefore the Gift of Wisdom leads to a godlike and explicit gaze at revealed truth, which mere faith holds in a human manner as it were disguised.

(*Scriptum super Sententiis* (Commentary on the Sentences), D. 35, q. 2, art.1, quoted in Knowles, D, *The Evolution of Medieval Thought*, p. 268.)

Aquinas on the cardinal virtues

Virtue is a habit (in the sense of disposition to act in certain ways) which is always for good. (*Summa Theologica*, 1a-2ae, lv.4)
Some faults are manifestly hostile to prudence – impulsiveness, inconstancy, also negligence which is against caution. Others are caricatures which abuse the features of prudence – worldly prudence, cunning and slyness, fraud, and over-anxiety. *(Summa Theologica, 2a- 2ae. liii, Prologue)*

In the display of courage two characteristics should be considered, the premeditated deliberateness and the habit of discipline; it is the latter that most appears in emergencies. (*Summa Theologica*, 2a-2ae. cxxiii.9)

Intemperance is superfluous concupiscence... A child is spoilt when left to his own devices: A horse not broken in becometh stubborn; and a child left to himself becometh headstrong. Concupiscence grows stronger with gratification; as Augustine says, when lust is served it becomes custom, and when custom is not resisted it becomes necessity. (*Summa Theologica*, 2a-2ae. cxlii.2)

References

1. Knowles, D, *The Evolution of Medieval Thought*, p. 265, 1962, Longmans, London. Josef Pieper also says that 'Thomas was neither Platonist nor Aristotelian; he was both' (quoted in Davies, B, *The Thought of Thomas Aquinas*, p. 16, 1992, Clarendon Press, Oxford).

2. Jolibert, B, introduction to D'Aquin, Saint Thomas, *De l'enseignement (De Magistro)*, 2nd edition, pp. 11-14, 17, 20, 2003, Klincksieck, Paris.

3. Aquinas, De magistro (On Teaching), in *Quaestiones Disputatae de Veritate (Disputed Questions of Truth)*. Aquinas Translation Project, De Sales University: www4.desales.edu/~philtheo/loughlin/ATP/index.html

4. Tate, N, *Conscience and the curriculum*, in 'Education for Good' (symposium proceedings of a conference held at Church House, Westminster, by St Gabriel's Trust), 2000; Hoffmann, T, *Conscience and Synderesis*, in Davies, B, and Stump, E, *The Oxford Handbook of Aquinas*, pp. 255-264, 2012, Oxford University Press, Oxford.

5. Aquinas, *Summa theologica, 2a-2ae.* cvii. 1 ad. 2, quoted in Davies, B, *The Thought of Thomas Aquinas*, p. 261, 1992, Clarendon Press, Oxford.

6. Aquinas, *Summa theologica, 2a-2ae. clxviii.2.*

Chapter 4

Donkeys laden with books: Michel de Montaigne

MICHEL DE Montaigne (1533-92), according to a recent French philosopher, 'is one of our great philosophers of education, with Plato before him and Rousseau after him'.[1] As a thinker Montaigne was not a creator of philosophic systems like Plato or Aquinas. The world for Montaigne was too diverse, and opinions about it too varied, for him to feel able to lay down many certainties. Nothing could have been further from his thoughts than the idea of creating some imaginary utopia, whether educational or political.

Yet his views about education were clear and strong and underpinned by powerful humanist ideals. His essay *De l'institution des enfans* (On the education of children), the main source of his views, is only 37 pages long, but contains enough to keep one thinking throughout a lifetime concerned with education.

Montaigne's great work is his Essays (*Essais*), published in stages from 1580 onwards. The word *essai,* which he invented as a literary term, and which then found its way from French into English and other languages, means 'trial' or 'attempt'. Montaigne, with these short non-fiction pieces, saw himself as *trying out* his opinions on a variety of subjects with a view to helping him to find out which were robust, which should be rejected, and which needed to be developed further.

There are essays on friendship, cruelty, the art of conversation, relationships, idleness, imagination, pedantry, the uncertainty of judgment, even on topics such as cannibals, smells and the custom of wearing clothes. Montaigne lived in the aftermath of the Renaissance, with its rediscovery of many aspects of antiquity and its challenge to traditional thinking, and of the Reformation, with its attacks on the position of the Catholic Church. It was also a time when Europeans were exploring many new parts of the world and bringing back accounts of very different ways of life. It was in this context that Montaigne strove to understand himself and his own opinions and, through this, humankind.

There have been many great works of self-reflection – and we will draw on another of the authors of these when dealing with Rousseau – but Montaigne's must be one of the most modest and truthful. As one reads his essays he comes across as clear-sighted, open-minded, endlessly curious, dispassionate about himself and his failings (not endlessly self-justifying as Rousseau can be), humorous, and an excellent *raconteur.*

His aim is self-enquiry in the context of learning and thinking about the world and how best both to live a good life and, when the time came, to die a good death. Although faithful to the Church and a practising Catholic, he saw reason and religious faith as separate domains and in matters unconnected with faith was sceptical about received opinions and orthodoxies. In this respect, as one of his recent translators and commentators has said, 'he seems to inhabit a world whose intellectual assumptions are close to our own'.[2]

Montaigne, born into a wealthy legal and landowning family in the south-west of France, was sent away to boarding school at the age of six and then attended the universities of Bordeaux and Toulouse. He held a number of legal posts and spent a year and a half at the court of Charles IX. On his father's death in 1568 he inherited the family estates at Montaigne in the Dordogne to which he moved in 1571 and where, in the tower of his chateau, surrounded by an extensive library, he gave himself up to study and the writing of his Essays.

But he was a man of action as well as a scholar and during the remaining 20 years of his life his seclusion was frequently disturbed: by the civil and religious wars raging at the time in France, in which he fought, by outbreaks of plague which forced him to flee from his home, and by his election as Mayor of Bordeaux, a post previously held by his father.

He also had a period of travel in Germany, Switzerland and Italy, searching for a cure to the gallstones that had begun to plague him. All these experiences provided food for reflection and are mirrored in his writings. His last years were spent revising and adding to his Essays, making them ever more personal and revealing.

★★★★★

> ...the most difficult and important challenge facing human beings is how to bring up and educate children. As in farming the preparations before planting are straightforward and sure, as is the planting itself; but once what is planted begins to grow there are all sorts of ways in which one can raise it, and it becomes difficult. It is the same with men: it is not troublesome to plant them, but as soon as they are born one takes on many cares, fears and tasks in order to train them and bring them up.
>
> Montaigne, M, *L'éducation des enfants. Du pédantisme et De l'institution des enfans*, p.39, 1999, Artea, Paris, translation by the author

> One must not just acquire wisdom, but benefit from it (Cicero). Dionysius mocked scholars who study the bad qualities of Ulysses but are unaware of their own; musicians who tune their flutes but do not

regulate their morals; orators who study how to talk about justice, but not how to act justly.

Montaigne, M, *L'éducation des enfants*, p.20, translation by the author

Introduction: Montaigne's own education

One reason why education is of enduring interest is because everyone has experienced it, or at least the effects of its absence. Montaigne's father, whom he greatly revered, took a close interest in Michel's education and had views about education that his son recounts in his *Essays*. Having been told that the sole reason why the moderns failed to reach the intellectual heights of the Greeks and Romans was the length of time it took them to learn these two languages (an opinion that the mature Michel did not share), his father employed a tutor, supported by two assistant tutors, to take charge of Michel when he was still a babe in arms.

They carried him and, as he grew up, accompanied him everywhere, speaking to him only in Latin. His father and mother were also only allowed to address him in whatever Latin they were able to come up with, as were the servants, with the result that the whole household in time, Montaigne tells us, became 'so latinised that it spilled over into the neighbouring villages, where, resulting from this usage, you can still find several Latin names for tools and for artisans'.

As a result Michel knew no French or Gascon until he was six but in Latin was totally fluent. '...Without art, without books, without grammar, without rules, without whips and without tears', he wrote, 'I had learned Latin as pure as that which my schoolteacher knew'.[3]

His father's plan for Greek was to have it *taught*, but 'in a new way, as a sort of game or sport'. His idea, Montaigne added, was 'to bring me to love knowledge and duty by my own choice, without forcing my will, and to educate my soul entirely through gentleness and freedom'.[4] Like many educational experiments, however, this second one fizzled out, partly because Michel's father was so 'extremely frightened of failure in a matter which meant so much to him (that) he finally let himself be carried away by the common opinion' and at the age of six sent Michel away to boarding school.[5]

Montaigne's seven years at the College of Guienne left him with strong views about how education ought *not* to be conducted. Despite the school having the reputation of being the best in France, and despite his father having hand-picked some outstanding tutors, 'for all that, it was still a school', observed Montaigne, in a dismissive aside worthy of the 20th-century de-schooler Ivan Illich.[6] He was free, however, to follow his own literary interests, devouring Ovid's *Metamorphoses* at the age of seven or eight, and quickly moving on to Virgil's *Aeneid* and to Terence and Plautus.He also took chief parts in performances of Latin tragedies, a practice he commended as a way of encouraging in children a love of learning. His school experiences were clearly not unpleasant, but his overall judgment, like that of some modern school inspector, was based solely on an evaluation of outcomes, and it was pretty harsh. 'I left College at 13', he concluded, 'having "completed the course" (as they put it); and in truth I now have nothing to show for it'. [7]

Educating for wisdom, virtue and character

Montaigne's interest was in the education of gentlemen, those who in his society were going to be in charge of land and property and of the affairs of state. His views need to be seen in this context. This does not make them any less relevant to a modern democracy which aspires to opening up the very best of education to all.

As with Aristotle and Plato, Montaigne's view of education was that it should make people better and wiser. This was the acid test. If it did not, if all it did was fill men's heads with knowledge, without forming their judgment and giving them the practical wisdom and virtue needed to enable them to respond appropriately and ethically to the many challenges of our lives, all was in vain. 'If our souls do not move with a better motion and if we do not have a healthier judgment', he wrote, 'then I would just as soon that our pupil should spend his time playing tennis: at least his body would become more agile.'[8] It is in this sense that Montaigne's view of education can be seen as 'utilitarian'. The test was whether or not the education fulfilled the aims for which it was intended and had practical and visible effects in everyday life.

This did not mean, however, that Montaigne was opposed to the transmission of knowledge. He had a deep veneration for the great thinkers of the past. References to Plato, Aristotle, Plutarch, Seneca, Cicero and St Augustine, and to contemporary writers, can be found on every page of his *Essays*. Studying these writings could make one better and wiser, but only if one read them actively, with an open mind, taking nothing on trust, deciding to what extent one agreed with them, making their opinions one's own, and thinking about the implications for one's own life.

It was a question not of how much one has learned but of how well one has learned it. Montaigne distrusted the kind of 'book learning' he found among teachers in his own day and in schools that flogged pupils 'into retaining a pannierful of learning'. If this is what you do, he wrote, all you produce are 'donkeys laden with books.'[9] He also valued the kind of learning that comes from ordinary experience. A fishwife on the Petit Pont in Paris, he wrote, will talk as clearly and well about the things she knows than any grammarian who has spent many years pointlessly learning linguistic rules.

Similarly, any experience can be a source of learning, even if it is simply a matter of observing other people's follies and weaknesses and using them as an opportunity for reflection about oneself. '...For such an apprenticeship', Montaigne said, 'everything we see can serve as an excellent book: some cheating by a page, some stupidity on the part of a lackey, something said at table, all supply new material.' Despite this, Montaigne did not reject books, nor did he suggest that people can learn solely on their own without the help of teachers.

Montaigne was keen that education helped to form character – a person's disposition to think and act in certain ways. A key component of character, as with Aristotle and Aquinas, was moderation or temperance. Throughout his *Essays* Montaigne shows by example what it is to think carefully before making a judgment, take into account all the circumstances of a particular case, be willing to listen to other points of view, change one's mind, and admit one's mistakes. These are the qualities, Montaigne thought, needed by people if they are to be virtuous and wise. They are the qualities needed by gentlemen and by rulers. They are also the qualities needed by all of us in the modern world, whatever our age, gender or status, in our private lives and in our role as citizens.

How to teach and how not to teach

Montaigne was devastating in his indictment of contemporary education: it failed to address education's key purposes; it bore little relation to life outside the classroom; it involved a great deal of pointless memorisation; it ignored personal experience; it failed to interest children in what they were doing; and, where it succeeded in its narrow pedantic aims, it gave pupils a false sense of achievement and made them arrogant and conceited. As someone who hated cruelty and violence, whether in France during the civil wars or in the brutal European conquest of the Americas, Montaigne was also damning about the prevalent use of corporal punishment in the education of the young:

> I condemn all violence in the education of tender minds which are being trained for honour and freedom. In rigour and constraint there is always something servile, and I hold that you will never achieve by force what you cannot achieve by reason, intelligence and skill... (had I had sons myself) I would have loved to make their hearts overflow with openness and frankness. I have never seen caning achieve anything except making souls more cowardly or more maliciously stubborn.[10]

Montaigne had no sons but six daughters, only one of whom survived more than a few months. With Leonor, his 'only daughter who ... escaped that calamity', he had corrected any childish faults with nothing 'but words – gentle ones at that'.

One area of study that Montaigne recommended was history, which he describes as his favourite pursuit, and especially for the stories of famous individuals that it contained. One book constantly quoted throughout the *Essays* is Plutarch's *Lives* of famous Greeks and Romans. These are not 'great men' in the sense of heroes; indeed Plutarch puts contrasting figures together in pairs so that the reader is better able to judge both their virtues and moral failings. For Montaigne they provided a never-ending stimulus to think about oneself and one's own life and to refine one's moral judgment. One of Montaigne's particular favourites was Plutarch's life of the legendary Spartan ruler Lycurgus, whom he praises for appreciating the crucial importance of education for the well-being of the state, focusing on practical, active learning rather than formal teaching, and creating a state whose people were noted for their simplicity of manners, brevity of speech, self-discipline, courage, and commitment to the common good.[11]

Educational realism

As well as being solely concerned in his essay *On educating children* with boys of good family *(enfants de maison)*, Montaigne also counselled teachers to be realistic about the limits of their ability to educate all children. Although believing that a person's disposition to wisdom and goodness could be enhanced, he also took for granted that individual children had a certain 'nature' which would play a major role in determining how they would end up.

There were noble souls (*grandes âmes*) and low souls (*basses âmes*) and the teacher would sometimes have to admit that there was little chance of the latter turning into the former. This distinction was less about intelligence than about character or personality. It had nothing to do with social class: Montaigne was quick to point out that folly and baseness could be found at the highest levels of society and virtue and wisdom among the lowest (including among peoples whom many of his contemporaries would have dismissed as 'savages' or 'heathen'). His views emerge in the following passage:

> Were our pupil's disposition so bizarre that he would rather hear a tall story than the account of a great voyage or a wise discussion; that at the sound of a drum calling the youthful ardour of his comrades to arms he would turn aside for the drum of a troop of jugglers; that he would actually find it no more delightful and pleasant to return victorious covered with the dust of battle than after winning a prize for tennis or dancing: then I know no remedy except that his tutor should quickly strangle him when nobody is looking or apprentice him to make fairy-cakes in some goodly town – even if he were the heir of a Duke – following Plato's precept that functions should be allocated not according to the endowments of men's fathers but the endowments of their souls.[12]

I quote this, both as revealing an aspect of Montaigne's thought and because it is no good simply reading those things that people in the past said about education which reinforce our contemporary viewpoint. If we do that we never step outside our own little world; we use the past simply as something to be mined in order to make us feel good about ourselves. Montaigne's amusing but possibly tasteless joke about strangling would probably never get past a nervous modern editor or, if it did, its author would be instantly, if metaphorically, battered to death under a hail of hostile tweets from jugglers, dancers, tennis players and the association of bakers of fairy-cakes.

Montaigne was tolerant of diversity, accepted that customs and beliefs were relative, supported religious freedom, was humane towards children, and saw merit in people of all classes. But, as this passage shows, he also had a clear vision of the kind of human beings we ought to be and what it meant to make best use of our lives, and this most emphatically did not include the 16th-century equivalents of watching *Big Brother* or thinking that participation in *Strictly Come Dancing* is the height of human achievement.

The confident public articulation of what constitutes the good life has characterised all previous societies, right up to recent times. Human beings have been habitually 'judgmental' in the ways that Montaigne is in this passage. With mass democracy, the spread of relativism and cultural permissiveness, and the decline of religious belief, this has become increasingly unacceptable. One may still criticise behaviours that adversely affect the body, as witnessed by the contemporary preoccupation with health and safety, but not – at least without peril – those which might damage what Montaigne would have called 'the soul'. This leaves the educator with two questions.

First, what impact does this wider culture have on the expectations of children and parents about education, and on teachers and how they see themselves and their role? Education is shaped by its social and cultural context much more than it shapes it, but if it wishes to be more active in its shaping it needs to know first how it is being shaped.

Second, what are the aspirations that modern education systems *should have* for the development of children's minds and sensibilities (or 'souls' if one wishes to stick with Montaigne's word) when the wider culture of the society is deeply egalitarian and terrified of seeming 'judgmental' about anything that is not illegal, unhealthy or unsafe?

*****

How Montaigne can help us think about education today

Modern progressive education is not as new as it likes to claim

Montaigne's main legacy as an educational thinker arises from his ability to get to the heart of the matter. First, the main aim of education is to help us lead better lives, to be happier, wiser and more virtuous. This should never be forgotten and should determine everything we do. Second, we should judge an education solely by its ability to achieve this end. The evidence for success will lie in people's characters, in their actions and in their lives, not in how well they have learned their grammar or how many quotations from Horace they can reel off. Third, these ends are most likely to be promoted and these outcomes achieved if pupils are treated respectfully, are active participants in their own learning, and are taught, above all through practice and repetition, to understand rather than just to memorise and to know.

It is often assumed within the educational world that the third of these features – a 'progressive' educational method – is a product of our own enlightened times or at least that its origins lie with relatively modern figures such as Rousseau, Froebel, and Dewey. This is clearly not so, as the writings of Plato, Aristotle and Aquinas, and most notably Montaigne, have now shown. The modern educational world can be insufferably self-satisfied. It is good for it to be reminded that others, long ago, already came to similar conclusions and often articulated them with greater wisdom and elegance than by parroting slogans about teachers having to become the 'sage on the stage' or the 'guide on the side' as if these were stating some new truth.

How modern education has contributed to the loss of a cultural heritage

Montaigne's account of his own education should make us think. By the age of seven or eight he was reading, by choice, Ovid's *Metamorphoses*, a lengthy verse narrative that, even in translation, can challenge educated modern readers. He then moved on to Virgil, Terence and Plautus, again not because he had to but because they gripped his attention.

This kind of early exposure to literature now often reserved for higher education (or even side-lined there because of its inaccessibility) was not uncommon in previous ages. The 19th-century philosopher John Stuart Mill had read most of the major Greek and Latin classics in the original language, as well as many works of history in English, by the age of ten. The 20th-century French philosopher and writer Simone de Beauvoir went to university at the age of 17 having read, outside her formal studies, more of the great writers of the past than most arts graduates of leading universities go on to do in the course of a lifetime. We know of these individuals' reading because they became famous and wrote autobiographies, but access to great and demanding literature at an early age was not in the past just reserved for the small group that these days is categorised as 'gifted' and provided with educational opportunities not available to others.[13]

Contrast the reading of a Montaigne, John Stuart Mill or Simone de Beauvoir with the requirements of the English literature examination taken in recent years at age 16 in England by those students who have chosen this as an option (the rest do not even have this much) and which is based on a two-year course that comprises the following: two relatively short modern texts (such as *Animal Farm*), one Shakespeare play, another 'literary heritage' text (such as *Pride and Prejudice*), and a poetry anthology.

More serious than meagre demands such as these – and one accepts that examinations cannot assess the whole of a student's reading – is the lack of encouragement from the surrounding environment to start undertaking, at this age, serious adult reading. Children may still read a great deal and may be keen, and even keener than in the past, to learn in all sorts of other ways, but this early and often life-changing contact with what for hundreds of years have been seen as the great pillars of western literary civilization has largely disappeared. The negative cultural consequences of this for the future, and whether anything can be done about them, raise issues for education one never sees discussed.

Monolinguals should be counted among 'the disadvantaged'

Montaigne's own education in terms of languages is also instructive. He was fluent in French, Gascon and Latin, well-read in Greek and, when on his travels, switched to writing in Italian in his diary the moment he crossed over into Italy. In this he was not unusual among educated people of his time.

Montaigne's ideas about language learning, based on how his own father had brought him up, involved exposure to other languages at an early age, total immersion, and an active pedagogy designed to make learning fun. Complete immersion in a language, having it as the language of instruction for half, most or all of the curriculum for at least part of one's schooling, rather than just learning it as a foreign language, remains the most effective, and probably the only, way outside the home of enabling children to grow up bilingual or multilingual.

Language learning is also very much a question of the attitude one has towards it. Montaigne and his educated contemporaries, and their successors over the following centuries, often saw it as the essential accomplishment of an educated person to be able at least to read in other European languages, and this at a time when travel to other countries was much more difficult and infrequent than it is today. Being able to read Virgil, Dante, and, in due course, Montaigne himself, in the original, was for some people an important part of that literary culture which 20th-century writers such as T S Eliot and Ezra Pound were still taking for granted but which has been largely lost outside the academic world.

The problems are particularly acute in English-speaking countries in which (Canada excepted) opportunities for dual language or immersion education are rare or non-existent. English-speakers may become fluent in a foreign language if they go to work or live in another country, or have a partner who speaks another language, but otherwise tend to remain firmly monolingual. For most practical purposes the global spread of English removes the incentive to learn other languages.

The loss that comes from monolingualism is, not surprisingly, rarely appreciated by monolinguals themselves. It is not just the practical and economic advantages of being able to converse in another language, but also the proven cognitive benefits of having a mind able to switch constantly from one language to another and the fresh insights that come from seeing the world, as Montaigne did, through the prism of a number of different thought systems.[14]

When I look back at the educational initiatives I have been involved in over the years one of those that gives me most satisfaction was the decision at the International School of Geneva, while I was its director-general, to move towards dual language provision for everyone, in other words towards a situation in which part of the curriculum (50% on one of our campuses) was taught through the medium of French and the rest through the medium of English. Teaching a foreign language as a subject has a poor track record of success unless one is also bombarded with the language outside school, as the Dutch and the Scandinavians tend to be but as English-speaking countries generally are not; using it as the medium of instruction puts it centre stage and gives it purpose.

Properly judging the outcomes of education

Montaigne felt that education should be judged by its outcomes in relation to its aims. This may be obvious, but it is a way of looking at education that many educational providers, over the centuries, have ignored. They have failed to think through the 'why' of what they have been doing, focusing instead solely on the 'how'. It was because Montaigne started with the 'why', and had a clear sense of what this meant, that he rejected many of the practices of his own time as not contributing to, and indeed as undermining, what he felt to be education's fundamental ends.

In recent decades a concern with the outcomes of education has become a feature of many national education systems around the world. The pressures are largely economic, arising from globalisation, but also, in an era of league tables, from the *amour propre* of nation states and politicians. It can be a healthy preoccupation, highlighting how vast sums of expenditure on education can achieve little or nothing and helping to identify factors that contribute to educational success. The problem comes from governments' almost exclusive focus on quantitative measures, and above all on ones that relate solely to levels of achievement in literacy and numeracy.

These are important indices but, if one takes a broader view of education's purposes, such as Montaigne's, do not reveal the whole picture. A highly literate and numerate population, or one with high levels of participation in post-school education, does not necessarily mean a population that, in Montaigne's terms, is wiser and more virtuous. This can only be judged by taking into account a much wider range of factors.

If a country is plagued by high levels of relationship breakdown, child abuse, drug-taking, drunkenness, gang-related crime, suicide, and pornography use, is witnessing a decline in civic responsibility, political involvement and manners, contains minorities reluctant to form part of a common culture, is over-preoccupied with individual rights, is drifting towards censorship and self-censorship in response to increasing diversity, is flooded with low quality mass entertainment, and swept by media-induced episodes of voyeurism and mass hysteria in response to natural disasters, the deaths of celebrities and comments that someone foolishly put in a tweet, what judgment, if any, does this pass on how that society has been educated during the previous 20 to 30 years? What does it tell us about how far education's fundamental purposes are being achieved? One might reply that education cannot solve all or most of the world's problems, which is true, but is it focusing on the right ones?

*****

Montaigne writes

Montaigne on judging the effectiveness of an education

> My pupil will not say his lesson: he will do it. He will rehearse his lessons in his actions. You will then see whether he is wise in what he takes on, good and just in what he does, gracious and sound in what he says, resilient in illnesses, modest in his sports, temperate in his pleasures, indifferent to the taste of his food, be it fish or flesh, wine or water; orderly in domestic matters: 'as a man who knows how to make his education into a rule of life not a means of showing off; who can control himself and obey his own principles' (Cicero). The true mirror of our discourse is the course of our lives.
>
> Montaigne, M, *The Essays of Michel de Montaigne*, translated by Screech, M A, pp. 188-9

Montaigne on active learning and listening to what pupils have to say

> Tutors never stop bellowing into our ears, as if pouring stuff down a funnel, and our job is just to repeat what they have been saying to us. I would want our tutor to correct that and, from the beginning, according to the type of mind he is dealing with, get it to show what it

is capable of by making it try things out, choosing and judging them itself; and with the tutor sometimes leading the pupil on and, at other times, letting the pupil lead himself. I do not want the tutor to come up with everything himself and be the only one to speak; I want him to listen to his pupil. Socrates and then Archesilaus made their pupils speak first and then spoke themselves. 'The authority of those who teach is often harmful to those who want to learn' (Cicero).

Montaigne, M, *L'éducation des enfants*, p.42, translation by the author

Montaigne on modesty and on sometimes holding one's tongue

In the social intercourse of men I have often observed this vice: that instead of trying to learn about others we put all our efforts into drawing attention to ourselves, and are more concerned with pleading our own goods than buying new ones. Silence and modesty are very proper qualities in our dealings with others. The boy will be trained to be sparing and frugal with his talents, when he has acquired some; and not to show offence at silliness or tall tales related in his presence, as it is rude and bad-mannered to complain about things not to one's taste. Let him stick to correcting himself and not come across as reproaching others for doing things that he would not do or as setting himself up against general custom. 'One can be wise without ostentation or arrogance, (Seneca). Let him avoid imperious and uncivil manners and that puerile ambition of wanting to stand out by being different, and of making a name for himself through being hypercritical or up-to-date with the latest fashions.

Montaigne, M, *L'éducation des enfants*, pp. 49-50, translation by the author

Montaigne on what philosophising should really be like

...things have now reached such a state that even among men of intelligence philosophy means something fantastical and vain, without value or usefulness, both in opinion and practice. The cause lies in chop-logic which has captured all the approaches. It is a great mistake to portray Philosophy with a haughty, frowning, terrifying face, or as inaccessible to the young. Whoever clapped that wan and frightening mask on her face! There is nothing more lovely, more happy and gay – I almost said more amorously playful. What she preaches is all feast and fun. A sad and gloomy mien shows you have mistaken her address.

Montaigne, M, *The Essays of Michel de Montaigne*, translated by Screech, M A, p. 180

Montaigne on learning from experience and from one's own mistakes

Were I a good pupil there is enough, I find, in my own experience to make me wise. Whoever recalls to mind his last bout of choler and the excesses to which that fevered passion brought him sees the ugliness of that distemper better than in Aristotle and conceives even more just a loathing for it...

When I find that I have been convicted of an erroneous opinion by another's argument, it is not so much a case of my learning something new he has told me nor of how ignorant I was of a particular matter – there is not much profit in that – but of learning of my infirmity in general and of the treacherous ways of my intellect. From that I can reform the whole lump.

With all my mistakes I do the same, and I think this rule is of great use to me in my life... To learn that we have done or said a stupid thing is nothing: we must learn a more ample and important lesson: that we are but blockheads.

Montaigne, M, *The Essays of Michel de Montaigne*, translated by Screech, M A, pp.1218-9

References

1. Vieillard-Baron, J-L, *Montaigne et l'éducation humaniste*, in Magnard, P, and Gontier, P (ed.), *Montaigne*, p. 205, 2010, Les Éditions du Cerf, Paris.
2. Screech, M A, *Montaigne and Melancholy*, p. 1, 2000, Rowman & Littlefield, Lanham, Maryland.
3. Montaigne, M, *The Essays of Michel de Montaigne*, translated by Screech, M, p. 195, 1991, Allen Lane, The Penguin Press, London.
4. Ibid, pp. 195-196.
5. Ibid, p. 196.
6. Ibid, p. 197. See Illich, I, *Deschooling Society*, 1995, Marion Boyars, London.
7. Ibid, p. 197. All the evidence, however, suggests that, as often when people look back over their education, Montaigne was wrong in this judgment.
8. Ibid, p.156.
9. Ibid, p.199.
10. Ibid, 'On the affection of fathers for their children', p. 437.
11. Vieillard-Baron, J-L, op. cit., pp. 216-25.
12. Montaigne, M, *The Essays of Michel de Montaigne*, translated by Screech, M, op. cit., p. 182. The reference to strangling was omitted by his adopted daughter Marie de Gournay in the posthumous 1595 edition of the Essays.
13. John Stuart Mill, *Autobiography*, ed. Ryan, A, 2006, Penguin, London; Simone de Beauvoir, *Mémoires d'une jeune fille rangée*, 1958, Gallimard, Paris.
14. One of the best introductions to bilingualism and bilingual education is Baker, C, *Foundations of Bilingual Education and Bilingualism*, 2011, Multilingual Matters, Bristol.

Chapter 5

Virtue, wisdom, breeding and learning: John Locke

JOHN LOCKE (1632-1704) is one of England's greatest and most influential philosophers. He also wrote a detailed treatise on education which went through many editions and was translated into other languages.

Locke's contribution to philosophy was wide-ranging, embracing philosophy of mind and language, epistemology, and moral and political philosophy. His two most influential works were *An Essay Concerning Human Understanding* and *Two Treatises of Government*. The impact of these on the subsequent development of philosophy and on political theory and practice was massive. He was also a proponent of ideas about toleration that have helped to shape the modern Western world.

But Locke was not just a philosopher and not just, or mainly, a scholar. As well as for many years an Oxford University lecturer in Greek and Rhetoric, he also qualified as a physician, was a member of the Royal Society, and a friend of some of the main scientists of his day such as Isaac Newton and Robert Boyle. He created a large Herbarium which contains some of the earliest surviving specimens of English wild flowers.[1] He also wrote about theology, economics, monetary policy, and, in some detail, education. He was simultaneously active in the public life of his time, holding a number of major public offices.

John Locke came from a family of the lesser gentry that had supported the cause of Parliament during the mid-17th century English Civil War. He was educated at Westminster School, where he received the kind of education of which later he was to be so critical, and Oxford University, which left him unimpressed. Despite taking up teaching posts at Oxford immediately following his graduation, his interests increasingly lay elsewhere: in medicine, science, philosophy and public life.

In the late 1660s Locke became the physician, personal secretary and adviser of the politician Anthony Ashley Cooper, later Lord Shaftesbury, remaining close to him for the next 15 years and sharing in his varying fortunes. Shaftesbury was one of the ablest and most controversial politicians of his day, a crafty opportunist who also genuinely believed in religious toleration (at least for Protestants) and in the need to limit the power of the restored Stuart monarchy. Partly under his influence, Locke's previously conservative views – characteristic of Oxford dons of his day – moved in a more liberal direction.

Shaftesbury's chequered career reached its climax in the late 1670s with his determined but unsuccessful attempts to get parliament to pass an Exclusion Bill designed to keep Charles II's brother and heir, James, Duke of York, a Catholic, from the throne. This, together with Shaftesbury's involvement in plots to overthrow the king and even murder him and his brother, forced him into exile in Holland in 1682, where shortly afterwards he died.

As Shaftesbury's associate, Locke also fell under suspicion. Though not involved in these plots, he too felt obliged to leave the country in a hurry, remaining in exile in Holland for the next five years. He was deprived of his posts at Oxford and even spent a time in hiding under an assumed name.

In1688 mounting opposition to the Catholic and autocratic James II, who had succeeded his brother in 1685, finally came to a head, precipitating the 'Glorious Revolution' that drove James from the throne. The Dutch leader William of Orange and his wife Mary, James's daughter, were invited to take over as joint monarchs on the basis of a new political settlement founded on the principles of constitutional monarchy, parliamentary government, toleration, and an independent judiciary.

As an associate and supporter of the new monarchs, who had a high opinion of him, Locke returned to England in their company, in a ship whose flag bore the motto: *Pro Religione et Libertate.* He turned down William's offer of an ambassadorship, though accepted a more minor post and later agreed to join a new Council of Trade, continuing in this latter role until 1700.

When Locke returned to England in 1688 he was aged 56. Although he had been writing intermittently for 30 years nothing of his had yet been published. In the next few years a flurry of publications ensued, including his *Two Treatises of Government* which, though written before 1688, provided a justification for the Glorious Revolution and for the right of peoples to withdraw their consent from governments that did not respect their rights. The publications included, in 1693, Locke's *Some Thoughts concerning Education.*

In the last years of his life, Locke, who never married, lived in Essex at the home of his friends Sir Francis and Lady Masham. He was particularly attached to Lady Masham, philosopher, author, correspondent of the German philosopher Leibnitz, and advocate of improved education for women, and who had sought Locke's advice on the education of her infant son. Appropriately, for a devout Christian who firmly believed in the God of Reason and of Revelation, it was while Lady Masham was reading to him from the Psalms that he died on 28th October, 1704.

*****

> That which every Gentleman (that takes care of his Education) desires for his Son, besides the Estates he leaves him, is contain'd

> (I suppose) in these four Things; *Virtue, Wisdom, Breeding,* and *Learning.*
>
> I place *Virtue* as the first and most necessary of those Endowments, that belong to a Man or a Gentleman; as absolutely requisite to make him valued and beloved by others, acceptable or tolerable to himself. Without that he will be happy neither in this, nor the other World.
>
> ...You will wonder, perhaps, that I put *Learning* last, especially if I tell you I think it the least part. This may seem strange in the mouth of a bookish Man; and this making usually the chief, if not only bustle and stir about Children; this being almost that alone, which is thought on, when People talk of Education, makes it the greater Paradox...
>
> *Learning* must be had, but in the second place, as subservient only to great Qualities. Seek out some-body, that may know how discreetly to frame his Manners: Place him in Hands, where you may, as much as possible, secure his Innocence, cherish and nurse up the Good, and gently correct, and weed out any Bad Inclinations, and settle him in good Habits. This is the main Point, and this being provided for, *Learning* may be had in to the Bargain, and that, as I think, at a very easie rate, by Methods that may be thought on.
>
> Locke, *Some Thoughts concerning Education*, ed. Yolton, pp.194, 195, 207, 208

Locke's philosophy

Locke's impact on the development of philosophy, and more broadly on the development of the modern Western mind, has been neatly summarised as follows:

> to set us free from the burden of tradition and authority, both in theology and knowledge, by showing that the entire grounds of our right conduct in the world can be secured by the experience we may gain by the innate faculties and powers we are born with.[2]

Locke was the founder of the philosophical tradition that came to be known as British empiricism, a tradition that has continued, through Berkeley and Hume in the 18th century to Bertrand Russell and A J Ayer in the 20th, and can still distinguish Anglo-American philosophy from many of its continental European counterparts. It is a view of the world that is keen to stay close to the common sense of ordinary people, avoids paradox, analyses carefully the words and concepts we use in everyday life, and distrusts notions that cannot be tested by the application of Reason. William James summed up Locke's contribution to this tradition by referring to his 'devotion to experimentalism, his common sense, and his hatred of obscure, misty ideas'.[3]

Locke rejected claims that there were innate ideas or principles, such as the idea of a divine authority exercised by kings and derived by descent from Adam, or the idea that words have some kind of intrinsic connection with the ideas they represent, or the notion of original sin. Claims like these are not based on evidence or the application of Reason. They block debate and further investigation and are open to abuse by those in authority who set themselves up as guardians of these alleged truths.

For Locke, by contrast, nothing should just be taken for granted. Knowledge should be established following scrutiny of the evidence, reflection, analysis and discussion. In the hands of other men and women this attitude could, and did, lead in radical directions that were to challenge traditional moral and religious beliefs. Locke, however, remained a devout Christian convinced that Reason and Revelation were compatible (his main theological work was entitled *The Reasonableness of Christianity*).

In his political philosophy Locke challenged the idea that authority was divinely inherited by the world's rulers. It was the people, not the rulers, who were ultimately sovereign. The people entrusted their individual rights to life, liberty and property to the community which in turn entrusted them to a government. If the government broke this trust and infringed these rights the people were entitled to resist and choose a new government, as they had done in England in 1688.

Locke's views had a huge impact throughout the course of the 18th century, including in continental Europe. He was one of the main shapers of the 18th-century Enlightenment, his influence on Voltaire and Diderot being particularly great. His *Essay concerning Human Understanding* was enormously influential, within and outside philosophy, in making people look differently at themselves and at issues of knowledge, identity and language. The arguments of his *Two Treatises of Government* provided the rationale for the parliamentary government established in England after 1688 and are at the root of the later development of liberalism and democracy (though Locke was no democrat).

In north America Locke's influence on the movement for independence, and the subsequent development of the USA, was considerable. One modern US writer has claimed that 'there remains a very real sense in which Americans can say that Locke is *our* political philosopher'.[4] Although the extent of his influence has been the subject of scholarly disagreement Locke was certainly one of the sources for the ideas that Thomas Jefferson put in the US Declaration of Independence.[5]

Locke's philosophy was kept largely separate from his thoughts on education, which were firmly based, in a characteristically common sense way, in educational practice. His view of the mind, however, by drawing attention to the need for understanding to be developed through the right experiences and the right habits, rather than by relying on the notion that there were innate moral truths, emphasised the crucial role of education. His view of politics, by placing the exercise of the rights and duties of the individual citizen at the centre of political life, did the same.

Locke's knowledge of children and of education

Although Locke had no children of his own, he probably had more first-hand experience of them, and of education in practice, than most of the other thinkers in this volume. As well as being a conscientious tutor of 13-18 year olds at Oxford, he also in the course of his life acted as the tutor of the 15 year-old son of Shaftesbury; supervised the education of Shaftesbury's grandson from the age of three to 12; was the tutor for two years of the son of Sir John Banks, travelling with him extensively in France to further his education; helped Lady Masham with the education of her infant son; and responded to many queries from friends and acquaintances about the best way of educating their children. Both his correspondence and his writings show the extent of his contact with, interest in, and close observation of, the children in the many families he visited.[6] There is evidence that some of these children liked him and appreciated the attention he gave them. There is also a clear indication in his writings that he enjoyed helping them to learn.

Locke's two main educational works are his lengthy and detailed *Some Thoughts concerning Education*, published in 1693, and his *Of the Conduct of the Understanding*, a guide to the possibilities and pitfalls in learning how to think, published posthumously in 1706.

Some Thoughts concerning Education went through many editions and was translated into French, Dutch, Swedish, German and Italian. It was based on a series of letters that Locke had written while in exile in Holland to his friend the future MP Edward Clarke, who was looking for advice about the education of his eight year old son. It is addressed to 'gentlemen' interested in knowing how best to educate their sons and, given Locke's low opinion of the schools of his own day and distrust of schools *per se*, focuses on how they might be educated at home, by the family and by a tutor.

It is very much a 'how to' or 'do it yourself' guide to education, full of practical advice but based nonetheless on a clear view of what education is for. One has a sense that Locke enjoyed writing it. Like anyone passionate about education, despite his deep reasonableness, he also gets carried away at times with his pet likes and dislikes: being made to write verses in Latin 'torment(s) a Child' and is 'the most unreasonable thing in the World'; 'Melons, Peaches, most sorts of Plumbs, and all sorts of Grapes…' should be banned as offering children 'a very unwholesome Juice' with a 'very tempting Taste', and indeed 'if it were possible, they should never so much as see them or know there were any such' (though gooseberries, strawberries and cherries are absolutely fine); learning how to dance is really important but 'excellency in Musick', he thinks, should probably have 'the last place' in his 'List of Accomplishments'.[7]

Why education is important and what it is for

Unlike Plato and Aristotle, Locke had little to say about the importance of education for the state or for society more generally. He took it for granted that it was in the interests of state and society to have a ruling class that had been educated in the ways he was recommending. His writings, however, are addressed to individual parents or, in the case of his *Of the Conduct of the Understanding*, to people in general. At no point does he so much as even hint that the state might be involved in educational provision. He has nothing to say in his writings about the education of the mass of the population.[8] He has little to say about the education of girls, although in letters to friends advised the same kind of approaches for girls as for boys. These omissions do not of course render irrelevant his recommendations about the aims and methods of education.

Locke's statement that the purposes of education are 'Virtue, Wisdom, Breeding and Learning', and that Learning is the least important of the four, sums up what he felt education ought to be trying to achieve. More important than books, reading, rhetoric, Latin and Greek, and acquiring a lot of knowledge, was the development of an individual's character and attitudes and his moral habits and principles.

If, as a result of his education, he had become a virtuous person, measured, capable of reasoning, able to control his desires, and had acquired 'breeding' (by which Locke meant being able to hold his own in company, neither forward nor bashful, and being considerate towards others), everything else would follow. He might not have a mind crammed with knowledge, but would have learned to appreciate its importance, how to acquire it, and want to continue learning and improving himself throughout his life.

About half of *Some Thoughts concerning Education* is about ways of developing the child's moral character. One of Locke's modern editors has analysed the positive traits that Locke tells us that he wants to develop in children and the negative ones he wants to avoid. Locke's aim was to turn children into 'persons'. The list below explains what Locke meant by a 'person' and also what it is to be to be deemed to fall short of this ideal.[9]

Praiseworthy traits	**Negative traits**
civility	captiousness
feeling of humanity	censoriousness
generosity	clownish shamefacedness
gracefulness of voice and gestures	contempt
honour	cruelty
humility	domineering
industry	hasty judgment
kindness	hypocrisy
love of God	indolence
love of study	lies
modesty	malice
politeness	negligence
prudence	rashness
reverence	sheepish bashfulness
self-control	stubbornness
self-denial	timidity

There are few of these positive traits that a modern educator, or parent, would not wish to promote and few of these negative traits that he or she would not wish to avoid. Modern democratic societies, with their emphasis on individual choice, their pervasive undercurrent of naïve ethical relativism, and their culture of 'respect', are, however, much less explicit about what constitutes 'virtue', 'character' and 'an educated person' and much more 'bashful' (to use Locke's word) about saying what it is they are trying to achieve.

Locke may not have believed in original sin, arguing that it was contrary to Reason, that there was no support for it in the Bible, and that it was unworthy of our idea of God, but he did believe in the existence of evil and the need to train children in virtue in order to keep evil at a distance.[10] His picture of children was a generally warm and beneficent one, but he did not idealise them, did not like the idea of them being given immodest images of themselves (by being called 'little princesses' for example), and admitted that some showed tendencies to cruelty to animals and to dominance over others.

An important element in Locke's concept of a virtuous person was self-control. Locke does not give a very positive account of desires and emotions, except for the access to virtue that comes to an individual in overcoming them:

> He that has not Mastery over his Inclinations, he that knows not how to resist the importunity of Present Pleasure or Pain, for the sake of what Reason tells him is fit to be done, wants the true Principle of Vertue and Industry; and is in danger never to be good for any thing. This Temper therefore, so contrary to unguided Nature, is to be got betimes; and this Habit, as the true foundation of future Ability and Happiness, is to be wrought into the Mind, as early as may be, even from the first dawnings of any Knowledge, or Apprehension in Children...[11]

As far as studying is concerned it is important that the mind should be trained not to give up when it feels like doing so and, where necessary, to defer other pleasures in order to concentrate on the matter in hand. If habits of this kind are established early on 'it will be an Advantage of more Consequence than Latin or Logick, or most of those Things Children are usually required to learn'.[12]

The formation of habits through education is very important to Locke, as it was to Plato, Aristotle and Aquinas. It is not, however, just an outward transformation that is required, despite the importance Locke attached to good manners. There must be an inward transformation too. 'Established habits' are linked in Locke's way of thinking to 'good Principles' and beliefs, including the central beliefs of the Christian religion.[13] It is part of Locke's common sense empirical way of looking at the world, however, to have little time for rules and lists of 'do's' and 'don'ts'. The Ten Commandments and the Creeds need to be learned by heart but even these will not have any effect unless internalised and turned into habits.[14]

The ultimate aim of education is to produce persons who are guided by Reason and live in accordance with the law of nature and the law of God, thus demonstrating 'Virtue' and 'Wisdom'. Those who live otherwise run the risk of turning into wild beasts and being treated as such.

The culmination of Locke's advice on how to cultivate a reasoning mind can be found in his *Of the Conduct of the Understanding*, a thinkers' manual which, 300 years after its publication, remains as relevant today as it was then. Our understanding is often weak, Locke argues, for three reasons: because we rely too much on the opinions of others, failing to check their assertions against the evidence and the arguments; because we are driven by our emotions and biases to adopt points of view that do not stand up to rational scrutiny; and because we often fail to see the whole picture.

We need practice in reasoning, learning how to avoid over-hasty generalisations, but also how not to get bogged down in the detail. We need to be critical reflective readers, not just spouting the opinions of the last book we have put down. Above all we need to respect Truth and be passionate about searching it out, not deferring to authority just because it says so, or to others' opinions, or to our own prejudices.[15]

The 'true secret of education'

Although he did not use the word Locke saw education as an 'art'. He knew enough about it at first hand to realise that the teacher needs to be highly adaptable, that what will work with one child on one day may not work with the same child the next day or may not work on any day with another child. '...there are scarce two Children, who can be conducted by exactly the same method', he wrote. This is why he recommended to teachers close observation of their pupils' behaviour and dispositions so that the best ways of getting them to learn might be found.[16]

Locke was convinced that children must be induced to want to learn, and to be in the mood to do so at the point when learning is due to take place. The 'true secret of education', as he referred to it, lay in manipulating the learning environment (though Locke did not use that modern phrase) in order to achieve this end. He had sufficient experience with children and empathy with teachers to realise that this would not always be easy. The complete failure of schools to master this 'secret' was one of the main reasons for his advice to try and avoid placing one's child in them if at all possible.

The key part of the 'secret of education' was not to turn the learning experience into a 'task' or a 'business'. This was a sure guarantee that children would quickly lose interest. They should be treated gently, dealt with as rational creatures, encouraged to ask questions, answered in their own terms, and never laughed at.[17] Locke also recognised their need to be able to play, as a way of restoring their strength and their spirit after study, though without arguing for the potentially educative nature of play. He did, however, encourage children to make up their own games rather than just using ones given to them and devised, in some detail, a game of his own, with ball and dice, to encourage young children to learn their letters.[18]

In keeping with his idea that human beings are driven by the pursuit of pleasure and the avoidance of pain, two of Locke's key motivating factors were 'esteem' and 'shame', and in particular 'esteem'. These were much more powerful in their impact on the child, he thought, than punishment, which he saw as the resort of lazy teachers who did not think through what they were doing. He particularly disliked corporal punishment which he saw as 'the most unfit of any (method) to be used in Education', though as a result of its inefficacy rather than its intrinsic inhumanity and he did not rule it out altogether in extreme cases.

Making use of 'esteem' – the praise and high regard of one's teachers, parents, peers and siblings – was Locke's constant recommendation to teachers. It both acted as a powerful incentive and reinforced the behaviours that one was trying to encourage. Unlike punishment it is 'a Principle ... which will influence (the child's) Actions, when you are not by ... and which will be the proper Stock, whereon afterwards to graft the true Principles of Morality and Religion.'[19]

Sometimes 'esteem' needed to be balanced by its opposite, 'shame', with clear messages being conveyed to the pupil that the people who mattered to him disapproved of the unworthy things he had done. Locke was keen that 'shame' was used sparingly and with care as to its effects. It is here that the modern educator, having nodded with approval (and self-approval) at Locke's stress on 'esteem', is likely to part company, the use of 'shame' having no place in the behaviour policies in current use in our schools.

For millennia recognised as an essential check on human behaviour, 'shame' for the last half century has had a bad press. We now look differently, and often more indulgently, at ourselves, our place in the world and the purpose of our lives. This does not prevent us from being unflinchingly 'judgmental' towards others in private, and about highly selective matters in public, but the prevailing mood music has changed. Locke, advocate of the occasional and careful use of 'shame', may have unwittingly contributed to the process by insisting that the moral impulse was not innate and by casting doubts on original sin.[20]

Locke's curriculum

Although the core of Locke's curriculum was an apprenticeship to virtue, and his aim was not to turn children into 'scholars', an introduction to a wide range of subjects was nonetheless important. Locke was particularly keen to help children develop fluency in their own language, English. He exclaimed at the prevalent attitude that Latin and Greek were 'the learned Languages fit only for learned Men to meddle with and teach' and that English was 'the language of the illiterate Vulgar'.[21]

As soon as a child can speak English Locke was keen that he start learning French through conversation and then, a year or two later, Latin. He was in no doubt that Latin was 'absolutely necessary to a Gentleman', but could not see the point of it for children whose future would be in trade. Even for gentlemen he had little time for Latin grammar, or for learning lists of words which he described as a 'very unpleasant Business'. Latin and French were both best learned by being used as the language of instruction for subjects such as arithmetic, geography, chronology, history and geometry. In this way children would both develop their subject knowledge and advance more rapidly in the language, not least because they would see the point of learning it.[22]

History is also important as the subject that teaches more and delights more than any other, 'which is the great Mistress of Prudence and Civil Knowledge', and which, in the case of the history of England, every 'English gentleman should be well versed in ... taking his rise as far back as there are records of it'. Before embarking on history children should study chronology so that they can place events in their different epochs. Geography should also be studied alongside history given the connections between the two subjects. The history of the ancient world was recommended, not least because of the knowledge of human character and behaviour that it would bring.[23]

As far as 'natural philosophy' or science was concerned, young people would be faced with views of the natural world that were very different from each other and with subject matter that was evolving. Some familiarity with science, however, was essential for a gentleman. Locke had little time for logic and rhetoric, key elements in the curriculum of the schools of his own day, and was particularly dismissive of the practice of disputing which these subjects involved.

His views on debaters 'priding (themselves) in contradicting others ... questioning every thing, and thinking there is no such thing as truth to be sought, but only Victory in Disputing' are worth a moment's thought on the part of teachers preparing young people for debating competitions today.[24]

Locke shows a less attractive side to British empiricism in his rather hasty dismissal of the arts. He distrusted the imagination, seeing it as a source of mischief. He is particularly dismissive of poetry. Should any child show a 'Poetick Vein' his view was that 'the Parents should labour to have it stifled, and suppressed, as much as may be'.[25] Painting and music are similarly brushed aside, partly because of the amount of time they take up and how this would distract students from more important matters. He is more favourable towards Drawing, which might be useful on one's travels.

The most radical of Locke's ideas was his recommendation, explored at length, that all boys be set to learn one or more manual trades such as gardening, carpentry, varnishing, perfuming, engraving or metalwork. These are skills worth having; they are good for one's health; and they provide activities for recreation that diminish temptations to waste one's time in gaming and idleness.

Locke was conscious that his view might not be shared by many gentlemen. He was probably right as there is no evidence that anyone paid any attention to this advice. The idea illustrates the utilitarian streak in Locke that led him to reject the traditional curriculum to be found in schools (he also recommended the learning of shorthand and Accounts). But it remains a bright idea that in most countries is still waiting to be put into practice.

*****

How Locke can help us think about education today

Is education really as important in shaping our lives as is often claimed?

Locke had a strong sense of the power of education to shape a young person for life. Put a boy in a school and the likelihood is that he will never recover in terms of virtue, wisdom and breeding even if he leaves having learned lots of (mostly useless) things. Put him with a tutor of good character and skill and he will be set up for life. Many politicians and teachers would share Locke's view of education's importance. But is this to exaggerate its impact?

At the very least, educational thinkers should be cautious about their claims. Plato did not get very far with the rulers of Syracuse whom he was trying to turn into philosopher kings. Aristotle's success with Alexander the Great was at least partial, given the trail of misery left behind by his pupil's conquests. The educational ideas of Seneca, the great Roman philosopher, clearly had little impact on his infamous pupil the Emperor Nero. Fifty years after Locke's death another educational experiment took place. The greatest European educators of their day took in hand the schooling of the young Duke Ferdinand of Parma with a view to making him their ideal of an 'enlightened ruler'. They were as unsuccessful as all the others. Although far from stupid, Ferdinand ended up a diehard reactionary, re-establishing the Inquisition and deeply disappointing those who had invested so much in him.[26] In our present day, if one wishes to complete the sorry list, the early International Baccalaureate education of the current North Korean dictator Kim Jong-un can also scarcely be said to have left much of a trace.

The difficulty in predicting the impact of an education is also shown by the way in which, down the ages, clever, profound and highly learned educational reformers have built their reputations on a rejection of the education that they themselves received. Both Locke and Montaigne, like many educational pundits today, were highly critical of the kinds of schools that they attended. One is left wondering both whether these schools were really as deficient as suggested and whether education is quite the determining factor in many people's lives that is often claimed.

The success of a child's upbringing depends on the company he keeps in schools

Locke's recipe for making sure that education really did work, however, was to get them young and to make sure that they avoided 'bad company'. The main reason why he advised parents to educate their children at home was because of the inability of the teachers, in establishments with 50 or 100 pupils, to give them the individual attention they needed or to ensure that they were not exposed to bad company and enticed into bad habits. Schools, Locke feared, were places where it was easy for boys to be swayed by 'the herd' into 'malapertness', 'tricking' 'violence', 'roughness' and 'vice'.[27]

In expressing concern about the 'company' that children kept, Locke reflects the anxieties of parents down the ages. His concern was not about separating the children of gentlemen from those of the rest of the population, but of making sure that they did not fall under bad influences *from those of the same class*. This is still a major concern of many parents today, whatever their social background and whether or not they have decided to put their children in state or private schools.

It is a concern that can no longer be avowed with Locke's frankness, for fear of being accused of 'snobbery' or thought 'judgmental'.[28] Trying to avoid bad influences on one's children is of course never going to be completely successful and is not in their interests if taken too far. It can also easily lead to misplaced judgments about the suitability of certain schools. It remains, however, a perfectly legitimate concern, and deserves respect. It will not disappear this side of utopia.

Avoiding the self-congratulation of the modern world

Locke's recommendation that children should, if possible, be denied all knowledge of the existence of melons, peaches and grapes (but only '*most sorts* of Plumbs') was quoted earlier as an example of how one generation's ideas about education can easily seem completely absurd to another. Locke's recommendation had a clear purpose, which was to promote self-control, though this somehow makes the idea even more preposterous to a modern mind because of the apparent disproportion between the objective and the proposed action.

It is important, however, not to start comforting oneself with the idea that what we have here is simply a contrast between modern sophistication and the naivety and dogmatism of a more backward society. In the preface to his play *Saint Joan* – one of my texts as an A level English literature student which has left a lasting impression on my vision of the world – George Bernard Shaw reminded his early 20th-century readers how the modern world could sometimes show 'grosser credulity' than that of the Middle Ages.

One hundred years later we are probably, if anything, even more apt to dismiss uncritically the ideas of previous eras (by contrast with Locke's world which was apt, uncritically, to revere them). We should bear in mind that it is more than likely that some features of current educational practice will seem completely absurd to people in the not too distant future, as indeed some of them, including some of the rapidly changing educational manifestations of technophilia, already do.

Teach children to dance properly

Locke was extremely keen that children learn to dance quite early on. I have failed to find any reference to whether he himself danced. None of the 35 portraits of him in the National Portrait Gallery's database make it seem very plausible, though that is almost certainly an over-hasty judgment on someone with so many other talents. Dancing, Locke felt, made children graceful and well-mannered but, above all, gave them confidence in themselves, thus helping their maturation into adults. Anyone, as I have done, who has worked in a school that brought in the company *Dancing Classrooms*, to give lessons in ballroom dancing will confirm that, as in so many other matters, Locke's judgment was absolutely spot on.

*****

Locke writes

Locke on learning how to learn

The business (of education), in respect of knowledge, is not, as I think, to perfect a learner in all or any one of the sciences, but to give his mind that freedom, that disposition, and those habits, that may enable him to attain any part of knowledge he shall apply himself to, or stand in need of, in the future course of his life.

Locke, *Of the Conduct of the Understanding*, p.348

Locke on making sure education is not seen as a burden or task

The right way to teach them those Things is, to give them a liking and Inclination to what you propose to them to be learn'd; and that will engage their Industry and Application. This I think no hard Matter to do, if Children be handled as they should be, and the Rewards and Punishments above-mentioned be carefully applied, and with them these few Rules observed in the Method of instructing them.

None of these things they are to learn should ever be made a Burthen to them, or imposed on them as a Task. Whatever is so proposed presently becomes irksome. The Mind takes an Aversion to it, though before it were a Thing of Delight or Indifferency. Let a Child be but ordered to whip his Top at a certain Time every Day, whether he has, or has not a Mind to it; let this be but required of him as a Duty, wherein he must spend so many Hours Morning and Afternoon, to see whether he will not soon be weary of any Play at this Rate? Is it not so with grown Men? What they do chearfully of themselves; Do they not presently grow sick of, and can no more endure, as soon as they find it is expected of them, as a Duty? Children have as much a Mind to shew that they are free, that their own good Actions come from themselves, that they are absolute and independent, as any of the proudest of you grown Men, think of them as you please.

Locke, *Some Thoughts concerning Education*, ed. Yolton, p. 134

Locke on the importance of observing individual children and adapting learning to meet their needs

Begin therefore betimes nicely to observe your Son's Temper; and that, when he is under least restraint, in his Play, and as he thinks out of your sight. See what are his predominant Passions, and prevailing Inclinations; whether he be Fierce or Mild, Bold or Bashful, Compassionate or Cruel, open or Reserv'd, etc. For as these are different in him, so are your Methods to be different, and your

Authority must take measures to apply itself different ways to him.
Locke, *Some Thoughts concerning Education*, ed. Yolton, p. 163

References

1. Jeffreys, M V C, *John Locke. Prophet of Common Sense*, pp. 24-25, 1967, Methuen, London.
2. Aarsleff, H, *Locke's influence*, in Chappell, V (ed.), *The Cambridge Companion to Locke*, p. 252, 1994, Cambridge University Press, Cambridge.
3. Aarsleff, *op.cit.*, p. 281.
4. Tarcov, N, *Locke's Education for Liberty*, p. 1, 1984, University of Chicago Press, Chicago.
5. Aarsleff, *op.cit.*, p. 281.
6. Yolton, JW and JS, introduction, pp. 5-8, to Locke, J, *Some Thoughts Concerning Education*, 1989, Clarendon Press, Oxford.
7. Locke, J, *Some Thoughts Concerning Education*, ed. Yolton, JW and JS, pp. 96, 230, 252-3.
8. (ed.) Adamson, J W, introduction to *The Educational Writings of John Locke*, 1922, Cambridge University Press, Cambridge. Locke's only reference to the education of the lower classes is in a memorandum on the reform of the Poor Law drawn up by him when working at the Council of Trade. This recommended that the education of pauper children aged three to fourteen consist of manual training and religious instruction only.
9. Yolton, op.cit., pp. 22-3.
10. Yolton, op.cit., p. 14; Tarcov, op.cit., p. 90.
11. Locke, op.cit., p. 111; see also pp. 114 and 136.
12. Locke, op.cit., p. 136.
13. Locke, op.cit., p. 90; Yolton, op.cit., p. 39.
14. Locke, op.cit., pp. 90, 120, 212.
15. Locke, J, *Of the Conduct of the Understanding*, in *The Works of John Locke*, volume 2, pp. 326-7, 347, 356, 364, 387, 1824, London.
16. Locke, *Some Thoughts Concerning Education*, op.cit., pp. 122, 162-3, 265; Locke, *Of the Conduct of the Understanding*, op.cit., pp. 325, 384; Yolton, op.cit., p. 14.
17. Locke, op.cit., *Some Thoughts Concerning Education*, pp. 98, 108, 134, 162-3, 183-4.
18. Locke, *Some Thoughts Concerning Education*, op.cit., pp. 108, 209-10; Jeffreys, op.cit., p.51.
19. Locke, *Some Thoughts Concerning Education*, op.cit., pp. 112-3, 116, 145-6, 168, 183, 255.
20. On 'shame' see Himmelfarb, Gertrude, *The De-Moralization of Society: From Victorian Virtues to Modern Values*, 1995, IEA, London.
21. Locke, *Some Thoughts Concerning Education*, op.cit., pp. 244, 226.
22. Locke, *Some Thoughts Concerning Education*, op.cit., pp. 216-7, 218, 227, 234-5.
23. Locke, *Some Thoughts Concerning Reading and Study for a Gentleman* in *The Works*

of John Locke, volume 2, p. 408, 1824, London; Locke, *Some Thoughts Concerning Education*, op.cit., pp. 219, 227, 237-8, 239.

24. Locke, *Some Thoughts Concerning Education*, op.cit., pp. 240-1.
25. Locke, *Some Thoughts Concerning Education*, op.cit., p. 240.
26. Badinter, E, *L'infant de Parme*, 2010, Fayard, Paris.
27. Locke, *Some Thoughts Concerning Education*, op.cit., pp. 128-9, 130-1, 207.
28. See London *Evening Standard*, 5th March 2014, in which, under the heading 'Private education is about snobbery, says Gove's wife', Sarah Vine, journalist and wife of the Secretary of State for Education, is quoted as accusing parents who pick fee-paying schools for their children of 'paying for their child to mix with the right kind of kids'.

Chapter 6

The child at the centre: Jean-Jacques Rousseau

When, in 1794 during the French Revolution, Rousseau's remains were transferred to the Panthéon, France's mausoleum for national heroes, the citation gave pride of place to his educational treatise *Émile*, a work, the citation read, 'that had led us to the Revolution, prepared, instructed and shaped us for it'. Putting aside the hyperbole of such occasions – many other influences shaped the revolutionary mentality – few educational writings have had such claims made for them. Rousseau himself also thought *Émile* his finest work.

Rousseau's views on education have probably had a bigger impact on educational practice than those of any of the other thinkers in this book. Although some of his main emphases were prefigured in Plato, Montaigne and Locke – to each of whom Rousseau acknowledges his debt – it is to Rousseau's direct influence that we owe much of the thinking behind the 'progressive' education that has become increasingly dominant in large parts of the western, and in particular Anglo-Saxon, world since the middle of the 20th century.

Rousseau was the mentor of progressive educators such as Pestalozzi, Montessori and Froebel. Echoes of his approach can be found in the work of the hugely influential 20th-century Swiss psychologist Piaget and of the great American educational philosopher John Dewey. Modern emphases on 'active learning', 'enquiry-based learning' and 'constructivism' (children constructing their own meaning rather than having it handed to them) all find support in Rousseau's writings. Rousseau is also an unacknowledged influence behind the educational approaches of the Geneva-based International Baccalaureate organization, whose educational programmes are taught in numerous schools in most countries of the world.

But Rousseau was a polymath who wrote about many things other than education. He is chiefly known for his *The Social Contract* which, in asserting the sovereignty of the people and theorizing about the nature of 'civic virtue', was a major influence on the leaders of the French Revolution. Rousseau's political views have also had a huge impact outside France.

They have continued to inform thinking right across the political spectrum up to and including the present day, being interpreted – not least because of their own internal tensions – in widely different ways.

His writings explore the phenomenology of the human mind, the roots of inequality, the nature of the arts and sciences, the origin of languages, religion and morality. Many of these themes are reflected in *Émile* which, appropriately for a book on education, is also about the whole of human life. In addition, Rousseau was the author of one of the 18th century's most popular novels, *Julie or the New Heloise*, and of a range of autobiographical writings, in particular his *Confessions*. He was a poet, author of operas and works for the theatre, and a man with strong views on music, contributing 200 articles on the subject to the great Enlightenment *Encyclopaedia* edited by Diderot and d'Alembert.

Rousseau was an immensely complex and sensitive thinker, full of profound insights but pulled by his thoughts and feelings in many different directions. This is why he has been subject to so many different interpretations. In many ways a thinker of the Enlightenment he nonetheless did not share its optimism or its rationalism. While rejecting conventional religion he also continued to assert the immortality of the soul and the existence of God. His emphasis on feeling made him one of the precursors of Romanticism.

Jean-Jacques Rousseau (1712-1778) was born in the small Swiss city state of Geneva, the son of a watchmaker. His mother died giving birth to him. He had virtually no formal education, though managed to learn how to read and, like Montaigne, developed an early enthusiasm for Plutarch's *Lives*. At the age of 12 he was apprenticed, first as a legal clerk and then as an engraver. Not enjoying either role he left Geneva for neighbouring Savoy where he became part of the entourage of a Catholic convert Mme de Warens. This relationship, which became sexual, continued on and off for the next 13 years.

During this time, between bouts of employment as a (hugely unsuccessful) tutor to two young boys and as a secretary, Rousseau continued to educate himself by reading. Finally breaking with Mme de Warens he moved to Paris where he set up house with a laundress Thérèse Levasseur who gave birth, over a period of six years, to five of their children. All were handed over to a home for abandoned children, a fact that Rousseau's critics later made public.

It was not until he was in his late 30s that Rousseau finally realised that he had things he wanted to say to the world. A brilliant and polemical prize essay on the harmful effects on society of progress in the arts and sciences, published in 1750, launched his career as an author. Other works, on music, the theatre and the origins of inequality, soon followed. In 1761 his novel *Julie or the New Heloise* was a huge success and this was followed in 1762 by the publication of *The Social Contract* and *Émile*. These last two works established his enduring fame, but their publication had devastating effects on his personal life. Both were felt to be seditious, *Émile* especially because of its critique of traditional religion.

The two books were burned in Geneva and *Émile* was condemned by the *Parlement* of Paris. Rousseau was forced to leave France, seeking refuge in two different Swiss cantons and, for a time after his house was stoned, in England. Although eventually able to return to France, under the protection of an aristocratic patron, he was henceforth convinced that he was surrounded by enemies and that plots against him were everywhere. Genuine persecution had induced paranoia. In his last years he regained a certain peace wandering the countryside, botanising and writing *Reveries of a solitary walker*, a moving final work in which his brilliant use of the French language reached new heights.

*****

> Make your pupil attentive to the phenomena of nature. Soon you will make him curious. But to feed his curiosity, never hurry to satisfy it. Put the questions within his reach and leave them to him to resolve. Let him know something not because you told it to him but because he has understood it himself. Let him not learn science but discover it. If ever you substitute in his mind authority for reason, he will no longer reason. He will be nothing more than the plaything of others' opinion.
>
> Rousseau, J-J, *Émile or on Education*,
> translated by Kelly, C, and Bloom, A, p. 312

> I do not tire of repeating it: put all the lessons of young people in actions rather than speeches. Let them learn nothing in books which experience can teach them… All the precepts of rhetoric seem to be only pure verbiage to whoever does not sense their use for his profit. Of what import is it to a Schoolboy to know how Hannibal went about convincing his soldiers to cross the Alps? If, in place of these magnificent harangues, you told him how he ought to go about getting his principal to give him a vacation, be sure he would be more attentive to your rules.
>
> Rousseau, J-J, *Émile or on Education*,
> translated by Kelly, C, and Bloom, A, p. 408

> Rousseau addresses each of his readers personally because he addresses the concerns, small and great, that each of us confront for ourselves, in our own daily existence. He writes about the everyday challenges of the moral life, about how hard it can be to live up to our own ideals, and about what steps we can take in order to live happier and better lives. He writes about the everyday challenges of our living together in political communities, about the difficulty of preserving our freedom, both from the powerful, institutional forces that threaten to overwhelm us from the outside and from our own vices, which threaten to destroy our liberty from within. And Rousseau addresses these concerns – my concerns – with passion and intensity, as if they matter more than anything else in the world.
>
> Reisert, J R, *Jean-Jacques Rousseau. A Friend of Virtue*,
> p.ix, 2003, Cornell University Press, New York

What type of book is *Émile?*

Émile is an extremely lengthy work – over 500 or 600 pages in most editions – and one reason for the frequent misrepresentations of Rousseau's views among those who comment on education may well be that the number of those who have actually read the whole of it is relatively small. Another reason may be that the work has internal contradictions that are not always easy to resolve.

Émile is both a manual of education and an exploration of a large number of wider philosophical issues. As one of Rousseau's translators, the US academic Allan Bloom put it, the book 'is a *Phenomenology of the Mind* posing as Dr Spock'.[1] Its theme is as much the nature of man and of woman, of society, of morality, and of God, as it is a treatise on how education should be conducted. All these wider themes, however, are always linked to the question 'how should we educate the young?' This is a major reason why, as an educational work, it stimulates so much reflection as education is impoverished when it is not seen as inseparable from these issues.

It is also both a treatise and a novel. It is the story of how a wise tutor – essentially Rousseau himself, though at times tutor and author are distinguished from each other – sets out and implements a plan for the education of his charge, Émile, to whom he devotes himself without interruption from the time of his birth to his marriage in his mid-20s to the young woman, Sophie, whom he has chosen as his lifelong partner.

The development of Émile's character and abilities, his relationship with his tutor, his love for Sophie, are all recounted, at least in part, in the form of stories. As a story, however, it cannot be taken literally. The notion of a tutor devoting 25 years of his life, day and night, without respite, to the education of one other person, in isolation for much of the time from the rest of the world, is absurd. It should instead be seen as a metaphor.

What Rousseau was trying to do was to show how a child could be educated, as he put it, as close to 'nature' as possible, so that he was formed by his own reactions to the world in the light of his own needs, and so that he would grow up, organically so to speak, as an autonomous and free individual able to think for himself, rather than having his mind imprinted, like some *tabula rasa*, with the opinions and vices of a corrupt society.

Rousseau rejected the materialism of most contemporary philosophers and the idea that the mind is just a product of the senses. He believed in the natural goodness of humanity, not in any sloppy sentimental way but arising from an analysis – most brilliantly expounded in his *Discourse on the Origin of Inequality* – of how contemporary society drove people into habits of in-authenticity that were the opposite of the life of virtue of which they were inherently capable. Rousseau's educational plans aimed not to help to create a more just society, but to enable a good man, and a good woman, to protect themselves from an unjust one and to find a way of living quietly and happily within it.

Émile ends with the tutor having apparently succeeded in his educational task and with Émile, now a young man of immense integrity and spirit, settling down with the loving and high-principled Sophie to a life of happiness and virtue. The ending of *Émile* did not, however, satisfy

Rousseau and he carried on working on a sequel whose conclusion he had still not finally determined at the time of his death 16 years later.

In this sequel Sophie is overwhelmed by the deaths of her parents and of her and Émile's daughter, the family moves to Paris, she is trapped into having a child by another man, the marriage breaks down, and Émile, captured on his travels by Barbary pirates, ends up a slave (though, thanks to his education, a resourceful and determined one who never loses his virtue – the kind of fantasy companion that any fantasy hostage would wish to have at their side). It was as if Rousseau had recognised both that the best of people, following the best of educations, could still be swept off their feet by unforeseen events and that his utopian dreams of arming individuals through education to resist the pressures of a debased society (and especially that of cities and of the rich) were destined to failure.

In his article on *Political Economy* in the Encyclopaedia and in his plan for the government of Poland (drawn up at the request of a leading Polish politician) Rousseau also implicitly recognised the limitations of the educational ideas of *Émile* to answer questions about the education needed in a state. He accepted that ideally one should learn simultaneously to be both an individual and a member of a political community of equals, and that these two roles should be compatible.

He admitted however that, though this might have been achievable in the city states of ancient Greece (Rousseau shared with Montaigne, one of his heroes, a particular fondness for Sparta), current states are not constituted so as to make this possible. His few thoughts about education in large states – the state's 'most important business', he called it – are directly focused on shaping young people into identifying with their country, its history and dominant values. There is little sign here of allowing children to flourish or construct their own meaning through enquiry.[2] Rousseau was both a communitarian and an individualist and his work is often most interesting when he is trying, and often not succeeding, to reconcile the two. Émile, whose moral sense and social conscience have been drawn out by his education, ends up as the kind of citizen who would be needed in the *ideal* society that Rousseau sketches in the *Social Contract*, but quite how such an individualist education could be adapted to meet the needs of this state is never fully explored.

The phases of education in *Émile*

Rousseau divided his story of Émile's education into five books which corresponded to the five stages of his life under the direction of his tutor: infancy (0-2); childhood (2-12); youth (12-15); adolescence (15-20); manhood (20-25). Each stage has its distinctive objectives and emphases.

The first two phases focus on the development of physical strength and of courage, learning to accept 'necessity' (being able to endure hardship and the occasional pains, and accepting that one cannot have all one wants), avoiding the formation of bad habits, and learning through the five senses. The child should not be introduced prematurely to reasoning or moral precepts that he will not yet fully understand, though must learn to accept 'No' without argument where this is appropriate. Reading and writing should emerge when the child needs them, but there should be no books.

Rousseau's concern above all is that the child should not be forced to do things for which he is not ready and that adults should refrain from trying artificially to cram into his developing mind all sorts of external stuff that does not relate to the world in which he is living. Delay in introducing new aspects of learning that do not naturally arise in the course of the child's life is not just nothing to worry about, it is actively recommended. Rousseau would recoil in horror from what he would see as the 'mechanistic' and deeply 'unnatural' interventionism of some contemporary governments with their testing of pupils at five, seven and 11 and their targets for ever-increasing pupil attainment at these ages.

Following such an education, Émile at age 12 'has come to the maturity of childhood'. He is strong, confident and independent, frank, curious and free of any pretention. He is a natural leader because of his talent, not through any sense of right or authority.

> His ideas are limited but distinct. If he knows nothing by heart, he knows much by experience. If he reads less well in our books than does another child, he reads better in the book of nature. His mind is not in his tongue but in his head. He has less memory than judgment. He knows how to speak only one language, but he understands what he says; and if what he says he does not say so well as others, to compensate for that, what he does, he does better than they do.[3]

The third stage, from 12 to 15, is one in which the young person's strengths begin to be outstripped by his desires. It is a time for turning 'sensations' into 'ideas', for developing Rousseau's 'sixth sense', which is 'common sense', and for being given a taste for the different sciences. It is a short 'peaceful age of intelligence' before puberty sets in and must be taken full advantage of. Where the first two stages accustomed the child to 'necessity', this phase focuses on 'utility'.

Émile should be introduced at last to a book, but to only one: Daniel Defoe's *Robinson Crusoe*. This should be the basis for doing practical science and for learning to be self-sufficient. Rousseau wished Émile to learn a trade, or indeed a number of trades: so that he could understand the satisfactions of living a simple and useful life among ordinary people away from the idleness and pretentiousness of the rich; so that he was not parasitic upon others; so that he could be independent of the vicissitudes of fortune; so that he was prepared for the revolution and the collapse of existing states that Rousseau was predicting nearly 30 years before they happened. These trades had to be 'honest' ones; however, like metalwork, shoe-making and agriculture, not crafts that pandered to the rich like those of varnisher, embroiderer or gilder as Locke had proposed.[4]

The fourth stage (15-20), that of adolescence, Rousseau sees as 'a second birth', 'It is now that man is truly born to life', he says, 'and now nothing human is foreign to him'. It is the stage in which Émile, as moral person, comes into being. Although this is the time when education is usually finished it is in fact just the time when it needs to begin.[5] Émile has so far learned to understand himself in relation to things. He must now understand himself in relation to others, without ever drifting into that kind of *amour-propre* (self-love) which has us endlessly comparing ourselves with others and wanting to be what we are not. He must now begin to shape his own moral nature, which will be a lifetime's work.

Rousseau particularly emphasises the importance in this phase of developing Émile's empathy, generosity and compassion for others. Though recognising the role of reason in decisions about right and wrong, Rousseau saw both feeling (the voice of the body) and conscience (the voice of the soul) as inseparable from the development of the moral sense. Efforts should be made to extend compassion to the whole of humanity, but we should not expect this to happen overnight.

This stage was also the one at which finally Émile begins to think about religion. Rousseau deals with this in Book IV through a lengthy aside in which he recalls an encounter that he had as an adolescent with a disgraced Savoyard priest in Turin. Through the words of this priest (*The Profession of Faith of the Savoyard Vicar*) Rousseau both states his own views about religion and illustrates the (inconsistently didactic) religious teaching that he felt it appropriate for Émile to receive.

It was above all this section of the book, with its advocacy of a simple theistic natural religion and distaste for dogma and ecclesiastical structures, which led to its condemnation. Book IV concludes by showing that Émile has been sufficiently well armed against society to be able to be exposed to Parisian society, not to be seduced by it, and to judge it according to its deserts.

Émile ends with an account of the hero's search for Sophie, his courtship of her and their marriage. This, however, is preceded by a discussion of the differences between boys and girls and the requirements for a girl's education (discussed below). In this final stage the tutor continues in his role only on the basis of Émile's explicit consent. A key objective in this stage is to ensure that, where the two clash, virtue triumphs over the passions. Before marrying, Émile is made to test his commitment to Sophie by a two-year absence and lengthy travels with his tutor, during which he learns about the nature of societies, is introduced to the ideal state as depicted in the *Social Contract*, and picks up two or three languages, and which, by developing in him further the seeds of 'wisdom' – the main leitmotif of this final stage – help to complete his education.

Rousseau's main thesis in Émile: what it is and what it is not

It is not, however, Rousseau's rather arbitrary division of human development into stages that has continued to be influential. It is the nature of his pedagogy. There are three fundamental principles underlying Rousseau's pedagogy.

The importance of studying children and childhood

First, childhood is a good in itself. It is not just a step towards adulthood. Children should be treated with goodwill and as equals with adults in terms of their humanity. The tutor shares Émile's discomforts, does physical work alongside him whenever this is part of Émile's learning, and consults and gives him decisions to make wherever it is appropriate to do so. Children's caprices and their desire to control others need to be thwarted, but punishments and rebukes do not work. Children have a variety of individual dispositions and their education should be adapted to their needs.

It is also important to study children carefully as a basis for deciding how best they should learn:

> I would want a judicious man to give us a treatise on the art of observing children. This art would be very important to know. Fathers and masters have not yet learned its elements.[6]

Rousseau had clearly observed children and on one occasion in *Émile* analyses in detail the gulf between a traditional teaching material (one of La Fontaine's *Fables*) and the understandings of children of the age with whom it was being used.

Active learning

Second, and this is at the heart of Rousseau's message and of his legacy to date, children need to learn by:

- following their own lines of enquiry, and discovering things for themselves;
- asking their own questions;
- posing hypotheses;
- testing them against the evidence;
- answering their own questions (rather than being given the answers by their teacher);
- being allowed to fail and learning from failure;
- correcting their own mistakes (rather than having them corrected by the teacher);
- seeing the consequences of their acts and learning from these (rather than being rebuked or punished for them);
- working with real things rather than just with symbols;
- going out into the real world – studying the night sky, orienteering in a forest, talking to local farmers and tradespeople, doing practical science, learning a trade – rather than being stuck behind a desk or with those 'instruments of their greatest misery – books'.[7]

Émile is full of practical examples of how its main character learns from direct experience: getting lost with his tutor in a large forest and being made to find his own way out by looking at the position of the sun in relation to its position on previous occasions when their location had been known; observing sunrises and sunsets, and the night sky, as an aid to astronomy; learning an important lesson, following an embarrassing incident, about one's judgment and about the dangers of *amour-propre*.

The approach is summed up by Rousseau's advice on the use of La Fontaine's *Fables* with children: use them if you must, if children have reached the appropriate level of understanding, but edit them so that you cut out the morals with which each of them ends and get your pupils to work these out for themselves.[8]

Clear aims and detailed planning of the learning process

What distinguishes all these examples is Rousseau's third fundamental set of pedagogical principles: total clarity on the part of the teacher about the aims and objectives of the education that he or she is providing and meticulous manipulation of the learning process by which these are to be achieved. Émile's tutor was undoubtedly a facilitator using active enquiry-based learning approaches (as we might call them today), and in no sense a traditional didactic educator, but neither can he be slotted into one of the axes of the antonymous 'sage on the stage/guide on the side' pairing discussed in the chapter on Plato and Socrates. If one wished to place him anywhere it would be as both 'sage' *and* 'guide'.

There is no sense in Rousseau that the autonomy that he so desperately wanted for his pupil was anything other than autonomy to live the kind of life that Rousseau felt that he ought to live. There was nothing ethically relativistic about Rousseau's educational aims. Rousseau was not just trying to give his imaginary pupil a chance of a good job, to enable him to pursue some 'dream' or 'passion' whatever it might be, or prepare him to enhance his country's economic competitiveness. The whole plan would have failed if Émile had not turned out to be a young man of integrity and truthfulness, with a strong sense of right and wrong, with compassion for his fellow human beings, and free from the sort of *amour-propre* that pushes people towards selfishness and self-promotion.

Rousseau would have been most unhappy if Émile had accumulated vast wealth and flaunted it in expensive clothes and furnishings or had taken up a career as a dancing master (a role that was an occasional target for Rousseau's contempt). What he would have made of contemporary celebrity culture, oozing at the pores with an *amour-propre* that makes the 18th-century French elite look like shrinking violets, or of democratic leaders cosying up to the owners and editors of newspapers which fuel celebrity culture's global publicity machine, is not hard to imagine.

There was similarly nothing non-interventionist about the way the tutor planned Émile's learning. Every piece of discovery learning is meticulously planned in such a way that it 'creates the effect of unmediated experience'.[9] Even the chance encounter with Sophie is stage managed. Émile was manipulated, but in a system of 'well-regulated liberty'. Behind the appearance of freedom the tutor is at all times firmly in charge, even more so, Rousseau would claim, than in school.

It is no coincidence that the contemporary primary education system which most shows Rousseau's continuing influence – the International Baccalaureate's Primary Years Programme – places huge demands on teachers' time and effort. Detailed planning is essential to ensure that children's ostensibly open-ended learning nonetheless produces the desired educational outcomes. The collaboration and pre-planning that this requires is not now that between Jean-Jacques and the gardener Robert, in helping

Émile to understand property rights, or between Jean-Jacques and Sophie's parents in throwing the two young people together, but across all teachers in a school in order to create a common environment for learning and allow smooth progression as children move up through the different classes.

The one drawback for teachers operating this system, Rousseau thought, was that its benefits – the production of sturdy, well-formed characters able to think – are 'perceptible only to clear-sighted men'. Other teachers put their energies into accumulating 'without distinction or discernment a rubbish heap in the child's memory'. This provides them with 'merchandise' – examination results or PISA results in contemporary parlance – with which to impress parents, governments and the world, thus doing wonders for their *amour-propre* but little for their pupils.[10]

Rousseau and women

Book V of *Émile* begins with a lengthy discussion of the differences between men and women and an account of the education of Sophie which is very much the opposite of that provided for Émile and close to the kind of contemporary education that elsewhere he condemned. This part of the book has attracted a great deal of understandably negative attention. It isn't just that some of it is offensive to many modern sensibilities, for example Rousseau's praise of ancient Greece where women, following marriage, disappeared from public view. 'Such', he wrote, 'is the way of life that nature and reason prescribe for the fair sex'.

He attacked Plato for educating both men and women to be 'philosopher kings', which in his view 'cannot fail to engender the most intolerable abuses' and, even more objectionably, argued that 'woman is made to yield to man and to endure even his injustice'. But one must expect to be offended as part of living in a liberal society, not rush to silence the offender so that henceforth all 'disrespectful' views are excluded from the public space. It is a defining characteristic of such a society that this be so. One must also learn to look at philosophers' views in the context of their times and in the context of the whole of their thought while reserving the right, once one has done so, to continue to disagree profoundly with them.

The main point, however, is not that it is offensive to the contemporary mind, but that a lot of it, at least taken literally, is simply wrong, for example 'In fact, almost all little girls learn to read and write with repugnance. But as for holding a needle, that they always learn gladly'. It is highly doubtful if this were true in Rousseau's time and, even if it were, we are now clear that this would be something that was socially rather than physically (as is implied) determined.

Rousseau, as ever, pulls us in different directions simultaneously. He also sees men and women as completely interdependent, women in many ways as superior to men, and women as the main teachers in the home (though this is hardly consistent with the education he has prescribed for them). 'Woe to the age in which women lose their ascendancy', he wrote, 'and in which their judgments no longer have an effect on men'.

What Rousseau has to say about the education of girls is irrelevant as a guide to practice. The value of *Émile* as a whole is that it lays down principles for education that we now know can apply equally to both boys and girls. Apart from this, all we can do is accept that, although Rousseau confronted the orthodoxies of his own times in many radical ways, there were some areas, including this one, where he did not. But even this may be to take Rousseau's account of female education too literally and to forget that, as Allan Bloom observed, '*Émile* is the canvas on which Rousseau tried to paint all of the soul's acquired passions and learning in such a way as to cohere with man's natural wholeness'.

One contemporary (female) commentator has argued that Rousseau's views about men and women and their different roles can perhaps therefore be better seen more as an extended metaphor which explores the relationships between a wide range of human characteristics in the context of a search for perfectibility, though to me this seems a bit like trying to get Jean-Jacques, for whom in other ways I have a great admiration, rather too easily off the hook.[11]

The best riposte to Rousseau on women's education came 30 years later from the radical English thinker Mary Wollstonecraft (1759-97) whose *A Vindication of the Rights of Woman* (1792) impressively pulls to shreds Rousseau's arguments for the separate treatment of women, while paying him the tribute of demanding for women the kind of education that Rousseau had advocated for men.[12]

*****

How Rousseau can help us think about education today

Rousseau's main legacy

Rousseau's relevance to the present day is four-fold. First, he taught us that education should focus on the development of durable qualities – a person's character, the kind of human being they are, the quality of their mind – rather than on secondary factors such as how much they know. Second, he was deeply conscious that one's chances of success as a teacher depended heavily on the social and cultural context in which one was operating, but that one should not just accept this context but help people to try to carve out an existence that was, if necessary, separate from it. Third, he showed us how we can get the best out of children by enabling them to learn actively, find out things by themselves, and construct their own knowledge. Fourth, he warned us that, in order to achieve this, great sophistication and skill on the part of the teacher would be required.

Contrary to some popular misinterpretations Rousseau did not idealise the child, did not allow the child to shape the aims and objectives of learning, and retained for the teacher a central, highly directive (and even more demanding) role. As Jean Starobinski, one of Rousseau's greatest interpreters has said, *Émile* should not be read, as it often is, as a book about the irrepressible spontaneity of a child but as an account of the reasoned reflections of a mature educator.[13]

For me, working for eight years in Rousseau's native city, Jean-Jacques's legacy was, in part, the pervasive reminder of his presence in my life. Most days I would drive across the Pont du Mont Blanc past the Ile Rousseau and Jean-Jacques's pensive statue overlooking the point where Lake Geneva flows out into the river Rhône. The school of which I was Head had been founded in 1924 by Swiss pedagogues hugely influenced by Rousseau and still rightly believed that in many ways it was following Rousseauite educational principles in its daily practice.

Jean-Jacques had also briefly lived in a house just across the road from the school. After reading Rousseau's *Confessions* I was keen to visit other places where he had lived: the house, Les Charmettes, near Chambéry in France, where as a young man he had his brief idyll with Madame de Warens, and the Ile St-Pierre in the Swiss Lac de Bienne, to which, after the public denunciation of *Émile,* he had retreated in 1765 and where, shortly before his death, he wrote that he had spent 'the happiest time of my life'.

I even organized a guided tour of places linked to his life in Geneva for those of the school's teachers who were interested enough to turn up, and many encouragingly did. By that time I had bid for the school to be part of the official programme of celebrations in 2012 for the tercentenary of Rousseau's birth, my bid had been accepted, and an exhibition of students' work illustrating aspects of Rousseau's pedagogy and his life and works was in preparation. By the time the exhibition took place, however, I had already left the school and the country.

Rousseau and amour-propre

Rousseau distinguished between *amour de soi* (love of self) and *amour-propre* (self-love). The first is good and necessary, allows one to protect one's rightful interests and gives one a sense of worth. It does not involve feeling that we need to get the better of other people. The second, especially in its most negative form, involves a desire to feel superior to others, a craving for domination and prestige, and a sense of worth which relies on one's status and on the opinions that others have of one. It is a main source of personal suffering and social evil.[14]

Dealing with the effects of *amour-propre* is central to a great deal of Rousseau's thought. He also knew from personal experience what it involved.

Helping young people to get the balance right between *amour de soi* and *amour-propre* is an extremely difficult one. Developing, *for all pupils*, the legitimate sense of self-worth that is at the heart of *amour de soi* was largely neglected by the kind of schools that Rousseau was familiar with. This neglect continued in schools in most countries until relatively recent times.

Schools of this type encouraged competition, placed pupils in rank order, awarded privileges selectively, and reserved praise for those who were successful academically and in sports. One might have been forgiven for thinking that the development of the *amour-propre* of a minority was indeed their main *raison d'être*. Schools of this type still exist in large numbers in certain parts of the world today.

In other parts of the world, and especially in Anglo-Saxon countries, there has been a huge reaction against this kind of educational environment, but has this reaction gone too far? The danger in eliminating arrangements that promote the *amour-propre* of a few is of two negative effects. First, by weakening competition, one may be removing useful stimuli to self-improvement and, second, by lavishing praise and fostering self-esteem indiscriminately in an 'all must have prizes' kind of atmosphere, one drifts into relativism, undermines the sense that one should always be trying to do better than one's previous best, gives people a false sense of their merits and talents, and turns a regime of selective *amour-propre* into a universal one.

Signs of this second effect can be found everywhere: in the all-pervasive use of social media for self-promotion, the availability of 'Personal Branding Workshops', the self-esteem 'Happy 2 Be Me' badges of Britain's Girl Guides, the banner 'Have pride in everything you are' that I saw held up recently in a Canadian city parade, and what a journalist has called the whole 'international gospel of self-belief'.[15] How to support *amour de soi*, while reasserting the moral and aesthetic benefits of modesty, humility and self-doubt, and how to set high expectations and encourage people to strive to meet them, without stimulating excessive *amour-propre*, remain educational and social objectives of supreme importance today just as they were when Rousseau wrote about them 250 years ago.

*****

Rousseau writes

Rousseau on understanding and memory

> When understanding appropriates things before depositing them in memory, what it draws from memory later belongs to it; whereas, by overburdening memory without the participation of understanding, one runs the risk of never withdrawing anything from memory suitable for understanding.
>
> Rousseau, J-J, *Émile or on Education*, p.358

Rousseau on how traditional pedagogy undermines autonomy

> Since everything which enters into the human understanding comes there through the senses, man's first reason is a reason of the senses; this sensual reason is the basis of intellectual reason. Our first masters of philosophy are our feet, our hands, our eyes. To substitute books for all that is not to teach us to reason. It is to teach us to use the reason of others. It is to teach us to believe much and never to know anything.
>
> Rousseau, J-J, *Émile or on Education*, p.264

Rousseau on learning how to learn

> *Émile* has little knowledge, but what he has is truly his own. He knows nothing halfway. Among the small number of things he knows and

knows well, the most important is that there are many things of which he is ignorant and which he can know one day; there are many more that other men know that he will never know in his life; and there are an infinite number of others that no man will ever know. Émile has a mind that is universal not by its learning but by its faculty to acquire learning; a mind that is open, intelligent, ready for everything, and, as Montaigne says, if not instructed, at least able to be instructed. It is enough for me that he knows how to find the 'what's it good for?' in everything he does and the 'why?' in everything he believes. Once again, my object is not to give him science but to teach him to acquire science when needed, to make him estimate it for exactly what it is worth, and to make him love the truth above all. With this method one advances little, but one never takes a useless step, and one is not forced to go backward.

Rousseau, J-J, *Émile or on Education*,
translated by Kelly, C, and Bloom, A, p.358

Rousseau on the rewards of a teacher who has taught his pupil to apply what he has learned

I heard the late Lord Hyde tell the story of one of his friends who, returning from Italy after three-years absence, wanted to examine his nine or ten-year old son's progress. They went for a walk one evening with the boy and his governor in a field where schoolboys were playing at flying kites. The father asked his son, in passing, "Where is the kite whose shadow is here?" Without hesitation, without lifting his head, the child said, "Over the highway." "And, indeed," added Lord Hyde, "the highway was between us and the sun." The father at this response kissed his son and, leaving his examination at that, went away without saying anything. The next day he sent the governor the title to a lifetime pension in addition to his salary.

What a man that father was, and what a son was promised him! The question suits the age precisely; the response is quite simple. But see what it implies about the incisiveness of the child's judgment!

Rousseau, J-J, *Émile or on Education*, p.307

Rousseau on not taking himself too literally

When told by a proud father that he had raised his child strictly according to the principles of *Émile*, Rousseau is reported to have answered, 'that's too bad for you and even worse for him!'

Gill, N, *Educational Philosophy in the French Enlightenment. From Nature to Second Nature*, p. 198, 2010, Ashgate, Farnham

References

1. Quoted in Kelly, C, in the *Introduction to Émile or on Education, The Collected Writings of Rousseau*, Volume 13, p. xv, 2010, Dartmouth College Press, Lebanon, New Hampshire.

2. Parry, G, *Émile: Learning to Be Men, Women and Citizens*, pp. 249-50, 263-4, and Riley, P, *Rousseau's General Will*, pp. 130-134, in (ed.) Riley, P, *The Cambridge Companion to Rousseau*, 2001, Cambridge University Press, Cambridge.

3. Rousseau, J-J, *Émile or on Education*, translated by Kelly, C, and Bloom, A, *op.cit.*, pp. 304-7, in The Collected Writings of Rousseau, Volume 13.

4. Rousseau, J-J, *Émile or on Education*, translated by Kelly, C, and Bloom, A, op.cit., pp. 332-347.

5. Rousseau, J-J, *Émile or on Education*, translated by Kelly, C, and Bloom, A, op.cit., p. 362.

6. Rousseau, J-J, *Émile or on Education*, translated by Kelly, C, and Bloom, A, op.cit., pp. 348-9. One feels inclined to add here, *contra* Rousseau, that even though 'fathers and masters' might not have learned how to fathom the individual characteristics of their children and pupils, Jean-Jacques might have found that some mothers had done so if he had ever thought to ask that question.

7. Rousseau, J-J, *Émile or on Education*, translated by Kelly, C, and Bloom, A, op.cit., p. 253. The discussion of La Fontaine is at pp. 248-53. The importance of learning to fail and not being insulated from the sufferings of this world is discussed in Bruckner, P, *L'euphorie perpétuelle. Essai sur le devoir de bonheur*, p. 243, 2000, Bernard Grasset, Paris.

8. Rousseau, J-J, *Émile or on Education*, translated by Kelly, C, and Bloom, A, op.cit., p. 404.

9. Bell, M, *Open Secrets. Literature, Education, and Authority from J-J Rousseau to J.M. Coetzee*, p. 21, 2007, Oxford University Press, Oxford.

10. Rousseau, J-J, *Emile or on Education*, translated by Kelly, C, and Bloom, A, op.cit., pp. 306-7.

11. Rousseau, J-J, *Emile or on Education*, translated by Kelly, C, and Bloom, A, op.cit., pp. 537, 542, 543, 570, 577; Shell, S, M, *Émile: Nature and the Education of Sophie*, pp. 272-301, in Riley, P (ed.), *The Cambridge Companion to Rousseau*. Shell quotes Bloom on p. 272.

12. Wollstonecraft, M, *A Vindication of the Rights of Woman*, (ed.) Poston, C H, 1975, Norton, New York.

13. Starobinksi, J, *Jean-Jacques Rousseau. La transparence et l'obstacle*, pp. 257-8, 1971, Gallimard, Paris.

14. Dent, N J H, *A Rousseau Dictionary*, pp. 30-36, 1992, Blackwell, Oxford.

15. Wakefield, M, *In defence of self-deprecation, The Spectator*, 29th April 2014, London.

Chapter 7

Encouraging a cosmopolitan disposition: Immanuel Kant

IMMANUEL KANT (1724-1804) has been regarded by many in recent times as the greatest philosopher since ancient Greece. Even though many of the fundamental principles of his impressive philosophical system have been challenged or rejected his views can still often be the starting point for debate. He was the first great philosopher of modern times to be employed as a university teacher of philosophy. One of his duties in this role was to give lectures on education, for which he was able to draw on his earlier experience as a full-time private tutor.

Kant's output over a long life was immense though his early works are now rarely read. His fame rests largely on works he published when he was in his late 50s and 60s, and in particular on four great works: *The Critique of Pure Reason* (1781 and 1787), *The Critique of Practical Reason* (1788), *The Critique of Judgment* (1790), and *The Fundamental Principles of the Metaphysics of Ethics* (1785).

Kant set out to answer three philosophical questions: What can I know? What should I do? What may I hope for?[1] At the heart of these questions was concern to explore the nature of knowledge and the extent of its objectivity, and to reconcile the methods of modern science with traditional ethical and religious convictions and thus with metaphysics.

Kant, mostly in *The Critique of Pure Reason*, tackled the first of these questions by distinguishing between the world of appearances or phenomena, which we can know about through our senses and minds, and 'things in themselves' about which we can know nothing and about which neither faith nor revelation can give us *knowledge*. The particular novelty of Kant's response to the question 'what can I know?' was his argument that there are necessary and universal propositions about the world of appearances that are neither true by definition nor derive from our observations, but which, like our in-built notions of space, time and causality, arise out of our own minds.

In answering the second question Kant was keen to be able to show that there are similarly necessary and universal maxims of morality, independently of the claims of religion, which cannot do other than command the assent of all rational beings. He had difficulty in explaining why this *must* be so. His ethical theory is chiefly known for his emphasis on the Categorical Imperative which lays down that one must 'act only according to that maxim by which you can at the same time say that it should become a universal law'. Only when we act morally in this way, out of duty, are we wholly rational, free and autonomous. Kant was well aware that this theory had major educational implications.

The third question was perhaps the most difficult. Kant's epistemology does not offer much scope for establishing knowledge about some of the main issues with which philosophy had been traditionally concerned: the question of man's free will, the immortality of the soul, the existence of God. He was reluctant, however, to give up on these, concluding that even though we could not *know* anything about such matters, we could nonetheless have *beliefs* about them, which can be neither proven nor disproven, and which do not contradict Reason.

Kant was born into a modest and deeply Christian family in the Prussian town of Königsberg (now the Russian enclave of Kaliningrad, between Poland and Lithuania, 'named in honour of one of the few of Stalin's henchmen to die of natural causes').[2] He had only praise for the moral education that he received from his parents, even though he later turned against their evangelical version of Protestantism and against all conventional religion. He went to two different schools and then, at the age of 16, to Königsberg University where he remained for eight years as a student. During this time both his mother and father died and, having been left with major responsibilities for his siblings and in need of funds, Kant spent the next six years away from Königsberg working as a private tutor. On his return he started to teach at the university, where eventually he became a professor and spent most of the rest of his life.

Kant is famous for his bachelor existence, his regular habits and the provincial seclusion of his life in Königsberg (he never moved out of his native province of East Prussia). His daily routine was demanding, being woken every day at 5am, working in nightcap and robe from 5 to 7, then lectures, then back to his desk (again in nightcap and robe), then lunch at a local pub where he mixed with ordinary townsfolk, followed by his famous daily constitutional walk.[3]

Though very particular about his routine, he was far from being a scholarly recluse. He dressed elegantly, had a wide range of friends and correspondents, dined out frequently, enjoyed the company of women, could be a brilliant conversationalist, and had a dry sense of humour. Königsberg, as a big trading centre with people of many different languages and nationalities, was also no backwater despite its distance from other parts of Germany.

In his final years Kant's mental and physical powers declined significantly, though his reputation as one of the greatest intellectual figures of the European Enlightenment remained undimmed. At his funeral in 1804 the bells of all Königsberg's churches rang in his honour and the whole town turned out to pay their respects to their very own 'philosopher king'. The day was bitterly cold but bright and sunny and the ground was frozen so hard that it was 16 days before Kant's body could be buried.[4] Kant is still commemorated in his native city by a bronze plaque, in German and Russian, with words from the *Critique of Practical Reason*:

> Two things fill the heart with renewed and increasing awe and reverence, the more often and the more steadily we meditate upon them: the starry firmament above and the moral law within.[5]

*****

> Many people think that the years of their youth were the best and most pleasant of their lives. But this is hardly so. They are the most arduous years, because one is under strict discipline, can seldom have a real friend, and even more seldom can have freedom.
>
> Kant, *Lectures on Pedagogy*, p. 472

> ...because we animal creatures are made into human beings only by education, in a short time we would see very different human beings around us if that educational method were to come into common use which is wisely derived from nature itself and not slavishly copied from old habit and unexperienced ages.
>
> Kant, *Essays regarding the Philanthropinum*, p. 102

> ...when a man dreads nothing more than to find himself, on self-examination, worthless and contemptible in his own eyes, then every good moral disposition can be grafted on to it, because this is the best, nay, the only guard that can keep off from the mind the pressure of ignoble and corrupting influences.
>
> Kant, *Critique of Practical Reason*, p.375

> A human being can be highly cultivated in physical terms, he can have a well-formed mind, but can still be poorly cultivated in moral terms, and thus be an evil creature.
>
> Kant, *Lectures on Pedagogy*, pp. 459-60

Kant's own experience of education

While attending his first school, a one-teacher school where he learned reading, writing and arithmetic, Kant's talent was spotted and at the age of eight his parents were recommended to transfer him to a school that prepared boys for high office in church and state. Although he clearly benefitted throughout life from the 18 hours a week of Latin that he received in the lower part of this school, and had at least one able teacher who made him want to read Latin authors outside the formal curriculum, he did not like to remember his schooldays. He described them as a period of 'slavery'. He was particularly critical in later years of the school's failure to develop the understanding and to teach pupils to think. As with Montaigne and Locke, his own educational views were very much in reaction against his own experiences.

Kant was also an experienced teacher. In his 20s, having finished at university, he spent six years as a private tutor living with three different families and being responsible for the education of boys of very different ages. Kant thought that he was probably the worst private tutor who ever lived and in later life had nightmares that he was once again back in this role.[6] He was likely, however, to have been unduly self-critical given the way in which the families continued to keep in touch with him once he had left. These years at least enabled him to learn about children and gave him first-hand experience of the challenges facing a teacher.

For the rest of Kant's life he was, by all reports, an outstanding lecturer, though his topics were sometimes difficult ones. One had to arrive by 6am if one wanted to be sure of a place for Professor Kant's 7am lectures. As well as being a 'spirited orator' who got across to his audience the seriousness and importance of the topics he was talking about and of scholarship generally, he also turned his lectures into a demonstration of the methodology of thought as well as of its conclusions. At different points he was also dean and rector of his university and did not at all enjoy the administration that this involved. It is impossible to imagine him in the managerialist world of contemporary higher education.

Kant and the Philanthropinum

Kant's views on education, as well as being shaped by his philosophy and his experiences as student and teacher, were also influenced by his admiration for Rousseau, and in particular for Rousseau's great educational work *Émile*, and by a contemporary educational experiment in Germany that was trying to put Rousseau's (and Locke's) educational theories into practice.

This was the Educational Institute or Philanthropinum of Dessau established by Johann Bernhard Basedow. Kant, keen to further 'enlightenment' in practice as well as in theory, was an enthusiastic supporter, writing two essays in a Königsberg journal in 1776 and 1777 extolling its principles and urging readers both to subscribe to the Institute's publications and to send donations to help with the initiative. He even did fund-raising for the Institute, inviting people to come to his house to pay their subscriptions, 'at Prof Kant's in the morning hours from 10 until the afternoons around 1 o'clock'.[7] Kant's excitement about the innovative nature of the initiative, and sense of the tremendous importance of education, comes across in the following reference, full of hyperbole, to be found in one of his surviving lectures:

> The present Basedowian institutes are the first that have come about according to the perfect plan of education. This is the greatest phenomenon which has appeared in this century for the improvement of the perfection of humanity, through it all schools in the world will receive another form, and the human race will thereby be freed from the constraints of the prevailing schools.[8]

What Kant liked about the Philanthropinum was its emphasis on learning from direct experience (by speaking and using languages, for example, not just learning their grammar and vocabulary), and on physical education, and that, in a religiously divided Germany, it was inter-denominational in its religious instruction, stressed morality rather than religion, and aimed at giving its pupils a 'cosmopolitan' outlook on the world. He also liked the way it had a plan for the dissemination of its ideas and practices through using its schools as training colleges for new teachers. The reality of the Philanthropinum turned out to be less than utopian, as usually happens with educational (and indeed all) utopias, and by 1790 the initiative had fizzled out.[9]

The 'many mistakes' of the Philanthropinum – accentuated, according to Kant, by the fact that Basedow 'drank too much Malaga' – nonetheless did not alter his view that radical changes to school education were needed. It was 'not a slow *reform*, but a swift *revolution*', he argued, that was called for. This required experimentation and he accepted that the effects of experiments were unpredictable. 'New experiments' are therefore 'always required' and 'no one generation can present a complete plan of education', he argued.[10] New ministers of education should not, however, cite Kant when feeling that they have *carte blanche* to turn everything upside down, as we shall find.

Kant's *Lectures on Pedagogy*

Knowledge of Kant's views on education comes largely from the lectures on practical pedagogy that he gave four times in 1776-7, 1780, 1783-4 and 1786-7. It was a requirement of the philosophy faculty at Königsberg that this course was offered and it rotated around the members of the faculty. Kant's great *Critique of Practical Reason* also begins to look at the educational implications of his views about the moral imperative, and there are passing references in other works too.

The *Lectures on Pedagogy* were edited by Kant's younger colleague Friedrich Theodor Rink and published the year before Kant's death. Kant's own lecture notes have not survived and it remains unclear to what extent they were edited by Rink and whether parts have been deleted or even added. The work has a rather unfinished feel to it, though nevertheless bears the mark of Kant's highly original mind.

Education should be about shaping the future

Kant had a strong sense of the social and political importance of education. It could not just be left to parents whose main or only concern was that their children 'get on well in the (present) world', however corrupt that world might be. Nor could it be left to governments which were only concerned with how they might best *use* their subjects to short-term advantage. If there was to be the progress in human affairs in which he believed, education needed to look to the future. He saw the final destiny of the human race as 'moral perfection' and this could only be achieved through education.

Unlike some other Enlightenment thinkers he did not see progress as inevitable, but nor did he share his contemporary Rousseau's pessimism about the potential power of education to transform existing societies. Though he believed that there were features in human nature driving us in that direction, progress might or might not happen. Human beings were capable of making free choices and through these choices were able to improve themselves. Education was crucial in order to help them to do this.[11]

Understanding one's moral duty and doing it

Kant was aware that there were many aims in education. He makes many distinctions about the different aspects of education: between 'discipline or training', which he sees as negative and, in very un-Rousseauite language, as 'the taming of savagery', and 'instruction', which is positive; between an 'instructor', who educates 'merely for the school', and a 'tutor', who provides guidance about the exercise of what has been learned and who educates for life; and between 'physical education' and 'practical education', a distinction which is perhaps not as clear as it might have been had Kant been able to edit these lectures himself.

All these different aspects of education have their purposes, whether to control negative impulses or to develop skills, to learn how to think or to acquire good habits. Behind all of them, however, there was one ultimate and overriding purpose of education, which reflects the ultimate and overriding end towards which Kant sees human beings as predisposed: the attainment of moral perfection.

Central to Kant's moral philosophy is the idea of the Categorical Imperative and the importance for human beings of understanding their moral duty and acting on it, not because their feelings prompt them to do so and not out of any calculation of the consequences of their actions, but because they understand the reasons why they must act in this way. If education helps individuals to reach this state it will have given them freedom, as freedom comes from choosing to do what one must do and not from doing simply what one's impulses tell one to do. It will also give them dignity.[12]

Kant had specific thoughts about how moral education was to be achieved. He shared with Rousseau a dislike of making children learn lists of moral precepts. He also opposed the kind of moral education that sets before people impossible ideals of saintly or heroic behaviour. He was keen instead to get pupils to explore specific ethical dilemmas in order to help them develop their understanding of the moral law, appreciate the pressures *not* to act morally, practise self-discipline, and ultimately acquire confidence in their ability to act with a good will as autonomous moral agents.

Imaginary situations could be used for this purpose but for preference Kant was keen on real case studies such as the one of Henry Norris, the servant of Henry VIII, who 'would rather die a thousand deaths than calumniate an innocent person', which ends the *Critique of Practical Reason* and which is quoted below. The teacher's role in these case studies, said Kant, echoing Socrates, was that of 'midwife of the pupil's thoughts'. In a process Kant called 'ethical gymnastics' pupils discuss, analyse and interpret in order to deepen their moral understanding, prompted by their teacher. The exercise is not open-ended and not quite the same as a Socratic dialogue. The moral understanding that is aimed at is pre-determined, at least in its fundamentals. The Categorical Imperative brooks of no opposition.[13]

Kant stressed the need to educate people to exercise their duties to others, respecting others' rights, but also to exercise their duties towards themselves. He put the latter first. The duty to oneself, a concept largely absent from contemporary educational writings, is not a question of satisfying one's wants and desires or (those contemporary favourites) 'following one's passion' and 'chasing one's dream', but of ensuring that one does not 'deny the dignity of humanity' in oneself through untruthfulness and immoderate and intemperate behaviour. The aim must be to ensure that 'a man dreads nothing more than to find himself, on self-examination, worthless and contemptible in his own eyes'. This, Kant felt, was 'the only guard that can keep off from the mind the pressure of ignoble and corrupting influences'.[14]

Many more specific characteristics must also be developed in order that the fundamental moral purposes of education might be achieved. Kant talks a great deal about character which, as distinct from temperament, can be developed and which, when it is successfully developed, gives the individual the aptitude to do what is right for the right reasons. Truthfulness is also central. For someone who placed Reason at the centre of his image of humanity and its moral life, lying was the ultimate outrage.

Kant had no time for those who prided themselves on their status and fortune. He stressed the fundamental equality of all human beings. Children should not give orders to servants under any circumstances and servants were not to be beholden to them. Similarly if a child showed contempt to a child poorer than itself it should be made to experience what it had inflicted on another until it came to understand what it had done. Only a person's inner worth should be allowed to count.

Kant also commended the practice of settling accounts with oneself at the end of every day, with a view to being able at the end of one's life to know oneself sufficiently to be able to estimate its value. It is on this noble, if somewhat chilling, note that Kant's lectures on education come to an end.

Education and work

Kant had a high regard for work. Human beings were the only creatures that must work. Work helped to give our lives a purpose and was able to give us great satisfaction. It was through work that we improved ourselves and came nearer to the perfection of which we were capable. It was through work that humankind would be able to bring about that progress in human affairs in which Kant believed.

It was therefore 'of the greatest importance' for Kant 'that children learn to work'. If in school they were led to believe that most things could be done through play, they would labour under a serious misapprehension which could harm them later. They need to learn early on that some things have to be done (i) by compulsion and (ii) whether one likes them or not. This lesson might not be appreciated at the time, but would be welcomed later in life when the child grows up to realise that these are the realities of the adult world. Kant's main point, however, was that work was good for one and should be embraced.

Although Kant in some ways here was distinguishing his position from those of Montaigne, Locke and Rousseau, he remembered the 'slavery' of his own school days and did not wish this to be inflicted on others. Unlike

Locke he had relatively little to say about the details of pedagogy – the title of the French edition of the lectures with its title *Réflexions sur l'éducation* gives a more apt description of their contents – but was clear that the focus should be on developing abstract thought, understanding and judgment and thus on helping children to think rather than on wasting a lot of time on rote learning.

Memorisation was an inferior faculty of the mind but an important one, to be occupied 'only with those things which for us are important to remember and which have a relation to real life'. The key to ensuring a good memory was not in learning things like speeches off by heart and then declaiming them, but in cultivating one's powers of attention and learning to avoid distraction.[15]

The teaching of geography

Different thinkers, have their own favourite subjects. So do different politicians involved in laying down the curriculum in national education systems. For Montaigne and Locke it was history. For Kant, like Dewey much later, it was geography. One of Kant's duties as a lecturer was to give lectures on physical geography, on which he became such an authority that he ended up boring even one of his best friends by constantly going on about it.[16]

Kant felt that a child's formal education might even begin with geography because, as a subject, it was an interesting route into other important parts of the curriculum such as mathematics, physics, zoology, botany and drawing. Physical geography could also lead on to political geography and to the geography of the ancient world and thus to history. The study and drawing of maps was particularly recommended as things that would always fascinate children (as they did Kant): 'when they are weary of everything else, they still learn something when maps are used'.

One of the major issues in drawing up a curriculum is which subjects to include and how much time to devote to each of them. There are always far more things that one would like children to learn than there is time in which to do it. Kant does not answer this question beyond saying, wisely, first, that 'it is better to know little, but to know this little thoroughly, than to know a lot and know it superficially', and, second, that it is best that the child ends up knowing 'thoroughly something of everything'. What Kant does illustrate is that a subject can merit its place in the curriculum both because it opens up links with a range of other subjects and because it can be taught in such a way that its importance and relevance are readily conveyed to pupils.[17]

Cosmopolitanism

Kant was possibly the first of the great philosophers who wrote about education to see one of its responsibilities as preparing young people to think beyond the borders of their state, not just as adherents of a universal faith or members of a single species but as members of an international community that needs to work together and have a sense of its own cosmopolitan identity.

In his *Idea for a universal history with a cosmopolitan aim* (1784) and his essay on *Perpetual Peace* (1795) Kant sketched a possible improved future for humanity in which there would be a diminution in the mutual aggrandisement of states, greater international harmony, measures in place to avoid further wars, and in due course the appearance of some kind of 'universal association of states'. He did not just recommend this but saw it as part of 'a hidden plan of nature' to enable human beings to develop their capacities to the full.

In order that humanity should move in this direction there were few things more important in education than helping children to develop what Kant called a 'cosmopolitan disposition'. 'One must make children familiar with this interest so that they may warm their souls with it', wrote Kant, 'they must rejoice at the best for the world even if it is not to the advantage of their fatherland or to their own gain.' We are already, in the last quarter of the 18th century, not far from the 'international-mindedness' and 'global citizenship' of contemporary bodies such as the International Baccalaureate, though it was to be a long time before such ideas were to have any wider currency.[18]

*****

How Kant can help us think about education today

Education for global and national citizenship

Developing a more 'cosmopolitan outlook' that sees beyond the interests of one's own state remains a pressing concern for many education systems around the world. The urgent need is to combat actions based on hatred of people from other countries, races and religions. Nothing could be further from Kant's vision of an improved and 'moralized' humanity than failing to take into account the viewpoints and legitimate interests of others. Education needs to address this so that, in the words of the International Baccalaureate's mission statement, children grow up learning that 'other people, with their differences, can also be right'.

In many countries encouraging this more 'cosmopolitan' or 'global' outlook is the main and overwhelming priority. But not in all. In some western countries the reaction against the nation state may well have gone too far and left some educators thinking that 'international-mindedness' and 'global citizenship' are all that now really matter. One reason for this attitude is the failure to distinguish between patriotism – the legitimate identification with, and pride in, one's country – and forms of nationalism, including colonialism and imperialism, with which patriotism has often been associated in the past.

Nationalisms can often be felt to be acceptable if they are an expression of minorities and of a supposed 'underdog', but where they are associated with efforts by major states to maintain themselves the contemporary Zeitgeist tends to turn up its nose in distaste. Another reason is more fundamental and is a defining feature of late modernity: the pervasive and unthinking distrust of all notions of borders, frontiers, barriers and distinctions as undermining of equality and limiting of freedom.

I encountered all of these attitudes when, as head of England's national curriculum body in the 1990s, I argued that one of the aims of education in the country's schools should be the fostering of a sense of national identity, not as the only identity that people should have, but as something that all must share for the sake of the coherence of both state and society. I made the point again and again in speeches, articles and radio programmes and was lambasted on all sides for doing so, being accused of 'neo-racism', 'neo-conservatism', 'cultural imperialism', and much more besides. I knew we were up against a profound and disturbing challenge within our society when a primary Head Teacher on one of our working groups told me how unhappy some of her teachers were going to be with a national curriculum history programme of study that gave priority to British history, seeing it as 'racist'.

The set of attitudes I encountered 20 years ago has not gone away, despite the fact that some politicians on the left, where these views mostly festered, have in the meantime woken up to its hugely dangerous consequences. Preparation for national citizenship remains just as important today as it was for Plato and Aristotle in the city states of ancient Greece. Nation states are still at the heart of the world order and look set to remain there for the foreseeable future. The vast majority of people in the world also still spend their lives within a short distance of where they were born. Despite mass migration only 3% of the world's population in 2010 was estimated to live outside its country of origin.

The decisions that most affect the lives of the world's seven billion inhabitants continue to be made within the nation states to which they belong. If a sense of civic responsibility in relation to the functioning at national level of nation states is lacking – and this *requires* a sense of national identity – nation states run the risk, behind a democratic façade, of turning into oligarchies run by small political elites devoted to the perpetuation of their own power. Even where decisions have to be taken internationally the quality of the decisions is largely dependent on the effectiveness of the governments of the different nation states involved. Nation states can also provide public recognition of the values that its citizens hold dear and give them a feeling of purpose and identity which helps to transcend their insignificance and transience in this world.

So, as well as a cosmopolitan outlook and a sense of responsibility for the global consequences of our decisions, we also need a national outlook, a sense of national identity, and a commitment to exercising our responsibilities as citizens of particular states. Kant would have wholeheartedly agreed. He had no wish for a withering away of the Prussian state and was a loyal subject of his king (even though he did not hide his preference for a republic). It was just that he wanted people to be educated so that they did what was right even if this sometimes meant not putting their country first.[19]

Who should make the decisions about education in a state?

Kant was firmly convinced that education should not be left to princes and governments. Governments are only concerned with educating their subjects so that they could be better used for their own purposes. Their interest is mostly in making their subjects 'skilful' rather than 'moral'. Neither parents nor governments 'have as their final end the best for the world and the perfection to which humanity is destined, and for which it also has the predisposition'.

Governments are also concerned solely for the well-being of their own state, not with the whole of the world which should be the object of a true education. Kant cited a scheme in Austria in which the government obliged all schools to follow the 'blindly mechanical' instruction offered in a network of training schools that it had set up, even refusing promotion to teachers who had not worked in those schools. In Kant's view 'nothing good can possibly thrive under such coercion'.

As neither parents nor governments can be trusted, Kant felt that 'the set-up of schools should depend entirely on the judgment of the most enlightened experts'. This is a recommendation that requires more attention than it has received in countries with strong political control over school education. It is rarely, if ever, followed.

The argument against Kant's recommendation is that 'enlightened experts', in practice, sometimes turn out to be less 'enlightened' than one might wish. There is often within the contemporary educational world a dominant way of looking at things – what the French call a *pensée unique* – that pushes aside all that is not in line and which those working in education ignore at their peril. It is also a world swept by ephemeral fashions – for 'creativity', 'blended learning', 'back to basics', 'data-driven decision-making', 'mixed ability teaching', 'streamed teaching', 'setted teaching' (and much more besides).

Rather than relying mainly on any one of government, parents or experts, a state-run education system in a democracy should probably be seen instead as involving a partnership between a range of different groups: popularly elected representatives, including ministers, who have a mandate to govern; civil servants who ought to be able to give impartial advice on the basis of their knowledge of what has worked or not worked in the past; those employed in the education system, in classrooms, schools, training establishments and research institutes, who inevitably know the most about the practical implications of proposed policies; parents, whose freedom is being limited by requirements to have their children educated in certain ways; and the wider public, whether or not they have children, who have a legitimate interest in the way in which, via education, the future of their country is being shaped.

Balancing all these elements is no easy task, but balance is clearly not being achieved when ministers of education by themselves decide what goes in and what comes out of a school history curriculum or when parental freedom, in a state desperately needing a common civic focus, extends to state subsidies for each and every faith group that puts in a claim for its own schools.

Education as both art and science

For Kant human beings, having freedom, are distinguished from animals in needing an education. They are not, for the most part, driven by instinct, as animals are, to behave in certain ways. They will only be able to develop their predisposition to be autonomous rational beings capable of understanding their duty and doing it if they are educated. Given the complexity of this task, 'education is an art', Kant said, 'the practice of which must be perfected over the course of many generations.' Despite his low opinion of current schools and his wish for 'revolution' rather than 'reform', he accepted that education needs to move forward step by step, with 'each generation transmit(ting) its experience and knowledge to the next'.

He also saw education as a science. If it just involves learning from experience on the basis of trial and error we will keep on repeating our mistakes and never make that progress in education that Kant, with the optimism of an Enlightenment thinker, felt was possible. Education must thus also become a science or, as Kant put it more precisely, 'the mechanism in the art of education must be transformed into science'. It is because of this that 'pedagogy must become a course of study'.

Kant would therefore have had little time for those who feel that teachers should be able to teach without being introduced to the body of knowledge that can be derived from experience and research into the nature of learning and are indeed sceptical about the very existence of such knowledge. He would equally have had little time for those who fill educational journals with jargon-laden research studies, based on an exaggerated notion of the potentiality of an educational 'science', that mostly lie unread and that do little or nothing to drive forward educational progress.[20]

*****

Kant writes

Kant on learning by doing

> The best way of cultivating the powers of the mind is to do everything that one wants to accomplish by oneself, for example, immediately to apply the grammatical rule that one has learned. One understands a map best when one can draw it oneself. The biggest aid to understanding anything is to produce it. One learns most thoroughly and retains best that which one learns as it were from oneself. Only a few human beings, however, are able to do this. They are called autodidacts.

Kant, *Lectures on pedagogy*, pp 465-6

Kant on the balance between constraint and freedom

> One of the biggest problems of education is how one can unite submission under lawful constraint with the capacity to use one's freedom. For constraint is necessary. How do I cultivate freedom under constraint? I shall accustom my pupil to tolerate a constraint of his freedom, and I shall at the same time lead him to make good use of his freedom.

...the following must be observed: 1) From earliest childhood the child must be allowed to be free in all matters (except in those where he might injure himself, as, for example, when he grabs an open knife) ... 2) The child must be shown that it can only reach its goals by also letting others reach theirs ... 3) One must prove to it that restraint is put on it in order that it be led to the use of its own freedom, that it is cultivated so that it may one day be free, that is, so that it need not depend on the care of others.

Kant, *Lectures on pedagogy*, pp 447-8

Human beings are only as good as their education has made them and their education is only as good as the educator who has provided it

The human being can only become human through education. He can only become what education makes out of him. It must be noted that the human being is educated only by human beings, human beings who likewise have been educated. That is also why the lack of discipline and instruction in some people makes them in turn bad educators of their pupils. If some day a being of a higher kind were to look after our education, then one would see what the human being could become. But since education partly teaches the human being something and partly merely develops something within him, one can never know how far his natural predispositions reach.

Kant, *Lectures on pedagogy*, p. 439

The acid test of a virtuous human being: a case study for a ten-year old

We will then point out the criterion of pure virtue in an example first, and imagining that it is set before a boy of, say ten years old, for his judgment, we will see whether he would necessarily judge so of himself without being guided by his teacher. Tell him the history of an honest man whom men want to persuade to join the calumniators of an innocent and powerless person (say Anne Boleyn, accused by Henry VIII of England). He is offered advantages, great gifts or high rank; he rejects them. This will excite mere approbation and applause in the mind of the hearer. Now begins the threatening of loss. Amongst these traducers are his best friends, who now renounce his friendship; near kinsfolk, who threaten to disinherit him (he being without fortune); powerful persons, who can persecute and harass him in all places and circumstances; a prince, who threatens him with loss of freedom, yea, loss of life. Then to fill the measure of suffering, and that he may feel the pain that only the morally good heart can feel very deeply, let us conceive his family threatened with extreme distress and want, entreating him to yield; conceive himself, though upright, yet with feelings not hard or insensible either to compassion or to his own distress; conceive him, I say, at the moment when he wishes that he had never lived to see the day that exposed him to such unutterable anguish, yet remaining true to his uprightness, without wavering or even doubting: then will my youthful hearer be raised gradually from mere approval to admiration, from that to amazement, and finally to the greatest veneration, and a lively wish that he himself could be such a man (though certainly not in such circumstances). Yet virtue is here worth so much only because it costs so much, not because it brings any profit.

Kant, *The Critique of Practical Reason*, pp.366-7

References

1. Hersch, J, *Emmanuel Kant, in L'étonnement philosophique*, pp. 199-251, 1993, Gallimard, Paris.
2. Scruton, R, *Kant*, p. 10, 1982, Oxford University Press, Oxford.
3. Scruton, *op.cit.*, p. 5.
4. Kuehn, M, *Kant. A biography*, p. 2, 2001, Cambridge University Press, Cambridge.
5. Scruton, *op.cit.*, p. 10.
6. Kuehn, op.cit., pp. 95-98.
7. *Essays regarding the Philanthropinum, in Lectures on pedagogy, Essays regarding the Philanthropinum,* and *Idea for a universal history with a cosmopolitan* aim, in Kant, I, *Anthropology, History and Education*, The Cambridge Edition of the Works of Immanuel Kant, pp. 98-104, 2007, Cambridge University Press, Cambridge.
8. Op.cit., p. 98.
9. Introduction by Philonenko, A, in Kant, I, *Réflexions sur l'éducation*, pp. 23-31, 2004, Librairie Philosophique J Vrin, Paris; Louden, R B, "*Not a Slow Reform, but a Swift Revolution*". *Kant and Basedow on the Need to Transform Education*, in (ed.) Roth, K, and Surprenant, C W, *Kant and Education*, pp. 39-54, 2012, Routledge, New York and London.
10. Kant, I, *Essays regarding the Philanthropinum, op.cit.*, p. 102; *Lectures on pedagogy, op.cit.*, pp. 445-6.
11. Kant, I, *Lectures on pedagogy,* op.cit., p. 442.
12. *Lectures on pedagogy*, op.cit., pp. 464, 468, 475-6.
13. Surprenant, C W, *Kant's Contribution to Moral Education*, in (ed.) Roth, K, and Surprenant, C W, *op.cit.*, pp. 1-11; Lovlie, L, *Kant's Invitation to Educational Thinking*, in (ed.) Roth, K, and Surprenant, C W, op.cit., p. 122; Guyer, P, *Examples of Moral Possibility*, in (ed.) Roth, K, and Surprenant, C W, op.cit., pp. 124-138.
14. Kant, I, *Critique of Practical Reason*, pp. 374-5, 1879, Longmans, London; Roth, K, and Surprenant, C W, *The Highest Good- the Moral Endeavor of Education*, in Roth, K, and Surprenant, C W, op.cit., pp. ix-xxiv; Kuehn, M, *Kant on Education, Anthropology, and Ethics*, in Roth, K, and Surprenant, C W, *op.cit.*, pp. 55-68.
15. *Lectures on pedagogy*, op.cit., pp. 460-5; Kant, I, *Réflexions sur l'éducation*, introduction by Philonenko, A, op.cit, pp. 52-3, 57-58, 73, 80.
16. Scruton, *op.cit.*, p. 3.

17. *Lectures on pedagogy*, op.cit., pp. 463, 465, 466, 474; Kant, I, *Anthropology, History and* Education, *op.cit.*, p. 2; *Réflexions sur l'éducation, op.cit.*, introduction by Philonenko, A, p. 78.

18. Kant, I, *Anthropology, History and Education, op.cit.*, pp. 14-16; *Idea for a universal history with a cosmopolitan aim*, pp. 114, 117, 118; *Lectures on pedagogy*, op.cit., p. 485.

19. Tate, N, *Challenges and pitfalls facing international education in a post-international world, in Journal for Research in International Education*, Volume 11, No 3, December 2012, pp. 206-8. The extent to which cosmopolitanism should be promoted was highly controversial at the time within Kant's own circle. His pupil Johann Gottfried von Herder, the German philosopher, poet, literary critic and nationalist, quarrelling with his former tutor on this issue, put a contrary view brilliantly when he wrote that the 'savage who loves himself, his wife and his child...and works for the good of his tribe as for his own...is more genuine than the human ghost, the citizen of the world, who, burning with love for all his fellow ghosts, loves a chimera. The savage in his hut has room for a stranger...the saturated heart of the idle cosmopolitan is a home for no one' (quoted in Kuehn, op.cit., p. 300). Rousseau was similarly dismissive of 'cosmopolitans' in *Émile* (Garnier-Flammarion edition, Paris, 1966, p. 39).

20. *Lectures on pedagogy*, op.cit., pp. 441-2.

Chapter 8

Education for authenticity: Friedrich Nietzsche

NIETZSCHE'S DIRECT impact on our contemporary cultural and intellectual scene is probably greater than that of any of the other philosophers in this volume. He is less well known as an educational thinker, but it was a subject in which he had an intense interest.

Many distinctive features of late modernity – individualism, hedonism, mass culture, ethical relativism, the decline of religion, the end of ideology and of metanarratives – are either prefigured in, or illuminated by, Nietzsche's writings. As the German philosopher Martin Heidegger put it, everyone who thinks today does so in Nietzsche's light and shadow whether they are 'for' or 'against' him.[1] Many major 20th-century literary figures – Thomas Mann, André Gide and George Bernard Shaw, among others – were deeply influenced by his writings. Nietzsche himself said that some people are born before their time and have a sense of the direction in which the world is moving long before others can see what is happening. He was right to assume that he was one of them. Unusually for a philosopher, his name crops up with a fair degree of frequency in everyday writing and conversation well outside the world of academia. There is a strong line in t-shirts with Nietzsche quotations.

Nietzsche also was, and is, almost certainly the most controversial of the philosophers with whom we are dealing. His educational views are no exception.

There are three reasons for the controversy surrounding Nietzsche. First, some of his ideas run counter to beliefs fundamental to western liberalism and democracy. Nietzsche attacks our most basic and often unexamined assumptions, and does so without mincing words. Second, Nietzsche was not a systematic philosopher. His view of philosophy was a wide one, embracing psychology, cultural anthropology and social critique. His writing is highly literary, some of it in aphorisms and epigrams, and open to varied and conflicting interpretations. He also changed his views over time. Third, early versions of some of his writings, published after his death by his sister Elisabeth Förster-Nietzsche, were so full of gaps and downright forgeries that the misunderstandings to which these gave rise cannot be said to have been cleared up over 100 years later.

Nietzsche's sister was a racist and a fascist. She later joined the Nazi party and was keen to enlist her brother's memory to her cause. Nietzsche was taken up by the Nazi regime and, despite his pan-Europeanism and his hatred of anti-semitism and nationalism (and especially German nationalism), was selectively quoted in defence of its ideology. An aura linked to this period still unfortunately surrounds his name.

Friedrich Nietzsche (1844-1900) was born in eastern Germany, the son of a Lutheran pastor who died when he was only four. He was brought up in a household consisting of his mother, grandmother, sister and two unmarried aunts, an environment against which he reacted and which left him throughout his life with ambivalent attitudes towards women.

After studying at the universities of Bonn and Leipzig, where his great talents were recognised, he was offered in 1869 the post of professor of classical philology at the University of Basel in Switzerland. He was only 24 and his doctorate had not yet been confirmed. A requirement of taking up the post was that he renounce his Prussian citizenship and apply for Swiss citizenship. He did this but lacked the necessary residential qualification to become Swiss, never renewed his application, and remained stateless for the rest of his life.

He remained at Basel for ten years, though was absent for long periods due to recurring bouts of illness which never henceforth left him. It was at this time that he became close to Richard Wagner, whose music and ideas influenced the development of his thinking about tragedy, the arts and the human condition, though by 1877 the friendship had come to an end.

In 1879, following another bad bout of migraine and sickness, Nietzsche was released from his duties at Basel, retiring on a pension. The next ten years, despite recurring illness, were incredibly productive, with major works being written and published in each of these years. For some of the time he was looked after by his sister and for some of the time he lived on his own. He travelled extensively, often living in France and Italy – Nice, Genoa, Venice, Turin – and, in summer, visiting Sils-Maria in the Swiss Upper Engadin, a small village, 6000 feet above sea level, of which he said 'I know nothing more suited to my nature than this piece of high land.'

1888 was Nietzsche's most productive year, with five works published or written and others in draft. Towards the end of the year his letters to friends began to worry them as to his mental state. On 3rd January, 1889, he collapsed in the Piazza Carlo Alberto in Turin, after creating a public disturbance, and when he finally recovered consciousness was found to be insane. It is reported that just before this incident he had walked past a cab driver in or near the square who was having trouble with his horse and had begun whipping it. Nietzsche was so distraught that he ran to the horse's aid and threw his arms around his neck to protect it from the blows.

The symbolism is powerful: the contrast between the private Nietzsche, kind, courteous and solitary, and the public persona of a philosopher who denounced compassion and justified cruelty. It is difficult to track down the source for the story. According to Nietzsche's views on knowledge, truth and history, it matters little, however, whether the incident took place. Knowledge, Nietzsche argued, should be seen in the light of its value and uses, not of its scientific accuracy, and this episode encapsulates aspects of our response to Nietzsche and has caught people's imaginations. It was the stimulus for the 2011 film *The Turin Horse* by the Hungarian director Béla Tarr.

Following his collapse Nietzsche was taken back to Germany where he was looked after by his mother and, after her death, once again by his sister. He sank further into dementia and finally died in Weimar in 1900 at the age of 55. By this time his sister had already carefully constructed the new identity for him that, posthumously, over a hundred years later, he is still striving to shrug off.

★★★★★

> During the seven years in which I taught Greek to the top form of the Basel grammar school I never once had occasion to mete out a punishment; the laziest were industrious when they were with me.
>
> (Nietzsche, F, *Ecce Homo. How One Becomes What One Is*, p.43)

> The educational system in large states will always be mediocre at best, for the same reason that the cooking in large kitchens is at best mediocre.
>
> Nietzsche, F, *Human, All Too Human*,
> aphorism 467, 1984, Penguin, London

> There are no easy answers in life, only difficult choices. To comprehend the weight of these choices it is necessary to pose the right kind of questions. This is what Nietzsche helps us to do. We err if we approach his work from some undeserved height of moral superiority. Labelling a thinker of his greatness a 'Fascist', on account of his confusions and excesses – and ignoring his nobility of mind and character, as well as the appositeness of a great deal of his political thought – is not a sign of insight, but of moral laziness and intellectual stupidity. We not only do Nietzsche a great disservice in this respect, but ourselves too.
>
> Ansell-Pearson, K, *An Introduction to Nietzsche as political thinker*,
> p.8, 1994, Cambridge University Press, Cambridge

> I (wished to) describe to you what I take to be the nature of the educational questions now attracting such enormous and pressing attention. It seemed to me that I must recognise two main directions in the forces at work – two seemingly antagonistic tendencies, equally deleterious in their action, and ultimately combining to produce their results: a striving to achieve the greatest possible expansion of education on the one hand, and a tendency to minimise and weaken

> it on the other. The first-named would, for various reasons, spread learning among the greatest number of people; the second would compel education to renounce its highest, noblest and sublimest claims in order to subordinate itself to some other department of life – such as the service of the State.

Nietzsche, F, *On the future of our educational institutions*, lectures delivered in 1872, in *The Complete Works of Friedrich Nietzsche*, Volume 6, pp.35-6, 1909, T.N. Foulis, Edinburgh

Nietzsche and education

Nietzsche had a fairly conventional schooling for his day and, although complaining later about the general state of education in Germany, does not appear to have been particularly unhappy at school or had much that he wished subsequently to complain about. After attending two schools in Naumburg, in Thuringia, where his family moved after his father's death, he transferred to the Gymnasium, the town's high school, where he did so well that at the age of 14 he obtained a scholarship to the nearby Schulpforta, one of Germany's leading boarding schools for boys founded in the 16th century.

Here he stayed until he was nearly 19, doing outstandingly well as a classicist though less well in other parts of the curriculum. Other distinguished former pupils included Leopold von Ranke, the founder of the kind of modern historiography that Nietzsche was later to loathe, as well as the philosopher Fichte. In Nazi times the school's Christian and humanist traditions were swept aside and it became an academy for preparing the Aryan elite of the 1000-year Reich. After the end of the Second World War it served instead to help educate the future leaders of communist East Germany. It continues to this day, in a reunified Germany, as a state boarding school for the academically gifted.

Nietzsche spent the next few years at university, first of all in Bonn and then, following one of his tutors who had taken up a post there, in Leipzig. It was possibly at Bonn that a visit to a brothel led him to contract the syphilis that may account for his later ill health and collapse (although the extensive writings on Nietzsche's medical condition leave one uncertain as to whether he suffered from syphilis or not).

He had begun as a student of theology and philology, but after a year abandoned the former having in the meantime lost his Christian faith. He went on to do a doctorate, interrupted for a year by military service, and then, as already mentioned, found himself at the University of Basel. Here one of his duties was to teach Greek to the top year in the local Gymnasium, which he seems to have done conscientiously. In one of his very last works, *Ecce Homo*, he claimed to have inspired all his pupils to industry, though like some other hyperbolic claims in this autobiographical work this must be taken with a pinch of salt.

Having committed himself to an academic career, Nietzsche clearly tried to make sense of the job and of the institutions in which he was now spending his time. The result was a series of five public lectures delivered at the University of Basel between January and March 1872 – *On the future of our educational institutions* – which is one of the main sources of our knowledge about his views on education.

These were followed two years later in 1874 by two long essays: *On the uses and disadvantages of history for life*, a critique of modern attitudes to history and of modern historical writing; and *Schopenhauer as educator*, a reflection on the thinker who had been, up to that date, one of the main influences on the development of Nietzsche's thought.

Although Nietzsche wrote no further works focused mainly on education, he continued throughout his active life to think about education, explore the educational purposes of philosophy and art, see himself, as a philosopher, in an educational role, and wonder what kind of education would be needed in a future world freed from all the negative influences within contemporary society that he had set out to analyse.

Education for authenticity

A major theme of Nietzsche's writings is the search for authenticity, in the sense of being able to understand all the beliefs, attitudes and conventions imposed on us from without, and, where necessary, to cast them off, so that we are able, so to speak, to 'become ourselves' or to 'make ourselves afresh', and thus so that we can be free.[2] The sub-title of Nietzsche's last and most autobiographical work *Ecce Homo*, significantly, is *How One Becomes What One Is*.

At the centre of Nietzsche's thought is a rejection of the West's Greek, Hebrew and Christian heritage. It is this that makes Nietzsche such a distinctive and radical thinker. Humankind took a wrong turn early on, he thought, first with the monotheism of the Old Testament, then with the rationalism of Socrates, Plato and the later Greek philosophers, and finally with the life-denying, ascetic ideals of Christianity and its 'slave morality'.

It is not just that the dominant attitudes of the last 2000 and more years are based on lies, and that we must now accept that 'God is dead', but that these lies have led us to refuse to face up to our human condition. The world is meaningless, Nietzsche believed. There is no God and no teleology. There is thus no over-arching narrative into which we fit, and, since Copernicus, nothing to lead us to believe that there is anything very special about man or the little planet on which he lives. Nietzsche was equally dismissive of the illusions about progress and the secular utopias of his liberal and socialist contemporaries. These are just a substitute for religious faith, part of the same pretence that there is some objective meaning to life.

Given that we find ourselves face to face with a meaningless world, and indeed with 'nothing', it is easy to sink into despair and 'nihilism'. But it was to avoid this despair, to suppress these intimations of what the world is really like, that all the false constructs of religion, morality and ideology were created in the first place. We must therefore shake off these constructs once and for all, face the harsh reality at the heart of our lives, accept our fate (*amor fati* or love of one's fate was one of Nietzsche's favourite phrases), joyously affirm our existence with all its suffering and tragedy, and stop whingeing. If we do this we will be able to move beyond nihilism. The real nihilism is that of those who cling desperately and pathetically to their illusions as comfort blankets protecting them from reality.

In his early work *The Birth of Tragedy* Nietzsche distinguished between the Apollonian (order, harmony) and Dionysian (disorder, passion) aspects of existence, associated with Apollo and Dionysus, the contrasting figures of Greek mythology. He argued that it was the lack of balance between the two, and in particular the neglect of the Dionysian, that had driven western civilization into a dead end.

The Greeks had given the Dionysian elements their due weight through music and dramatic tragedy, only for this to be neglected within the Judaeo-Christian tradition with its denial of sensuality and its debilitating self-denigration and altruism. It is this Dionysian view of the world that helps to explain Nietzsche's early enthusiasm for the music of Wagner. It is also one of Nietzsche's themes with a strong resonance in subsequent literature, most notably in Thomas Mann's 1912 novella *Death in Venice*.

From a Dionysian perspective the Christian virtues of humility, compassion and self-denial are the opposite of what Nietzsche felt that human beings ought to be, which is self-confident, self-affirming and egoistic. Nietzsche believed that we always need to ask of moral codes not whether they are right or wrong in themselves – these questions are unanswerable – but instead the purposes they serve. In his *On the Genealogy of Morals* Nietzsche sees the origins of the Christian virtues in the age-old struggle of the 'herd', as he calls the mass of humankind, against the strong. The 'herd' – the weak and the powerless – are unable to combat the strong head-on but adopt the Christian virtues as a way of getting their revenge, denigrating the qualities that they do not have but envy in others.

Nietzsche was particularly damning about the dominant attitudes of his own time, and especially its materialism, the self-satisfaction of the bourgeoisie, and the movement towards democracy. He believed passionately that all that was good about humanity, and the highest expressions of its culture, was the work of a small number of free spirits who were able to stand above 'the herd', to make their own meaning, and thus to live authentically. At different times he talked both of 'higher men' and of 'over men' (*übermensch*), the latter being one of the themes of his *Thus Spake Zarathustra*. He contrasted both with the 'last men' who seek only comfort and security and are happy to live boring lives based on illusions that they are too unreflective ever to challenge.

What are the implications of these thoughts for education? Like many lay commentators on education Nietzsche had more to say about what it ought not to be than what it should be. What is most educationally fruitful in Nietzsche's thought is the way he deconstructs the ideas, assumptions and language through which we habitually see the world. The notion of exploring the 'genealogy' of morals and truths is central to Nietzsche's thought. A well-educated person is able to stand back from his or her beliefs and values and subject them to re-examination, and likewise to take a critical stance with regard to the language – and above all the clichés, metaphors and what the French call *langue de bois* (language which evades the reality of the issues under discussion) – through which they are expressed.

To do this requires, as part of his or her education, both the development of appropriate attitudes of mind, whatever the topic under examination, and opportunities to engage with issues that transcend the subjects into which the curriculum is usually divided and in particular to engage with the kind of philosophical and ethical issues that, in the traditional education that Nietzsche lambasted in his lectures *On the Future of our Educational Institutions*, are most marked by their absence.

Education by 'breadwinners' and 'old maids'

In his lectures *On the Future of our Educational Institutions* Nietzsche attacked two trends in the German education of his own day: the increasing emphasis on education for utilitarian and economic purposes, which he called education by 'breadwinners', and the emphasis in academic education on a scholarly induction into the major disciplines, which, with his usual lack of political correctness with regard to gender-related terminology, he called 'education by old maids', the 'old maids' that he had in mind being the kind of dry-as-dust academics satirised in the character of Edward Casaubon by George Eliot in *Middlemarch*.[3]

Although the targets of these criticisms were more general, and reveal Nietzsche's views on much more than education, they also corresponded with the two main types of secondary education then current in Germany: the relatively new *Realschulen*, with their emphasis on the natural sciences and German studies; and the traditional *Gymnasien*, at which Nietzsche himself had been educated and which focused on providing a liberal education with a stress on the classics.

Nietzsche's objection to the utilitarian education of the *Realschulen* was that it posited as the prime good material advancement and man's increasing dominance over Nature and that it involved subservience to the state, which had taken over these aims as its own. Its aim, as he saw it, was simply socialization, to produce performers of certain social functions (what he called the rearing of the most 'current' man possible).[4] Education based on such aims was hostile both to Nature and to Life, and did not count as education at all. Nietzsche did not deny the need for preparation for work, but objected to the idea that this was all or mostly what education was for.

Underlying these objections was a view of Nature not that distant from Rousseau's, which saw it as something with which human beings should have a relationship that was not simply of domination. Also underlying it was distaste, shared by other 19th-century thinkers such as John Stuart Mill and Alexis de Tocqueville and later, in the 20th century, by Nietzsche's fellow German Hannah Arendt, for the increasing domination of politics by economic issues.

Nietzsche saw dangers in the politics emerging out of modern capitalist economies and out of democracy, and in particular in how this was leading to a growth in state power and in bureaucracy. He was also, like Mill and de Tocqueville, acutely conscious of the tension between liberty and equality and the threat to freedom posed by the 'tyranny of the majority' in democratic societies. Nietzsche saw politics as a means to an end, which was the production of culture and human greatness, objecting strongly to the idea of the English Utilitarians that it was just about promoting 'the greatest happiness of the greatest number'.

Nietzsche's critique of the education provided by the *Gymnasien* and by contemporary German universities was equally damning. Again, the objection was that this was not an adequate preparation for Life in the sense of a life authentically lived. Nietzsche's objection to an education based on an induction into the major disciplines was that this involved a focus on the acquisition of knowledge *for its own sake* rather than as a means to the end of learning how to live.

His criticism was partly of the specialisation that this kind of education involved, which prevented students from looking at life and the world more generally, and partly because its aim seemed to be to form scholars rather than men, but above all because the wrong things were being studied. Nietzsche, in his essays on Schopenhauer as educator and on history, contrasts the pursuit of knowledge for its own sake with the study and practice of both philosophy and art. Only the latter enable people to engage with the kind of issues that they need to face as human beings.

The study of history for its own sake, for example, distracts students from the emotional encounter with personalities and events in the past that might have an impact on their development as human beings. The direct encounter with great literature, music and drama is similarly much more important than literary history, musicology or the history of art. Philosophy and the arts moreover leave one free to respond as one sees fit, whereas induction to a discipline is intrinsically conservative and forces our thinking into inherited frameworks.

But Nietzsche's objections to liberal education are even more profound than this. First, he saw the 19th-century expansion of science, in which he included not just the natural sciences, but the new historiography developed by Ranke, the social sciences, and some types of philosophy, as yet another manifestation of the Christian ascetic ideal. The obsession with the accumulation of knowledge is just the latest example of the flight from life. It is an evasion of all the issues thrown up by philosophy and art.

Second, Nietzsche's epistemology suggested that the pursuit of knowledge, and the idea of the possibility of truth which this assumes, was a chimera. Nietzsche's epistemology is far from systematic, changed significantly in the course of his life, and is interpreted by Nietzsche scholars in different ways, but seems generally to point in the direction of a 'perspectival' view of truth, by which truths are true for those who hold them but are unable to claim universal validity. As with morality, so too knowledge needs to be understood in terms of its origins and the function it is serving. It is these views that made Nietzsche so influential with French structuralists such as Foucault and Derrida and have led to him being seen as a precursor of postmodernism.[5]

In his essay *On the uses and disadvantages of history for life* Nietzsche provides a case study of the negative effects of science and scholarship. Historical study and writing have their uses, he argues: to inspire us with the great achievements of the past and to provide the chronological framework that gives us a sense of our place in time. In practice, however, the effects of a preoccupation with history are often stultifying.

In order to live it is important that we can forget about the past, that we are 'un-historical' (forgetting was important for Nietzsche as a way of enabling us to overcome guilt and self-pity). It is also important that we are 'supra-historical', that we focus on those few people in the past whom it is impossible to see just as a product of their times. Nietzsche also implied that it was sometimes more important for history to serve our needs in the present, and to be written with this in mind, rather than to be obsessed with meeting Rankean criteria for truth.

Nietzsche's scepticism about history as a 'truth-telling' subject underestimates the dangers of ceasing to see it as one that is at least 'truth-seeking'. He nonetheless does us a service in highlighting how history is inevitably shaped by the perspective of the historian, how all accounts of the past are a dialogue between past and present, and how the changing nature of history and its changing function within a society (what Nietzsche might have called its 'genealogy') are worthy objects of study in themselves. He thus anticipates some of the changes in historiography and in historical education that were to become important 100 years later. As far as school history is concerned he also reminds us that it is legitimate for the study of past events and individuals to inspire and motivate us to action.

The education of the higher man

Nietzsche believed neither in equality nor in democracy. Although he was not the kind of thinker to come up with a specific agenda for social and political action, his interests were in the kind of qualities to be found in aristocracies, and not in the mass of humanity. His interest was in creating the conditions in which a small number of men – the 'higher men', the free spirits, the geniuses capable of seeing the world afresh – are able to flourish. 'The education of the masses cannot, therefore, be our aim', he said in his Basel lectures on the future of educational institutions, 'but rather the education of a few men picked for great and lasting works'. Posterity will judge an age by the creative achievements of such men, not by how far it extends an inferior education to the masses.

What he disliked about the German educational scene of his day was that it involved both an extension of education to more and more people and a simultaneous watering down of its content. The effect of this, he argued, was to create 'a culture false to the root'.[6] What was needed was less education, fewer institutions of higher education, less dependence on the state, and a greater concentration on education for the few in all the ways necessary to create the 'authentic' man.

Nietzsche had little interest in liberating or enlightening the masses. An education that equipped them to fulfil the kinds of roles that they had to occupy in life was all that was needed. Their function was above all to facilitate the work of the creative few.

Although Nietzsche's views are profoundly alien to most people living in contemporary democracies, he highlighted the problem of catering simultaneously for the 'highly able', or the 'gifted and talented' as they are sometimes known, and the rest of the population. Countries tackle this issue in different ways: by segregation at some point within the secondary phase of a state education system; by 'differentiated' learning within state comprehensive schools attended by the whole of the population; by allowing, and encouraging, the existence of a selective private education sector with staffing and resources that enable some schools to focus more exclusively on the formation of an educated elite; by strict criteria for entry into a hierarchical system of higher education. In some ways, at times covertly, we do what Nietzsche recommended, while studiously avoiding his anti-egalitarian rhetoric.

Even more generally Nietzsche also drew attention to the difficulties within a democracy, given the potential 'tyranny of the majority', in sustaining the kind of artistic and intellectual culture responsible for many of the achievements of western civilisation and traditionally associated with the small and leisured aristocratic elites that had formerly set the tone for society.

His particular *bête noire* were journalists whom he saw as parasitic on real artists and men of genius and whose role was to create or reinforce the dominant clichés and assumptions of the 'herd'. To Nietzsche they represented the conformity, shallow thinking, and instant opinions that he loathed. One wonders what he would have made of the world of Twitter and Facebook, journalistic pundits who sing the merits of this world, and newspapers which publish a list of 'tweets of the day'.

★★★★★

How Nietzsche can help us think about education today

Nietzsche and education in a democracy

There were few, if any, fully fledged democracies in Europe in Nietzsche's time, but in many countries the trends were in that direction and, like de Tocqueville earlier in the century, Nietzsche had a nose for what the future implications of democratic societies were likely to be. This is one of the areas where his thought has powerful lessons for education today.

Nietzsche feared that, in democratic societies, the lowest common denominator tastes and values of the majority would swamp all that was noble and creative in human life, impose a stifling conformity, reinforce a morality of pity and envy, and make it difficult for people to live in a way that was authentic and free or to be educated to live such a life.

Unlike de Tocqueville who shared the first of these two concerns, but also saw the advantages of democracy, believed in its overall desirability and inevitability and focused his thought on how its disadvantages might be overcome, Nietzsche remained unrelentingly negative. This is one reason why there is such a strong strain of anti-Nietzsche criticism, with books like the one by the French philosopher Luc Ferry – *Why we are not Nietzscheans* – popping up from time to time. Distaste for Nietzsche's political, social and cultural preferences should not, however, lead us to ignore his analysis of the very real problems that democracies face.

Nietzsche thought that the 'slave' or 'herd' morality that he disliked was based on what he called *ressentiment*, borrowing a French word that had no equivalent in German. *Ressentiment* means resentment or envy and is used by Nietzsche to describe and explain the way that the discontented, the unhappy and the weak can be apt to envy and resent others, blame them for their problems, and try to make themselves feel better by bringing down those who are more successful than, or have other and different qualities from, themselves.

This is a process that is both degrading for the perpetrators of *ressentiment* and damaging for society. It is also a process that is much more likely to occur in the democratic world in which the masses have acquired the power to make their opinions heard and their (to Nietzsche's eyes) false values prevail.

Nietzsche could not have anticipated the technological means now at people's disposal to give full rein to their *ressentiment*: opportunities to batter into submission with 1000 tweets anyone who steps out of line with opinions that are not those of the majority or, more often than not, of the oppressive minority that has set itself up as the guardian of *mores*; petitions and denunciations that threaten the careers of politicians, footballers and anyone in the public eye when they infringe currently approved conventions of behaviour or language; outpourings of ersatz grief at the deaths of people one has never met; relief from boredom and routine when, thanks to the hundreds of reporters and photographers on site making sure that our appetites are catered for to the full, the news breaks on the latest 'humanitarian' or natural disaster.

'Media studies' have often been mocked as a school subject, as a low level alternative to the study of great literature. But there can be few things more important than getting young people to engage thoughtfully with these phenomena and to understand the psychology that lies behind them – envy, sentimentality, hypocrisy, indignation, hysteria, voyeurism, whingeing, *ressentiment* in spades, alongside more positive qualities such as empathy and generosity – and to see how their own views and attitudes are being shaped (sometimes consciously, sometimes unconsciously) by media that have adopted a particular viewpoint on national or global issues as if it were the only way of looking at them.[7] In doing all this we would be helping them to live lives that are authentic and free.

We would not need to call it 'media studies'. Indeed it is much more important than this. It is 'philosophy', in Nietzsche's sense of the word. It is the element of the curriculum traditionally most neglected in education systems throughout the Anglo-Saxon world.

Nietzsche on values and virtues

In her book *The De-moralization of society. From Victorian Virtues to Modern Values*, Gertrude Himmelfarb gives Nietzsche an important role in the process by which some western societies have moved from thinking in terms of a set of 'virtues', which everyone should aim to acquire, to feeling that what matters are not 'virtues' but 'values' and that the latter are are not immutable but things that you choose to have or not to have as you see fit. Nietzsche, she claimed, was one of the first to drop the idea of 'virtues' and to start talking instead about 'values'. She draws attention to Nietzsche's use of the phrase 'transvaluation of values' by which he meant the rejection of Christian morality.[8] This is how he put it at the end of *The AntiChrist*:

> ...I call Christianity the one great curse, the one great intrinsic depravity, the one great instinct for revenge for which no expedient is sufficiently poisonous, secret, subterranean, petty – I call it the one immortal blemish of mankind...
>
> And one calculates time from the *dies nefastus* (fatal day) on which this fatality arose – from the first day of Christianity! Why not rather from its last? From today? Revaluation of all values![9]

To Himmelfarb, Nietzsche's legacy – his contribution to the de-moralization of society – has been disastrous. In a de-moralized society, as she describes it, there is a perception among many people that there is no longer good and evil, virtue and vice, just values, and the consequence of this moral relativism is an emphasis on the individual's choice of his or her values, a fear of being thought 'judgmental' towards others, and a collapse of that transmission of attitudes and behaviours that has been at the heart of civilization.

One may contest the extent to which society has been de-moralized in the way that Himmelfarb suggests, argue that since the date of her book (1995) there have been some movements in an opposite direction, and make a case for saying that, despite alleged de-moralization, schools have continued to be some of the most moral places in society – they are difficult to run if they aren't – and have been doing their bit to combat this process. The spread of a pervasive ethical relativism is, however, incontestable and it is difficult to argue that this is not what Nietzsche had wanted to achieve. Whether he would have welcomed its consequences is another matter.

There are some messages from these ethical debates for the moral education of the young. One might summarise them as follows:

> the importance of keeping an eye open for both the 'genealogy' and the consequences in practice of moral principles (though remember that Kant fundamentally, and impressively, disagreed with this approach to ethics). These enquiries may not invalidate the moral principles but will make you think about what you are doing when you adhere to them;
>
> the need to be aware of the self-interest that may lurk behind one's most principled decisions. As Socrates said, 'Know thyself';
>
> not to ignore the aesthetic element in morality. This is something that Nietzsche emphasised. Some things just don't look, feel or smell right. Nietzsche's nose helped him to sniff out what he saw as the hypocrisies of Christian morality. We should feel free to respond similarly to some of Nietzsche's uglier preferences such as his

acceptance of the inevitability of cruelty and slavery;

not to confuse moral decisions and principles with tastes, even if Nietzsche sometimes seems to see them as very much the same. Moral positions can be argued for and against rationally, in a way that tastes cannot, in terms of whether they are consonant with other moral decisions and other principles and in terms of their effects;

not to give up on the idea that some things are simply and incontestably wrong in themselves, like the systematic murder of people just because they belong to a particular race (Nazism) or social class (Communism). *Contra* Nietzsche the world is not liberated but a much more dangerous place, as the 20th century showed us, when basic moral imperatives and interdicts are brushed aside.

*****

Nietzsche writes

Nietzsche on education systems whose driving force is 'money-making'

The goal (of education is) to create as many current human beings as possible, in the sense in which one speaks of a coin as being current; and, according to this conception, the more of these current human beings it possesses the happier a nation will be. Thus the sole intention behind our modern educational institutions should be to assist everyone to become current to the extent that lies in his nature, to educate everyone in such a way that they can employ the degree of knowledge and learning of which they are capable for the accumulation of the greatest possible amount of happiness and profit...
Here there is a hatred of any kind of education that makes one a solitary, that proposes goals that transcend money and money-making, that takes a long time... Precisely the opposite ... is held in esteem: namely, a speedy education so that one may quickly become a money-earning being.

Nietzsche, *Schopenhauer as educator*, in *Untimely Meditations*, pp. 164-5, 1983, Cambridge University Press, Cambridge

Nietzsche on educational guff

Let anyone examine the pedagogic literature of the present; he who is not shocked at its utter poverty of spirit and its ridiculously awkward antics is beyond being spoiled...

I don't deny, of course, that they (educationists) can find pompous words with which to describe their aims: for example, they speak of the 'universal development of free personality upon a firm social, national and human basis', or they announce as their goal: 'The founding of the peaceful sovereignty of the people upon reason, education, and justice'.

Nietzsche, *On the Future of our Educational Institutions*, in *The Complete Works of Friedrich Nietzsche*, Volume 6, pp 45 and 112, 1909, T.N. Foulis, Edinburgh

Nietzsche on education that, as well as freeing the spirit, inculcates habits of discipline

The most desirable thing remains, under all circumstances, a hard discipline at the right time; namely, at that age when it still makes one proud to see a lot demanded of one ... there are no good scholars who do not have the instincts of a capable soldier... What does one learn in a hard school? Obeying and commanding.

Nietzsche, quoted in Cooper, D E, *Authenticity and Learning. Nietzsche's educational philosophy*, p. 5, 1983, Routledge and Kegan Paul, London

Nietzsche on science and scholarship

...science rests on the same foundation as the ascetic ideal: both presuppose a certain impoverishment of life – a cooling of the feelings, a slowing of the tempo, dialectic in place of instinct, the impression of seriousness upon face and gestures... Take a look at the periods in the history of a people in which the scholar comes to the fore: they are times of exhaustion, often of twilight, of decline – the overflowing strength, the certainty of life, the certainty of the future are things of the past. The predominance of mandarins is never a good sign.

Nietzsche, *On the Genealogy of Morals*, trans. Smith, D, p.129, 1998, Oxford University Press, Oxford

Nietzsche against the self-righteousness of the modern world, humanitarianism, nationalism and racism

...can we really be at home in an age that loves to claim the distinction of being the most humane, the mildest, and most righteous age the sun has ever seen? It is bad enough that precisely when we hear these beautiful words, we have the ugliest misgivings. What we find in them is merely an expression – and the masquerade – of a deep weakening, of weariness, of old age, of declining energies! What can it matter to us what sequins the sick use to cover up their weakness? Let them parade it as their virtue; after all, there is no doubt that weakness makes us mild, so righteous, so inoffensive, so 'humane'! The 'religion of compassion' to which one would like to convert us – oh, we know these hysterical little men and women well enough today need just this religion as a veil and finery. We are no humanitarians; we should never dare to allow ourselves to speak of our 'love of humanity' ... No, we do not love humanity; but on the other hand we are not nearly 'German' enough, in the sense in which the word 'German' is constantly used nowadays, to advocate nationalism and racial hatred and to be able to take pleasure in the national scabies of the heart and blood poisoning with which European peoples nowadays delimit and barricade themselves against each other as if with quarantines.

Nietzsche, F, *The Gay Science*, (ed.) Williams, B, pp 241-2, 2001, Cambridge University Press, Cambridge

References

1. Ansell-Pearson, K, *An Introduction to Nietzsche as political thinker*, p. 1, 1994, Cambridge University Press, Cambridge.
2. For a discussion of the educational implications of Nietzsche's emphasis on authenticity, see chapter 8 of Cooper, D E, *Authenticity and Learning. Nietzsche's educational philosophy*, 1983, Routledge and Kegan Paul, London.
3. Nietzsche had read George Eliot but, despite her having exemplified his thoughts on the conflict between scholarship and life, attacked her for believing that it was possible to have morality without God, dismissing her in characteristic fashion as a 'little bluestocking'. He may have been influenced by the fact that George Eliot was one of the favourite novelists of his mother and sister. See *Nietzsche and the "English", The Agonist*, Volume II, Issue II, July 2009.
4. For a discussion of the role of education in mass socialization see Oakeshott, M, *The Voice of Liberal Learning*, ed. Fuller, T, pp. 78-85, 1989, Yale University Press, New Haven and London
5. Schrift, A D, *Nietzsche's French legacy*, in Magnus, B, and Higgins, K M, *The Cambridge Companion to Nietzsche*, pp. 323-55, 1996, Cambridge University Press, Cambridge
6. Nietzsche, F, *On the future of our educational institutions, in The Complete Works of Friedrich Nietzsche*, Volume 6, trans. Kennedy, J M, pp. 13 and 75, 1909, T.N. Foulis, Edinburgh
7. Ferry, L, *L'Innovation destructrice*, pp. 40-2, 2015, Flammarion, Paris. Luc Ferry defines the 'democratic passions' of modern secular societies as indignation, fear, jealousy and anger.
8. Himmelfarb, G, *The De-moralization of society. From Victorian Virtues to Modern Values*, p. 10, 1995, IEA, London.
9. Nietzsche, F, *The Anti-Christ*, in *Twilight of the Idols and The Anti-Christ*, pp. 186-7, 1968, Penguin, London.

Chapter 9

Education for democracy: John Dewey

JOHN DEWEY (1859-1952) is probably the philosopher in this volume whose educational views had the greatest impact on practice in schools during his lifetime. He is also the one for whom education was most central to his philosophy, describing education as 'the laboratory in which philosophic distinctions become concrete and are tested'.[1] He was, and remains, immensely controversial and – these things often go together – frequently misrepresented.

One reason for the extent of Dewey's impact was that he was active intellectually, politically and educationally for most of a life that started before the American Civil War and ended in the early years of the Cold War. His influence was greatest in his own country, the United States, which was always at the centre of his political and educational concerns, but he was also an international figure, spending a couple of years teaching at a Chinese university, conducting educational surveys in a range of different countries, and being involved in many international causes.[2] He has been aptly described as a 'rooted cosmopolitan'.[3]

He was one of the most important figures of the US intellectual scene in the first half of the 20th century, his writings covering many aspects of philosophy, including epistemology, ethics and theory of mind, as well as religion, aesthetics, political thought, psychology and education. His academic writing and journalism spanned 70 years and fills 37 volumes in his collected works.

Much of this was directed at an audience outside academia and, though not always as elegant as Montaigne and Rousseau or as pithy as Nietzsche, was nonetheless highly accessible. Many of his educational writings – *My Pedagogic Creed, Experience and Education, Education Today* – were written with teachers and ordinary citizens in mind.

Dewey was born in Vermont into a modest family and brought up by a Congregationalist mother who instilled in him a feeling that God was watching his every action. Although he turned his back on his religious upbringing, and in particular the notion that humankind was *fallen* and intrinsically flawed, he remained strongly influenced by Christian ethics.

Like many other 19th-century figures who had lost their faith, he was keen to hold on to that deeper sense of purpose and meaning that Christianity had given to people's lives.

This, optimistically but cautiously and without utopian exaggeration, he felt might be achieved through a combination of science and democracy. The scientific spirit and scientific modes of enquiry, together with a deep commitment to democracy as a way of life for a community, and not just a set of political arrangements, are at the heart of Dewey's philosophy.

Dewey appears to have found his own experience at his local public school in Vermont less than exciting, but went on to benefit from a broad liberal arts education at his local university in which he was first exposed to some of the philosophical issues he was to spend his life addressing. After graduation he taught in schools for a couple of years while keeping in touch with his philosophy tutor who encouraged him to continue with his philosophical reading. It was partly this tutor's influence that led Dewey in 1882 to seek and gain a place in the graduate school of the recently established Johns Hopkins University in Baltimore.

Two years later he had gained a doctorate with a dissertation on Kant and was on his way to the University of Michigan as an instructor. From Michigan he moved to the University of Minnesota and then in 1894 to the University of Chicago as professor and chair of the philosophy department.

Dewey remained in Chicago for eight years and, throughout this time, was closely associated with the university's Laboratory School which he had established on his arrival and used to test out his educational theories. The school did exciting and innovative things, but this required a generous teacher-pupil ratio that had to be funded by high fees and philanthropy. The school was an elementary one with a plan to extend upwards into the high school years, though this only happened after Dewey had left. Much of Dewey's writing, as a result, focuses on primary rather than secondary education. Dewey had in the meantime married and his wife Alice, with whom he had six children, became principal of the school.

Like other subsequent educators in prominent positions, Dewey was soon to find that mixing the professional and the personal – having one's spouse as a member of one's staff or one's child as a pupil in one's school – is a disaster waiting to happen. A bitter dispute ensued between Dewey and the university's president over Alice's terms and conditions as a result of which Dewey resigned, moving immediately in 1904 to a new post at Columbia University, New York.[4] Here he was to stay for the rest of his career. According to one of his former students, himself a distinguished philosopher, Dewey showed no interest as a university teacher either in course content or pedagogy at university level, teaching orthodox philosophy courses boringly and badly.[5]

Dewey's reputation as a philosopher has fluctuated since his death in 1952. The increasing ascendancy of Anglo-American analytical philosophy made Dewey's approach to philosophy seem out of date, one US philosopher describing him patronisingly in the 1970s, in the way that only certain academics can, as 'a nice old man who hadn't the vaguest conception of real philosophical rigor or the nature of a real philosophical problem'.

Richard Rorty, the most famous US philosopher of recent times, has, however, encouraged a major reappraisal, describing Dewey as one of the three most important 20th-century philosophers, alongside Wittgenstein and Heidegger.[6]

Some of the misconceptions about Dewey's educational philosophy have proved harder to eliminate, partly because (like Rousseau) he is so frequently cited and so rarely read. Dewey was not an uncritical champion of 'child-centred' education and was often as damning about the excesses of 'progressive' education as he was about 'traditional' education, refusing to see educational debates in terms of such a polarity. He was an enemy of 'sentimentalism' which he saw as one of the great evils that threatened education, along with 'dullness, formalism and routine'.[7]

He was similarly in no way 'anti-intellectual', describing his aim as trying to get children ever closer to 'nothing but the best': he was just asking that thinking and subjects be taught differently. He was also incredibly demanding of teachers, insisting on levels of reflection about aims and implementation never previously required. This is not to say that there was not a lot in his writings to disagree with, which there was, as we shall see.

★★★★★

> ...education is a process of living and not a preparation for future living.
>
> Dewey, J, *Education Today*, p.6, 1941, George Allen and Unwin, London

> ...education is the fundamental method of social progress and reform.
>
> Dewey, J, *Education Today*, p.15

> The teacher is not in the school to impose certain ideas or to form certain habits in the child, but is there as a member of the community to select the influences which shall affect the child and to assist him in properly responding to these influences.
>
> ...every teacher should realize the dignity of his calling; that he is a social servant set apart for the maintenance of proper social order and the securing of the right social growth.
>
> ...in this way the teacher always is the prophet of the true God and the usherer in of the true kingdom of God.
>
> Dewey, J, *Education Today*, pp.8 and 17

> To imposition from above is opposed expression and cultivation of individuality; to external discipline is opposed free activity; to learning from texts and teachers, learning from experience; to acquisition of isolated skills and techniques by drill is opposed acquisition of them as means of attaining ends which make direct vital appeal; to preparation for a more or less remote future is opposed making the most of opportunities of present life; to static

> aims and materials is opposed acquaintance with a changing world.
>
> Dewey, J, *Experience and Education*, pp. 19-20, 1963, Collier Books, New York

> There is, I think, no point in the philosophy of progressive education which is sounder than its emphasis upon the importance of the participation of the learner in the formation of the purposes which direct his activities in the learning process, just as there is no defect in traditional education greater than its failure to secure the active co-operation of the pupil in construction of the purposes involved in his studying.
>
> Dewey, J, *Experience and Education*, p. 67

Dewey's pragmatism and scientism

Dewey is the chief representative of the American school of philosophy known as 'pragmatism', founded by Charles Sandars Peirce (1839-1914), although Dewey preferred to call himself an 'instrumentalist'. Dewey criticized traditional philosophy for its obsession with the search for a universal knowledge of absolutes. Philosophy, he argued, was detached from those things that matter to human beings and looked set to be marginalised unless it 'ceases to be a device for dealing with the problems of philosophers and becomes a method, cultivated by philosophers, for dealing with the problems of men'.[8]

For Dewey the key criterion for determining the meaning, truth and value of ideas was whether they were found in practice to help tackle and solve the problems that faced human beings. Ideas were thus seen as 'instruments' for responding to problematic situations. Philosophical ideas about knowledge, mind and ethics, for example, need to be tested out in the context of education, social relations, nation states or inter-state relations in order to see whether or not, as prisms through which we see the world, they help, or fail to help, to solve problems. It was in this sense that Dewey saw schools as 'laboratories'.

Dewey's use here of the term 'laboratories' is revealing in that it illustrates another aspect of his thought: his 'scientism'. Dewey was deeply conscious of the transforming effect of science on the world in which he lived and believed that the scientific method could be applied to all situations and was the central way in which one could and should learn. It is in this context that Dewey can rightly be criticised for having a cavalier attitude towards the possibility of error, ignoring the limitations of the scientific method, and failing to do justice to the numinous.[9]

Dewey and enquiry-based education

In educational circles Dewey is associated above all with 'enquiry-based learning'. Along with Rousseau and his many European disciples, whose core ideas are not dissimilar, Dewey's thinking underpins much of the educational theory and practice currently dominant in the English-speaking world. It also underpins the pedagogy promoted by the educational programmes of the International Baccalaureate (IB), possibly reaching its purest form in the IB's Primary Years Education Programme which revolves around a sequence of 'units of inquiry'.

Dewey's impact has been greatest in North America but everywhere within the English-speaking world his basic ideas concerning enquiry-based education have been embraced by a majority of those whose voices are most heard in university education departments and teacher education colleges, in specialist education journals, and at education conferences. Enquiry-based education has also been, and still is, fiercely contested (see Hannah Arendt on this issue, pp149-150) and at times has given rise to what one can only describe as 'culture wars' between progressives and traditionalists, wars that – as wars do – make people very angry on both sides but generate little light.[10] It is important therefore, both for supporters and opponents, to be clear what Dewey meant by 'enquiry' and why it was so important to him.

The importance of enquiry for Dewey arose from his beliefs about growth, progress and democracy. Dewey talked a great deal about growth and saw people's lives as a process in which they continued to grow in ways that were not pre-determined externally but which needed to be shaped by them by the use of their intelligence. If individuals were able to grow by developing their intelligence and to use this intelligence cooperatively with others the societies in which they live would be able to improve themselves.

Dewey was no utopian and, like Kant, did not believe in the inevitability of progress but he was an optimist convinced of the improvability of humankind and of the world, in particular through the reflective application of the scientific method. For growth and progress to take place, however, democracy was essential. Dewey has been described, 'among liberal intellectuals of the 20th century (as) ... the most important advocate of participatory, deliberative democracy'.[11]

His view of democracy was broad and ambitious and involved fostering a democratic culture within which everyone was given the opportunities and resources they needed to take part in social, cultural and political life and, in doing so, to develop their capacities to the full. Democratic societies, he felt, needed people who were critically open to new perspectives, willing and able to take part effectively in debate, flexible and creative.

Enquiry, for Dewey, was the route to achieving these ends. It was the means by which one would be able to develop within people the habits of mind needed to keep on bringing about further intellectual and moral growth, within the individual and within society as a whole. Enquiry was also at the heart of Dewey's pragmatism or instrumentalism as it was methods of enquiry that would give one the tools with which to edge one's way towards finding rational and workable solutions to one's problems. If enquiry was the route to human improvability, social progress and the creation of a genuine democracy, it is no surprise that for Dewey it should be placed at the heart of education.

The essence of enquiry is identifying a problem and working one's way carefully and rationally through stages to a proposed solution. The five steps of enquiry Dewey identified as follows:

> (i) a felt difficulty; (ii) its location and definition; (iii) suggestions of possible solutions; (iv) development by reasoning of the bearings of the suggestion; (v) further observation and experiment leading to its acceptance or rejection; that is, the conclusion of belief or disbelief.[12]

Although not made explicit here, Dewey's assumption was that for much of the time, and to ensure that it was most effective, enquiry should be a cooperative process. Dewey saw the development of what he called a 'cooperative intelligence' as one of the key challenges facing a democracy. Although this aim is arguably even more important today than it was in Dewey's time, given the growing complexity of our world, it has led to the criticism that an emphasis on cooperative learning downplays those aspects of education that are likely to involve, and benefit from, a great deal of isolated individual effort and that in doing so it reduces opportunities for the intellectual excitement that comes to individuals faced with the challenge of mastering difficult subjects.

Given the centrality of enquiry, both to education and to democratic society, the key task of the teacher was therefore to create an environment in which children would be confronted with problems that were real and significant, arose out of familiar situations, stimulated their interest, stretched their thinking to the utmost, and for which they would be able to find, or helped to find, the necessary resources, including knowledge from traditional subjects.

This is of course a highly demanding role for the teacher. He or she not only has to manipulate a complex environment to achieve the desired ends (as the tutor is shown doing throughout Rousseau's *Émile*, and in this case with only one child to focus on), but also to be familiar with a wide range of subject matter as well as with the needs and capabilities of each individual child. This is why the IB's Primary Years Programme, structured around a series of enquiries, guided by teachers but with high levels of pupil choice at different stages, is so challenging for teachers and requires such a high level of skill.

The criticism of this kind of approach, when applied to national education systems, is that not all teachers, in a mass workforce, are likely to be capable of rising to this challenge. They may end up providing an even weaker educational experience for pupils than in a more teacher-led programme and it would therefore be better for pupils, it is argued, if their teachers were to be given much tighter direction as to what they should teach, when and how. Dewey would have seen this response as overly pessimistic and a denial of the improvability of people and systems in which he so firmly believed, but direct experience of setting teachers' salaries within tight budgetary controls, or of recruiting staff in times of high employment, might have led him to think differently.

The other criticism of enquiry-based learning is that it can be very time-consuming and that there are ways of acquiring essential knowledge and skills that are more efficient and can be achieved without putting children off the idea of learning. Certainly Dewey has little to say about how best to teach routine skills. The model of scientific investigation from which enquiry-based learning derives is also less applicable to some kinds of literary and artistic production, does not have an obvious place for the cultivation of awe and wonder, and while encouraging creativity may not accommodate all the kinds of creativity one might wish to promote.

Dewey, however, was confident about the universality of his enquiry method, extending it even to ethics. His pragmatism prevented him from believing that there was a set of values that were determined for all time and he felt that his five step process could apply equally to solving the kind of problem where one was testing out the strength of one's values, their compatibility with each other, and their consequences as applied in different ways, in one's imagination, to the situation under consideration.

This is incontestable, given that values are not the same as tastes and are subject to rational discussion in exactly the ways that Dewey suggests. It fits well with utilitarian calculations of the greatest happiness of the greatest number where these are an appropriate basis for ethical solutions to problems, but has no place for those who residually believe that some things either are (or should be seen to be, even if they are not) good or bad in themselves.[13]

Dewey on education as transmission

In the 'progressive' versus 'traditional' education debate the criticism of 'progressives', such as Dewey, is that they downplay the importance of transmission which for 'traditionalists', and even for some more radical thinkers such as Hannah Arendt, is at the heart of education. The criticism, at least of the enquiry-based approach, is valid insofar as the transmission of what has been called 'cultural literacy' is concerned. An enquiry-based approach is much more likely than one based on a rich and detailed formal curriculum to leave to chance whether a child acquires the full range of cultural reference on which any common culture is based: the historical events, literary and artistic references, geographical locations, sayings and customs that educated adults take for granted when communicating with others.

Writers such as E D Hirsch argue that children are being sold short by the absence of this kind of transmission, and especially children from backgrounds unable to compensate through the kind of transmission that occurs spontaneously in the home and the local community.[14] The absence of this cultural literacy not only diminishes children's life chances but also impoverishes them intellectually, depriving them of the cognitive benefits that come from a 'well-stocked mind' able to make creative connections between the multifarious pieces of knowledge it has acquired.

Dewey's counter-argument was that it is more important to retain children's interests, and to focus on the development of modes of reflective thought that will continue into adult life, than to cram lots of information into the child's mind at an early stage. He also had a more fundamental point to make about education as transmission. To him this was one of education's central functions though he saw it differently. For Dewey what mattered was the transmission of the 'like-mindedness' of the aims, expectations and dispositions that help to hold a democratic society together.[15] This was what schools should focus on instead of being over-concerned with ticking off topics on a curriculum list. This focus was best assured, he felt, through having enquiry-based learning, and in particular cooperative enquiry-based learning, at the heart of what they did.

Dewey and the school curriculum

It is not surprising that the curriculum was not the primary focus of Dewey's educational writings. The enquiry-based approach prescribes a broad educational programme, with principles relating to methodology, objectives and ultimate outcomes, but leaves considerable flexibility as its application. The IB's Primary Years Programme, which I have observed in detail in five of the schools for which I have been responsible, is based on this principle. The programme specifies the different types of enquiry to be covered and lays down the approaches to be used, but imposes no formal curriculum. The content of the programme's units of enquiry are for schools to determine.

Dewey, however, did not deny the importance of the curriculum. 'The child and the curriculum', he said, 'are simply two limits which define a single process'.[16] In the primary curriculum, which was his main interest, his main concern was to reduce the dominance of formal language learning before the age of eight or nine. Learning to read and write should not crowd out other subjects and should ideally wait until children themselves, to support their enquiries, feel an urgent need to do these things.

This is probably Dewey's most fiercely contested idea. It has been hugely influential though most efforts today are directed towards ensuring rapid progress in literacy in the early years in ways that retain interest and, wherever possible, are integrated with the rest of the curriculum.

Space needed to be found at this early age, Dewey felt, for a great deal of manual work and for science, nature study, art, history and geography. He is full of ideas about manual work – for horticulture, elementary agriculture, cooking, sewing, weaving, work with cardboard, wood and iron, and clay modelling – and for how using the tools needed for these activities can help to develop children's problem-solving skills.[17]

Reading Dewey's thoughts on manual work has helped to explain an episode in my own childhood that had always puzzled me. Out of the blue and seemingly unrelated to the curriculum, a request had come home from school for pupils in my class to try to acquire a small hand loom on which we might begin weaving at home. Coming from a family keen to support school requests, a carpenter we had used on house repairs was promptly asked to construct the loom; a shuttle, heddle and wool were purchased at a craft shop, and the weaving began. I remember it being quite fun. I eventually produced a rather uneven and very short piece of material (it was a very small loom) which I decided *post hoc* was a scarf. I did not know what to do with it but finally put it round the neck of my ancient teddy bear where it remains, in excellent condition, to this day.

I never knew, or even wondered, what the purpose of this exercise had been. I learned only the most basic principle of weaving and nothing about the textile industry which was the dominant industry of the town in which I was living. Only now, over 50 years later, have I at last realised that I had probably been a guinea pig for some Deweyan 'laboratory' experiment which failed to get off the ground. Dewey was particularly keen on weaving, wanted children to design and construct simple apparatus themselves, and saw manual work of this kind as a way of getting them to learn about the range of occupations on which society depended.

None of this, however, got through to me. The school was a traditional one but with an excellent and thoughtful Head. I can imagine him getting hold of one of Dewey's many short works published in the UK and, over a cup of cocoa one evening (definitely not a glass of wine in that 1950s north of England bastion of Nonconformity), deciding that he would launch a little experiment to help us learn more about how the inhabitants of our town earned their living.

Like many educational experiments over the years, however, it had not been thought through. It was only some years later, during a university long vacation when I worked in a woollen textile mill operating a large and noisy carding machine, that I really began to understand where the wealth and employment of my home town came from and what this kind of work involved.

★★★★★

How Dewey can help us think about education today

What do the people want from education, and what do they need?

As an advocate of radical educational change and at the same time a passionate democrat, Dewey was exercised by the question of how such change might be effected while at the same time enabling the people, and in particular parents, to feel that they were getting what they wanted. His observation was that generally what people wanted was what they were accustomed to getting but that what they *wanted* was not necessarily what they *needed* within a rapidly changing economic and social context.

His response, as a democrat, was not, as often happens, to go ahead on the basis that we, the experts, or we, the government, know better, but to set about 'help(ing) the people to a clearer and more systematic idea of what the underlying needs of modern life are, and of how they are really to be supplied'. He was not, he said, advocating 'breaking into people's educational houses in order to provide them with the agencies, the instrumentalities, they really want, but of the need of which they have not become aware'.[18]

This raises the question of where decisions about the nature and content of education provided by the state should lie and the nature and extent of the educational choice, if any, that it offers to parents. If parents want state-funded faith schools (Christian, Jewish, Muslim, Hindu, Sikh, *etc*) should the state be willing to provide and fund them, as long as they meet certain common criteria, as is happening in England, or should state schools provide the same education for all students irrespective of their background, with faith-based education left firmly outside the public domain, as in France? The one set of arrangements privileges the individual's choice; the other puts first the overall cohesion of the community.

Should there be mechanisms for parents and members of the public to be involved in school governance, as in US school boards and UK school governing bodies, or should the role of parents be confined to membership of advisory bodies without executive or decision-making functions? The first approach requires Heads to be accountable to those they serve, but risks the domination of the supervisory mechanism by those with individual agendas, sectional interests and little knowledge of what they are trying to govern; the second may allow 'the provider interest' – the employees of the education system – to manage things in ways that fail to take into account the parent voice.

Should parents also form a majority of the governing body of a school, as was the case with the international school I ran in Switzerland, or should they just be included (if at all) as a minority voice as happens in most English independent schools? The one approach recognises the fact that the school would not exist without the parents' fees but risks weakening the power of those in classrooms who tend to know best what works and what doesn't. The other may ensure a more impartial attention to strategic school issues but also enable governing bodies in a cavalier fashion to keep on awarding their schools above inflation fee increases (as happened over a long period in England), raising them to levels that put them out of the reach of the domestic communities that they have been trying to serve.

These issues will continue to be argued over. The one group sometimes overlooked in all this is the pupils. Ministers are concerned for their careers and the impact of their decisions on their party's fortunes (as well as trying selflessly to do good for the nation). Teachers care about their pay and conditions of work (as well as being highly professional and devoted to their charges). Parents have their own wishes for their children that may not be what these children either want or need (as well as loving them to bits and caring about their welfare above all else in the world). The general public may be grossly ill-informed about education and influenced by distorted media coverage (as well as genuinely concerned about the future of a part of the national infrastructure with a major role to play in shaping the country's future).

In the midst of all this who or what is ensuring that the decisions are ones that best meet the needs of young people? It cannot be any one of these groups, but a set of arrangements that enables all to have their say, arrangements that are likely to vary from country to country in the light of differing histories and political and educational cultures.

The problems of educational change in a democracy were brought forcibly home to me when living in Geneva and confronted by educational decision-making by referendum. 'Progressive' educational influences in the 1990s had led to the abolition of end-of-year overall marks for primary school pupils in the canton of Geneva. These had been replaced by written reports. A minority of teachers, some parents, some business people, together with members of the wider public, were unhappy with this situation and launched a campaign to get it reversed. They wished to return to the old system of marking each pupil out of 6 at the end of each school year. This, they argued, was crucial to enable parents to see how well their children were doing by comparison with the average for the population as a whole.

The campaigners managed to get the required number of signatures on a petition that would enable them by law to have a referendum on the issue. This took place in 2006 and was preceded by fierce debates. On the one side was the 'conservative' 'pro-marks' coalition and on the other Geneva's able socialist minister of education, supported by the 'progressive' teachers' unions and most 'expert' educational opinion.

There was a vigorous poster campaign funded by wealthy backers of the 'conservatives', with Monsieur X, taxi driver, and Madame Y, nurse, beaming at one from the back of trams telling one how important it was that they knew how their child was doing in relation to others. My own views on this issue fluctuated, inclining towards the 'progressives', given that theirs was the practice in my own school, but I tried hard to keep my head down, keen that a private international school should not be seen to be poking its nose into cantonal affairs.

In the referendum voters responded massively in favour of change, with the well-heeled communes being much more supportive of the change than the poorer ones, and, although one of the teachers' unions announced peevishly that the people had not a clue what they were doing and had acted like 'turkeys voting for Christmas', the minister of education accepted the popular verdict with grace and turned immediately to planning the implementation of the approved change.

I was left impressed with direct democracy in action but still wondering, irrespective of the outcome, whether this was the best way to ensure that pupils' interests were well served in a situation in which the wisdom of alternative approaches was never going to be determined wholly by facts and evidence. My wondering continues and I am not sure that even Dewey's five step enquiry process is going to help me bring it to an end.[19]

Making sure the teacher's voice is heard

As a democrat Dewey was keen that teachers, like other workers, had 'some regular and representative way in which (they) can register judgment upon matters of educational importance'.[20] However it is done, their voice must be heard when important educational decisions are being made, whether these are inside the school or at higher levels in local authorities and national departments of education.

As an educator he also believed that the best way of providing an education that met the needs of individual pupils was to give teachers considerable freedom as regards both subject matter and methods used in lessons, enabling them to adapt what and how they taught to pupils' changing needs, capacities and interests. By making teaching an intellectually challenging profession one would also be able to attract the 'best minds' into schools and keep them there, with beneficial consequences for pupils' well-being and levels of achievement.

Modern research into the factors that correlate with high pupil achievement, such as a 2007 McKinsey education survey, fully endorses Dewey's emphasis on the central importance of recruiting the best teachers. The survey studied what works in system reform in the world's best performing education systems and came up with three main factors: getting the right people to become teachers; developing teachers to become effective instructors; and ensuring that every child succeeds.[21]

Although the message has got home, some national education systems have failed simultaneously to absorb Dewey's message that detailed prescription, lack of meaningful consultation, heavy bureaucracy, and oppressive accountability are some of the biggest deterrents both to recruiting the 'best minds' in the first place and to keeping them. A favourite ploy of governments is performance related pay. This may work as an incentive in some areas of employment but a study of the research into the relationship between performance related pay and raising pupil attainment undertaken by Durham University's Centre for Evaluation and Monitoring (CEM) has failed to come up with any evidence of a positive effect.[22]

Multiculturalism: good and bad hyphens

The largest part of Dewey's life was spent in two cities, Chicago and New York, in which two-thirds of the population were either foreign-born or the children of immigrants. He was very happy that people should have multiple identities and had no problems with the idea of 'hyphenated' Americans (African-Americans, Nigerian-Americans, Japanese-Americans, and so on). He was keen, however, that the hyphen joined rather than separated, arguing that 'good hyphens join; bad hyphens separate'.[23] He had no time for the kind of 'plural mono-culturalism' described by Amartya Sen, in which quite separate cultures live side by side with each other within the same state.[24]

Even if such cultures were able to do so harmoniously, the lack of a shared identity and a sense of common culture was no basis, in Dewey's eyes, for the kind of democratic society he wished to see. This common culture might be perceived differently by the various groups but there needs to be enough in it that they share for them to be able jointly to exercise effective citizenship.

The experience of the United States in this respect is not the same as that of those European countries that over the last 50 years have experienced high levels of immigration both from outside Europe and, more recently, from other parts of the European Union. An almost entirely immigrant country such as the USA is in a very different situation from European countries, however traditionally diverse internally, with settled populations, and in some cases identities, that go back over 1000 years. The extent of diversity in the USA is also much greater.

It is perhaps these differences that help to explain why building a common culture and a common civic identity has been a much more explicit aim of the education system in the USA than it has, for example, in England where, only belatedly, have governments woken up in recent years to the fact of a burgeoining and potentially dangerous and divisive plural mono-culturalism, and the need to tackle it with 'citizenship education' or through the promotion of 'Britishness' in schools.

The measures taken so far, however, only scratch the surface, especially as they concern the implications for British society as a whole of the presence of a large and growing Muslim minority, some of whose members have social and cultural assumptions very different from those of the majority. These measures fail in particular to address the inherent incompatibility between, on the one hand, the government's commitment to parental choice, faith schools and community involvement in school governance and, on the other hand, its Deweyan belief that a key function of schools within a state-funded education system should be to educate children to take their place as citizens within this state, feel a strong sense of identity with it, and share a common culture.

The conflict here is between the claims of the state and those of individuals and cultural sub-groups. It will require a particularly skilled application of Dewey's five-step process even to begin to disentangle it. Some of the obstacles to possible solutions lie within education but, as in so many other educational issues, the biggest ones lie outside it, in society, demography, the economic situation and the long and complex legacies of the past.

Bridging the academic-vocational divide

Dewey had strong views on the unity of the educational aims that we should set for all young people. He saw all education as both 'vocational' and 'liberal' or 'cultural' and was impatient with those who tried to polarise the two and in particular with suggestions that employment-related education inherently lacked intellectual demand. Most previous education, he argued, had been implicitly 'vocational': liberal or cultural education for the elite being prepared for ruling and leisure and an education based on the three Rs and moral maxims for the masses destined for mechanical work and obedience.

This state of affairs should be replaced by an education which prepared everyone for the various 'occupations' that they faced in life. These would include both the different kinds of employment that people might experience in a world in which the nature of employment was changing, as well as all the roles associated with membership of a democratic community, including how best to make use of one's leisure.

Schools and universities offering liberal education should bear in mind that they were preparing young people to take their place as workers, not just as scholars or leisured gentlemen, and focus their teaching accordingly. Similarly, it was crucial that those offering 'vocational' courses directed at specific areas of employment, insofar as these were needed, saw their role as more than just 'training' people to perform certain tasks.

Such courses should include a substantial element of 'liberal education'. This was not simply because employers and the modern economy needed workers to be reflective, flexible and cooperative, and thus more productive. Dewey had no interest in providing employers with an obedient and passive workforce. He also wanted to enable workers to play active and critical roles within their workplace and the wider society. Dewey argued that:

> Any scheme for vocational education which takes its point of departure from the industrial regime that now exists, is likely to assume and to perpetuate its divisions and weaknesses, and thus to become an instrument in accomplishing the feudal dogma of social predestination.

An education, however, which sees vocations in their wider context:

> would include instruction in the historic background of present conditions; training in science to give intelligence and initiative in dealing with material and agencies of production; and study of economics, civics, and politics, to bring the future worker into touch with the problems of the day and the various methods proposed for its improvement.[25]

Efforts to bridge the vocational-academic divide over the years have taken many forms, some tokenistic or inappropriate (as lampooned in accounts of teaching 'liberal studies' to plumbers and butchers in the novels of Tom Sharpe), a few successfully breaking down barriers that should never have existed. One of those closest to Dewey's concept is the relatively recent IB Career-Related Programme (IBCP) which I planned to introduce at my school in Geneva and with whose development I was closely associated between 2010 and 2014 as governor of the IB and chair of its education committee. This programme places academic study, foreign language learning, self-reflection and problem-solving skills alongside a course of specific vocational preparation of the student's choice.

*****

Dewey writes

Education as preparation for a changing world

> With the advent of democracy and modern industrial conditions, it is impossible to foretell definitely just what civilization will be 20 years from now. Hence it is impossible to prepare the child for any precise set of conditions. To prepare him for the future life means to give him command of himself; it means so to train him that he will have the full and ready use of all his capacities; that his eye and ear and hand may be tools ready to command, that his judgment may be capable of grasping the conditions under which it has to work, and the executive forces be trained to act economically and efficiently.

Dewey, J, *Education Today*, p.5

Dewey on the importance of the school as a moral community

...much of present education fails because it neglects (the) fundamental principle of the school as a form of community life ... moral education centers upon this conception of the school ... that the best and deepest moral training is precisely that which one gets through having to enter into proper relations with others in a unity of work and thought. The present educational systems, so far as they destroy or neglect this unity, render it difficult or impossible to get any genuine, moral training.

Dewey, J, *Education Today*, p.8

All subjects can require profound reflection: it depends how you teach them

It is desirable to expel ... the notion that some subjects are inherently 'intellectual' and hence possessed of an almost magical power to train the faculty of thought... Thinking is ... a power of following up and linking together the specific suggestions that specific things arouse. Accordingly, any subject, from Greek to cooking, and from drawing to mathematics, is intellectual, if intellectual at all, not in its fixed inner structure, but in its function – in its power to start and direct significant inquiry and reflection. What geometry does for one, the manipulation of laboratory apparatus, the mastery of a musical composition, or the conduct of a business affair, may do for another.

Dewey, J, *How We Think*, pp.211-12, quoted in Cochran, M, *The Cambridge Companion to Dewey*, p.271, 2010, Cambridge University Press, Cambridge

Education ignores the nature of young children at its peril

Every respectable authority insists that the period of childhood, lying between the years of four and eight or nine, is the plastic period in sense and emotional life ... it is pre-eminently the time when the child wishes to do things, and when his interest in doing can be turned to educative account. No one can clearly set before himself the vivacity and persistency of the child's motor instincts at this period, and then call to mind the continued grind of reading and writing, without feeling that the justification of our present curriculum is psychologically impossible. It is simply a superstition: it is a remnant of an outgrown period of history.

Dewey, J, *Education Today*, p.31, 1941, George Allen and Unwin, London

A pedagogical revolution is overdue

Let the community once realize that it is educating upon the basis of a life which it has left behind, and it will turn, with adequate intellectual and material resources, to meet the needs of the present hour.

Dewey, J, *Education Today*, p.35

Dewey on the obstacles to getting the best minds into teaching

> The dictation ... of the subject matter to be taught, to the teacher who is to engage in the actual work of instruction, and frequently, under the name of close supervision, the attempt to determine the methods which are to be used in teaching, mean nothing more or less than the deliberate restriction of intelligence, the imprisoning of the spirit...
>
> If teachers are incapable of the intellectual responsibility which goes with the determination of the methods they are to use in teaching, how can they employ methods when dictated by others, in other than a mechanistic, capricious, and clumsy manner?
>
> ...The system which makes no great demands upon originality, upon invention, upon the continuous expression of individuality, works automatically to put and to keep the more incompetent teachers in the school. It puts them there because, by a natural law of spiritual gravitation, the best minds are drawn to the places where they can work most effectively. The best minds are not especially likely to be drawn where there is danger that they may have to submit to conditions which no self-respecting intelligence likes to put up with; and where their time and energy are likely to be so occupied with details of external conformity that they have no opportunity for free and full play of their own vigor.
>
> Dewey, J, *Education Today*, pp. 65 and 67

References

1. Dewey, J, *Democracy and Education*, p. 384, 1916, Macmillan, New York.
2. Cochran, M, *Dewey as an International thinker*, in Cochran, M, *The Cambridge Companion to Dewey*, pp. 209-336, 2010, Cambridge University Press, Cambridge.
3. Bernstein, R J, *Dewey's vision of radical democracy*, in Cochran, M, *The Cambridge Companion to Dewey*, pp. 288-308. The reference is to an article by Cohen, M, *Rooted Cosmopolitanism: Thoughts on the left, Nationalism, and Multiculturalism, Dissent, 1992, pp. 478-83.*
4. Westbrook, R, *The making of a democratic philosopher: the intellectual development of John Dewey*, in Cochran, M, *The Cambridge Companion to Dewey*, pp. 13-33; Ryan, A, *Liberal Anxieties and Liberal Education*, pp. 92-3, 1999, Profile Books, London.
5. Ryan, A, *Liberal Anxieties and Liberal Education*, p. 107.
6. Quoted in Westbrook, R, *The making of a democratic philosopher: the intellectual development of John Dewey*, in Cochran, M, *The Cambridge Companion to Dewey*, pp. 16-17.
7. Dewey, J, *Education Today*, p. 15, 1941, George Allen and Unwin, London.
8. Westbrook, op.cit., p. 13.
9. Noddings, N, *Dewey's philosophy of education: a critique from the perspective of care theory*, p. 267, and Levi, I, Dewey's logic of inquiry, pp.99-100, in Cochran, M, *The Cambridge Companion to Dewey*, pp. 16-17.
10. Ryan, A, *Liberal Anxieties and Liberal Education*, pp. 10-11.

11. Westbrook, op.cit., p.18.

12. Dewey, J, *How We Think* (pp. 236-7 in vol.6 of the Middle Works cited in Ryan, p. 110).

13. Welchman, J, *Dewey's moral philosophy*, in Cochran, M, *The Cambridge Companion to Dewey*, pp. 166- 186; Boydston, J (ed.), *Guide to the Works of John Dewey*, pp. 278-9, 1970, Southern Illinois University Press, Carbondale and Edwardsville.

14. Hirsch, E D, *Cultural Literacy: What Every American Needs to Know*, 1987, Boston, Houghton Mifflin.

15. Dewey, J, *Democracy and Education*, pp. 4-5, 1916, Macmillan, New York.

16. Quoted in Noddings, N, op.cit., p. 269.

17. Dewey, J, *Education* Today, pp. 72-3.

18. Dewey, J, *Education* Today, p. 37.

19. Tate, N, *Where X hits the mark, The Times Educational Supplement*, 6th October 2006.

20. Dewey, J, *Education Today,* p. 64.

21. http://pragmaticreform.wordpress.com/2013/01/05/mckinsey/

22. Durham University, Centre for Evaluation and Monitoring (CEM).

23. Ryan, op.cit, pp. 115 and 161-2.

24. Sen, A, *Identity and Violence*, 2006, W. W. Norton, New York.

25. Dewey, J, *Democracy and Education*, p. 372, 1916, Macmillan, New York.

Chapter 10

The need to 'stop and think': Hannah Arendt

As an educational thinker, Hannah Arendt is chiefly known for her damning, but nuanced, critique of modern progressive education, but the whole of her work is about an exploration of the kinds of human beings we ought to be.

Hannah Arendt (1906-1975) is one of the 20th-century's greatest political thinkers, better known, and perhaps generally more highly regarded, in continental Europe and North America than she is in Britain.

She saw herself as an 'independent thinker' rather than a professional philosopher. Like Nietzsche, who was one of many influences on her thought, she was sometimes a less than systematic theorist whose thoughts are open to a wide range of interpretations. Her writings are nonetheless a rich source of ideas about the human mind, the nature of the political life, and equality, elitism, morality, revolution, nationalism and totalitarianism. She wrote little about education, but her brilliant essay on *The Crisis in Education* (1954) is still hugely relevant today, and possibly more relevant than when she wrote it given the even greater dominance within the western world of the progressive educational ideas that she so bitingly attacked.

Hannah Arendt was born in Hannover in Germany into a secular, highly educated and left wing German Jewish family, but spent most of her childhood in Königsberg, Kant's home town, where her extended family had long lived. Although excelling at school she was expelled for 'insubordination', showing at an early age that fearlessness with regard to received opinions that was to make her such a creative thinker. She benefitted from her expulsion by preparing her *Abitur* (university entrance examination) at the University of Berlin, where she studied classics and Christian theology as a special student. Much of her thought bears the stamp of her admiration for the political thought and practice of Greece and Rome, and in particular of Socrates.

In 1924, at the age of 18, and having obtained her *Abitur*, she went to study philosophy at the University of Marburg. Here she fell under the influence of one of her tutors, the philosopher Martin Heidegger who, at the age of 35, had already made a name for himself as one of the leading German philosophers of his day. Heidegger was immediately attracted to her and it was he, as a married man, who took the initiative in starting an affair, which lasted for over a year, and a troubled friendship that lasted on and off for the rest of their lives.

Arendt greatly respected Heidegger as a philosopher, being influenced especially by his critique of modern technological society. In later life she did much to disseminate his works in the USA. She was also intermittently highly dependent on their relationship, despite eventually recognising the unattractive aspects of his character. She was revolted by his support for the Nazi regime, by the fact that he remained a member of the Nazi Party right up to 1945, by his subsequent failure to express regrets for what the Nazis had done, and by how he had treated some of his Jewish academic colleagues. Despite this she made excuses for him after 1945 to aid his rehabilitation and kept in touch until the end of her life.

After the affair with Heidegger was over she moved to Heidelberg where she completed a dissertation on St Augustine. It was around this time that she began to be more interested in her Jewish identity and to become active in left wing Zionist circles. In 1933, when Hitler came to power, she fell under suspicion and, following a week's interrogation by the Gestapo, escaped to Czechoslovakia from where she made her way to Paris. Here she worked for the next few years with organisations supporting Jewish emigration to Palestine. In 1940 the German invasion of France drove her from France as well, along with her second husband (a German political refugee) and her mother. In the chaos of France's defeat they succeeded in escaping from the internment camp in which they had been placed and, via Portugal, were able to reach the USA. Here Arendt remained until the end of her life, acquiring US nationality and writing most of her books in English.

Arendt's first hand experience of Nazism, and her knowledge as an active Zionist of the fate of European Jews, shaped much of her political thought. Her first great work, *The Origins of Totalitarianism*, published in 1951, was original in showing how Nazism and Soviet Communism under Stalin were fundamentally one and the same thing. Its main thesis was that this was a wholly novel type of regime, based on ideology and terror, quite different from the tyrannies of the past.

After the end of the war Arendt was employed in trying to salvage some of the archives that testified to the millennium-old Jewish culture in Europe that Hitler had set out to destroy. Her relations with some of her fellow Zionists, however, were often strained. She had criticised them during the war for their concentration on Palestine rather than on rescue operations in Europe. She criticised them after the war for insisting on setting up a Jewish state in Palestine and for their attitude towards Palestinian Arabs.

Tensions between Arendt and parts of the worldwide Jewish community came to a head in the early 1960s after she attended the trial in Jerusalem of the Nazi war criminal Adolf Eichmann on behalf of *The New Yorker* and published her thoughts about the trial in her book *Eichmann in Jerusalem: A Report on the Banality of Evil.* As well as being highly critical of the role of some Jewish community leaders during the Holocaust she also caused offence by the use of the phrase 'banality of evil' to describe Eichmann's participation in the planning of the Holocaust.

This was misunderstood as saying that the evil was in some ways 'banal'. This, however, was not what she meant. She was not saying that the evil of the Holocaust was 'banal', nor that Eichmann did not deserve the supreme penalty, but that the most monstrous evil could be committed, as it were mechanically, by 'banal', ordinary and insignificant people who had no comprehension of the enormity of what they were doing.

Arendt's life from the 1950s until her death in 1975 was filled with writing, lecturing and teaching at different US universities, interspersed with European lecture tours and the occasional visit to Heidegger. She followed closely the political developments of her own times – the US civil rights movement; the student protests of 1968; the campaign against the war in Vietnam; third world revolutionary movements. These further stimulated her thoughts about the nature of political activity in its many different forms.

While giving the Gifford Lectures – on the nature of 'thinking' – at the University of Aberdeen in 1974 she suffered a major heart attack in the middle of her first lecture. She recovered but had a further attack which killed her at the end of the following year.

★★★★★

> ...the answer to the question of why Johnny can't read or to the more general question of why the scholastic standards of the average American school lag so very far behind the average standards in actually all the countries of Europe is not, unfortunately, simply that this country is young and has not yet caught up with the standards of the Old World but, on the contrary, that this country in this particular field is the most 'advanced' and most modern in the world. And this is true in a double sense: nowhere have the education problems of a mass society become so acute, and nowhere else have the most modern theories in the realm of pedagogy been so uncritically and slavishly accepted. Thus the crisis in American education, on the one hand, announces the bankruptcy of progressive education and, on the other, presents a problem of immense difficulty because it has arisen under the conditions and in response to the demands of a mass society.
>
> Hannah Arendt, *The Crisis in Education*, pp.178-9, 1961, New York

> These ruinous measures (*ie* the spread of progressive educational ideas in the USA) can be ... traced back to three basic assumptions... The first is that there exists a child's world and a society formed among children that are autonomous and must insofar as possible be left to them to govern. Adults are only there to help with the government... By being emancipated from the authority of adults the child has not been freed but has been subjected to a much more terrifying and truly tyrannical authority, the tyranny of the majority.

> The second basic assumption ... has to do with teaching. Under the influence of modern psychology and the tenets of pragmatism, pedagogy has developed into a science of teaching in general in such a way as to be wholly emancipated from the actual material to be taught. (This) has resulted in recent decades in a most serious neglect of the training of teachers in their own subjects.
>
> But this pernicious role that pedagogy and the teachers' colleges are playing in the present crisis was only possible because of a modern theory about learning... This basic assumption is that you can know and understand only what you have done yourself, and its application to education is as primitive as it is obvious: to substitute, as far as possible, doing for learning.
>
> Hannah Arendt, *The Crisis in Education*, pp.180-2

The connection between thinking and the sense of right and wrong

When attending Adolf Eichmann's trial in Jerusalem Arendt was struck by the utter insignificance of a man responsible for so many deaths. Eichmann was not a 'monster', she argued, but someone who thought and spoke in clichés and never questioned what he was told to do. This was her point about the 'banality' of the perpetrators of evil. What they did was indeed monstrous and evil, but they failed to see it themselves. They showed an utter inability to think. This in no way excused them but understanding the nature of their actions helped one to explain why such appalling events could have occurred and to think about what might be done to ensure they did not happen again.

The Eichmann trial led Arendt to ask whether 'our faculty of telling right from wrong' might be related to 'our faculty of thought'.

> Could the activity of thinking as such, the habit of examining whatever happens to come to pass or attract attention, regardless of results and specific contents, could this activity be among the conditions that make men abstain from evil-doing or even actually 'condition' them against it?[1]

She did not argue that thinking by itself necessarily produced usable practical wisdom or by itself gave one the power to act. It might, however, enable one to exercise better one's judgment in difficult situations, especially when others were being carried away by misguided convictions and enthusiasms. Arendt saw the power of mass opinion – 'the mob' which only 'acclaims' or 'stones' – as a major threat to modern societies and a major source of the totalitarian danger. If people could find the time and solitude to stand back from majority opinion, understand the pressures upon them, and put themselves in the position of others, some of this might be avoided.

This did not mean that Arendt was urging people to become philosophers wrapped up in their own thoughts and detached from their everyday world. Indeed she saw this detachment from and distaste for the actual world of politics as the reason why so few political theorists, from Plato onwards, could in her opinion be trusted.

In her own times she criticised German intellectuals for the fact that so many of them, including her mentor Heidegger, had come to some kind of accommodation with the Nazis. "I never forgot that", she said in an interview in 1964, "I left Germany dominated by the idea (of course somewhat exaggerated): Never again! I shall never again get involved in any kind of intellectual business. I want nothing to do with that lot."[2]

Her ideal of a thinker was neither Plato nor Aristotle, nor any of their philosophical successors, but Socrates because he did not write anything down, had no truths to try and impose on others, and focused his efforts on helping others to understand why they were perplexed. Socrates gave himself the time he needed for thinking and self-examination, withdrawing from the world as necessary, but did not retreat into an ivory tower. He was out there in the marketplace talking to people and showing them *how* to think rather than telling them *what* to think.[3]

Arendt's views on thinking and evil, forged from her personal engagement with 20th-century totalitarianism, have major implications for education and in particular for how schools might best help pupils to reflect on *how* they learn as well as on *what* they learn. Elite German education in the early part of the 20th-century had been focused on the transmission of high culture and took place in an atmosphere which emphasised the authority of the teacher. It may have served Arendt well, but failed to prevent some of the country's most highly educated men during the Nazi period from assuming responsibility for acts of gross barbarity without protest or even qualms (many of the leaders of the *Einzatzgruppen*, the German squads that roamed eastern Europe killing hundreds of thousands of Jews in 1941, had doctorates, and one had two).

Thinking and the Socratic approach were particularly important given the ease with which, without it, morals, habits and customs could so easily be transformed. This had been one of the lessons of totalitarianism:

> Almost overnight and with scarcely any resistance the traditional commandment, 'Thou shalt not kill' was transformed into a new imperative, 'Thou shalt kill for the sake of the Führer.'[4]

Arendt was emphatic about the kind of thinking she was envisaging. This was not the kind of thinking that would enhance our empirical or scientific understanding. It was self-examination, 'nothing more than to think what we are doing', as she put it, in order to move beyond the 'thoughtlessness' that she saw as a characteristic of her times.[5] One of the implications for school education is that children need time to 'stop and think', a clichéd phrase that she injected with fresh meaning.

The emphasis placed by progressive education on group work and cooperative learning brings many benefits, prepares pupils for a life of collaboration with others, and can aid many kinds of learning. It risks, however, closing off routes to individual thought. It can also lead to the kind of group mentality in which majority opinion, rather than new thinking, takes over. One of Arendt's favourite quotations was from the Roman statesman Cato: 'Never is one more active than when one does nothing: never is one less alone than when one is by oneself.'[6]

Preparation for the political life

Political activity played a central role in Arendt's vision of 'the human condition' (the title of one of her most important books) or of what she felt 'the human condition' should be like. As a political theorist she distanced herself from most of her predecessors, from Plato onwards, whom she criticised for 'telling the people how to be virtuous' and for seeing political activity as a means to some kind of utopian end rather than as an end in itself.

She was not of course neutral about what emerged out of political activity, but her focus, and what she saw as the value of the political life, lay in the nature of political activity itself. It was her view that human beings were able to achieve the best of which they were capable through shared activities, engaged in as equals, each with their different views and perspectives, towards common ends. Political activity, in her eyes, should be about what all the people do together, not what others do to the people. Though not advocating her own utopia, Arendt was setting out criteria against which political systems could be judged.

Her vision of the political life was based on the fifth century BC Athenian city state or *polis*. She used this, in somewhat idealized form, as the basis for her concept of political activity whose defining features were equality among citizens, open debate, the acceptance of differences of opinion, the possibility for all of active participation in common concerns, and a sharp distinction between the public and the private sphere. Judging modern political systems by this standard left them seriously wanting. Totalitarian regimes met none of the criteria and were, by Arendt's definition, the very antithesis of 'political'.

Liberal democracies, however, were also deficient. First, they were dominated by representative rather than direct democracy. Arendt shared the view of Benjamin Rush, one of the US Founding Fathers, who summed this up by saying: 'although power is derived from the people, they possess it only on the days of their elections. After this it is the property of their rulers'.[7] For Arendt this stripped politics of its benefits to individuals and of its dignity.

Second, echoing the views of Matthew Arnold and J S Mill, politics in modern liberal democracies had come to be preoccupied by economic, rather than political, legal and constitutional, issues. It was the latter that ought to be its core. Politics had come to be seen as the centralized administration of the needs of life and the modern state as 'little more than a national or collective household'.[8] As a result of this politics had become the prey both to private interests and to the dominance of the expert, both of which were the enemies of civic engagement.

It was not just in totalitarian regimes that people were happy to abandon their freedom as long as the state continued from time to time to toss them some economic benefits. This was a feature of liberal democracies too. Arendt saw this 'political infantilization of citizens', as she called it, as an inherent feature of modern mass democracy and a serious danger to freedom in the modern world.

She traced it to the lowering of expectations about what a human being should be arising from capitalism's 'life of endless consumption, which converts all things into means out of an unappeasable desire for gratification', as well as to the alienation of modern men and women from a world of rapid social and cultural change in which scientific and technological processes have ceased to be under human control.[9] The freedom left in modern democracies was the negative 'freedom *from*', not the positive 'freedom *to*' which would allow the possibility of civic engagement for all.

Frustratingly, Arendt says little about how these problems in liberal democracies might be tackled in order to bring about the kind of political involvement she so passionately advocates. She had positive things to say about the US Founding Fathers and about US federalism and local self-government, but did not feel that even they put in place adequate structures to maintain the Athenian spirit of the original revolutionaries.

One likes to think that she would have seen the potential for citizen involvement arising from recent developments in mass communications, though the dangers of 'mob rule' that these present, and the 'infantilizing' demands that the state steps in to protect people from any kind of public offence to their sensibilities, would also no doubt not have escaped her.

Despite Arendt's failure to chart a way forward for liberal democracies her message about the importance of politics and of civic engagement by all citizens remains a powerful one. The implications for education are immense and include: fostering a sense of identification with, and responsibility for, the state in which one happens to live; encouraging young people to see the state and its institutions as the basis for the common life of a national community and as something which, in the public or civic domain, transcends other allegiances (Arendt had no time for states based on ethnicity or religion, beginning with Israel); and practising civic engagement, within the life of the school (school councils and other consultative arrangements) and within the wider community ('service learning' both locally and elsewhere in the world).

The 'crisis in education'

Arendt's 1954 essay on 'The Crisis in Education' arose out of concerns in the USA that the country's education system was failing to maintain educational levels and, in doing so, at the time of the Cold War, falling dangerously behind those of other countries. The 'crisis', however, was not, she argued, confined either to the USA or to education. It assumed greater proportions in the USA for two reasons: first, because it was in the USA that progressive education had made its biggest advances; and, second, because the USA was a country of mass immigration and depended crucially on its education system to mould immigrants into one nation.

It was because the USA had such high expectations of education in helping to create 'a new world', and because of its thirst for novelty in general, that it had embraced with such enthusiasm progressive educational ideas, described by Arendt as 'that complex of modern educational theories which originated in Middle Europe and consist of an astounding hodgepodge of sense and nonsense'.[10]

Arendt was referring here to the child-centred enquiry-based 'constructivist' ideas that have their origins in Rousseau and his many disciples such as Froebel, Montessori, Pestalozzi, Ferrière and Claparède and that have subsequently been so influential throughout the western world, and which still shape much of educational practice today. She nowhere mentions the American educational philosopher John Dewey, whose direct impact on the USA must have been greater, but she can hardly have failed to have had him in mind as well.

The 'crisis in education', however, is deeper even than this. It is also a result of the development of a 'mass society', of which the USA at the time was the most advanced example, and of the pressures that emerge from such a society for equality and thus to 'erase as far as possible the difference between young and old, between the gifted and the ungifted, finally between children and adults, particularly between pupils and teachers'.[11]

The pedagogical ideas that seemed so attractive, partly because they could be harnessed in the service of egalitarianism, involved three assumptions: a new conception of childhood that gave children greater freedom and involved a degree of adult withdrawal from their world, leaving children open to the potential tyranny of majority child opinion; new ideas about teaching, which turn it into a general pedagogical science and play down the importance of knowing and understanding one's subject; and the notion that one learns actively by doing rather than in ways that give teachers a more central role.

Arendt cites, as an illustration of the baleful influence of this modern pedagogy, learning a modern foreign language, where the serious study of grammar and syntax is abandoned in favour of 'active' learning through play and talk. Given that one has only a few periods a week in which to do this the dismal results of using a method based on the way one picks up one's maternal language, chosen misguidedly because it is a more 'natural' one, are entirely predictable.

Arendt mentions in passing possible US responses to the 'crisis in education': reducing the element of play; re-establishing teacher authority; playing down the relative importance of extra-curricular activities; reforming teacher training. She admitted, however, that she was not an educationist and the rest of her essay is an analysis of what the 'crisis in education' tells us about modern attitudes towards authority, the alienation of adults from their world (the source of the crisis in authority), and the intractable problems of ensuring cultural transmission in a world that has turned its back on tradition in many aspects of life.

*****

How Hannah Arendt can help us think about education today

Education is more than just preparing people for employment and leisure

Arendt's essay *The Crisis in Culture* puts her thoughts on the crisis in education in a wider context. Her concern here is to examine the implications for the kind of human beings she wishes to see of some of the key features of 'modernity', and in particular of the collapse of tradition in culture, morals and religion and the coming of a mass society.

Traditional 'high culture' – the transmission of Matthew Arnold's 'the best that has been thought and said' – is under threat from two quarters: first, from the 'educated philistines', those who treat 'high culture' as objects that support their status in society; and, second, from 'mass society' which is focused on entertainment and leisure and which, where it touches 'high culture' at all, experiences it in 'dumbed down' mode, as when efforts are made to tempt the masses to listen to *Hamlet* by persuading them that it can be as much fun as *My Fair Lady*.

In this situation, where 'the thread of tradition is broken ... we must discover the past for ourselves, that is, read its authors as though nobody had ever read them before'.[12] In saying this, Arendt is not just suggesting an approach to the study of great literature which liberates it from any kind of passive acceptance of an inherited canon – we must teach it, she is saying, in all its plurality and subversiveness – but is also pointing to the key purposes both of education and of life.

Education, at any stage, is about shaping us as human beings, and continuing to do so throughout our lives. It is not just about preparing us for employment, enabling us to be wise consumers, or giving us hobbies to engage with during our leisure time. It is about enabling us to think profoundly about what it means to come to terms with the finite existence in which we find ourselves. It is about preparing us to have not just what Arendt called the *vita activa* (the active life) but also – something that had been pushed aside by the modern world, and which required periods of solitude for it to be achieved – the *vita contemplativa* (the contemplative or thinking life). Education, seen from this perspective, whether directed for us by our teachers or done by ourselves, is something noble, not simply a utilitarian exercise.

The tyranny of majority opinion within the world of children

Arendt is unusual among those concerned about the potential 'tyranny of the majority' in mass societies and in modern democracies in extending the notion to children. The idea will resonate with all those adults, and I include myself here, for whom leaving school was a welcome liberation not from adult tutelage but from the tyranny of the peer group. The advances in mass society, and mass communication, in the last half century have added to the pressures of conformism. Schools have a responsibility to help children understand these pressures and to resist them.

Their Arendtian duty to protect children from the world also extends to ensuring that the eccentric, quirky and different among their pupils (and above all those who resist the officially endorsed pressures to be subversive, daring and rebellious, *ie* to conform to the stereotype of the adolescent) have the space and the confidence to forge their own path in life even while languishing under the hegemony of peer group opinion. One of the things that I most liked about Winchester College, where I was Headmaster, was the way in which it tried to provide this space and this confidence and on the whole seemed to succeed.

The removal of all barriers

Arendt put her finger on a key characteristic of the modern western world when she talked about the passion in the USA for removing all barriers to equality. Arendt in many ways was a staunch egalitarian but saw the march of equality as going hand in hand with a diminution of liberty. Under the influence of capitalism and the growth of mass society this was taking two forms with people becoming the slaves of a dynamic self-perpetuating consumerism on the one hand and of an increasingly oppressive bureaucratic state on the other.

During the 60 years since her essay was published, egalitarian pressures have had a major impact on almost all aspects of life, affecting radically the position of women, children, and cultural, ethnic and sexual minorities, though with little effect on where equality, for many people, matters most which is income. In England, for example, comprehensive secondary schools have largely replaced selective ones, private schools are pressured to use their resources to support those who cannot afford their fees, universities have targets for admissions from 'disadvantaged' groups, and Free Schools have been urged by a Conservative Secretary of State for Education to develop admissions policies that give priority to poor children over those from better-off families even where the latter live closer to the school.

Although it would probably be denied by government, equality is now being promoted in England through positive discrimination in favour of the 'disadvantaged', as in the United States, in other words through measures that infringe traditional liberties and that create new inequalities with a view to tackling old ones. The implications of this situation for the relationship between justice, equality and liberty are just the kind of ones that Arendt wished to see debated in a healthy modern *polis* – there is a wholly understandable plurality of views on these issues – though the debate in England has been chiefly noticeable by its absence.

The removal of barriers, however, is not confined to issues of equality, though this is its most prominent manifestation. It is indeed a distinguishing feature of the modern western world to distrust frontiers and barriers of all kinds, as I have noted previously, along with the conventions and rules that go with them. Arendt was concerned about the breaking down of barriers between the public and the private spheres, both because of the intrusion of the public world into childhood and the value of maintaining distinctions about how the two areas of existence functioned.

The French intellectual (and former guerrilla fighter) Régis Debray has analysed these issues brilliantly in his essay *In Praise of Frontiers* (*Éloge des frontières*). He quotes the Martiniquan writer Aimé Césaire as saying that there are two ways in which a human being is able to lose himself – 'by walling oneself up within the particular and by dissolving oneself into the universal' – and adds that 'of these two suicides the second is today the most tempting' and the most dangerous, culturally, intellectually and psychologically.[13] The consequences of this mind-set in some education systems, in downplaying the study of 'national' history and culture and elevating 'global citizenship' over national citizenship, have been considerable, within a world in which nation states show little sign of losing their central role.

Education is essentially a conservative activity

Education in the second half of the 20th century and in the early 21st century has been affected by a series of 'culture wars', with the post-Rousseau and post-Dewey progressives, keen on child-centred, enquiry-based learning on the one hand, and the conservative defenders of the transmission of 'the best that has been thought and said' on the other. At first glance Arendt, with her withering criticism of the progressive education 'hodgepodge of sense and nonsense', seems to come down firmly on the conservative side.

She regards authority as generally constructive and enabling rather than negative and limiting, distinguishes clearly between how authority should be exercised among adults and what it means with children, and sees the authority of the teacher as based on an assumption of responsibility for the world and on a duty both to show children '(this) world as it is' and to protect them from it (and also, she argued, where necessary, to protect the world from children). For Arendt therefore a key part of education was an induction into the past and present world. Children would be ill-prepared to take their place in the world, or to start critiquing it, unless they knew what it was and how it had come about. Schools should not teach as if the world were already other than it is, she argued, as this conveys the message to pupils that the world has already been changed for them and that therefore there is little for them to do.

Arendt differed from other conservatives in her longer term objectives for the kind of conservative education that she was advocating. Her interest was not in ensuring the maintenance of existing political and social traditions, or of continuity with the past, but in giving the kind of education to children that would best equip them as adults to shape the world anew in ways that they saw fit. Arendt talked a great deal about 'natality', by which she meant that new generations of children keep on coming into the world and, once ready as adults, both want and need to act in ways that will change it, often radically.

A key function of education should be to enable them to do this. In protecting them from the world we need to ensure that they are not so stifled by existing conventions and attitudes that the new and the potentially revolutionary in them are suppressed. Arendt distinguished clearly between *what we are*, with all the accumulated baggage of the past and of our own identities (as a woman, German, Jew, *etc*) into which we need to be inducted, and *who we are*, which we must be left to be free to create ourselves. This is a radical message for someone who simultaneously insisted on the role of cultural transmission and on the centrality of the teacher and his or her authority in the process of learning.[14]

Arendt's synthesis of radical objectives and conservative pedagogy deserves greater attention than it has received. It is relevant to contemporary debates in England, France, the USA and elsewhere. Her thoughts about the need to maintain childhood as a separate phase and to protect children from the world are also important. Educators need to take care about creating situations that *encourage* young children to come to moral and political judgments about contemporary world events (as opposed to these arising spontaneously, which omnipresent mass media will ensure happens anyway from time to time) before they have learned much about 'the world as it is' and as it has been.

They will have a better understanding of the current issues affecting their country's relations with other parts of the world once they have learned something about its history. There needs to be even greater care about anything that might burden children with a sense of responsibility for the world, before they are in a position to exercise this responsibility. The curriculum should be used to help children understand about the world as it is and as it has been. It should not be packed with topics – environmental, social, political, cultural – the main purpose of which is to ensure that the next generation of young adults, when it acquires responsibilities, has the opinions and attitudes currently approved by those in charge of schools (whether these be ministers or teachers).[15]

Education to make the world 'a better place'

If one Googles 'making the world a better place' one finds a very large number of schools that have this phrase as part of their strapline (though why schools bother to display these, content-free, 'feel good' and wince-making slogans is beyond me). Some of these schools are ones that follow the programmes of the International Baccalaureate (IB) whose mission statement includes aiming to develop young people 'who help to create a better and more peaceful world'.

Hannah Arendt did not talk about making a 'better world' through education and I suspect that she might have felt that this phrase, with its hints of the utopianism which had done so much damage in the first half of the 20th century (both Communism and Fascism had promised a radically different and 'better world'), was as if the existing generation were continuing to call the shots in terms of what a future world might be like. She did, however, talk about making 'a decent world', by which she meant in particular a world in which it was no longer possible for totalitarianism to develop.

In *Eichmann in Jerusalem* Arendt recounts an episode in the trial which gave her a glimpse of what this world would be like.

> At this slightly tense moment, the witness (Mr Kovner) happened to mention the name of Anton Schmidt, a ... sergeant in the German Army. Anton Schmidt was in charge of a patrol in Poland that collected stray German soldiers who were cut off from their units. In the course of doing this, he had run into members of the Jewish underground, including Mr Kovner, a prominent member, and he had helped the Jewish partisans by supplying them with forged papers and military trucks. Most important of all: 'He did not do it for the money.' This had gone on for five months, from October, 1941, to March, 1942, when Anton Schmidt was arrested and executed... During the few minutes it took Kovner to tell of the help that had come from a German sergeant, a hush settled over the courtroom: it was as though the crowd had spontaneously decided to observe the usual two minutes of silence in honor of the man named Anton Schmidt. And in those two minutes, which were like a sudden burst of light in the midst of impenetrable, unfathomable darkness, a single

> thought stood out clearly, irrefutably, beyond question – how utterly different everything would be today in this courtroom, in Israel, in Germany, in all of Europe, and perhaps in all countries of the world, if only more such stories could have been told.[16]

Arendt does not go on to discuss how education might contribute to creating a world in which the decency of an Anton Schmidt had become more common. Martin Gilbert's book *The Righteous*, which chronicles the efforts of that tiny minority of Gentiles, all over Europe, who helped Jews escape Nazi persecution during the Second World War, often at the risk of their own lives, while the rest of the population turned a blind eye or were actively hostile, finds little correlation between these people and the information that we have about their social or educational background or their religious beliefs.[17]

As may well have been the case with Anton Schmidt, the sources of moral action are likely to have had more to do with personality and family upbringing than with the education these people received at school. The potential of the latter to mould ideas and feelings and attitudes, to develop empathy and to shape character, should not, however, be overlooked. It is one of the main things that makes the teacher's job so tremendously important.

★★★★★

Hannah Arendt writes

Arendt on education's losing battle with the consumer society

> The ... trouble with mass society is ... because this society is essentially a consumer's society where leisure time is used no longer for self-perfection or acquisition of more social status, but for more and more consumption and more and more entertainment... The result is, of course, not mass culture which, strictly speaking, does not exist, but mass entertainment, feeding on the cultural objects of the world. To believe that such a society will become more 'cultured' as time goes on and education has done its work is, I think, a fatal mistake. The point is that a consumers' society cannot possibly know how to take care of a world and the things which belong exclusively to the space of worldly appearances, because its central attitude toward all objects, the attitude of consumption, spells ruin to everything it touches.
>
> Hannah Arendt, *The Crisis in Culture*, p.211, 1961, New York

The threat to cultural transmission

> There are many great authors of the past who have survived centuries of oblivion and neglect, but it is still an open question whether they will be able to survive an entertaining version of what they have to say.
>
> Hannah Arendt, *The Crisis in Culture*, pp. 207-8, 1961, New York

Education is not about instructing children in the art of living

...the function of the school is to teach children what the world is like and not to instruct them in the art of living. Since the world is old, always older than they themselves, learning inevitably turns toward the past, no matter how much living will spend itself in the present.

Hannah Arendt, *The Crisis in Education*, p. 195, 1961, New York

The need to tackle 'thoughtlessness'

(Eichmann) merely ... never realized what he was doing. It was precisely this lack of imagination which enabled him to sit for months on end facing a German Jew who was conducting the police interrogation, pouring out his heart to the man and explaining again and again how it was that he reached only the rank of lieutenant colonel in the SS and that it had not been his fault that he was not promoted. In principle he knew quite well what it was all about... He was not stupid. It was sheer thoughtlessness – something by no means identical with stupidity – that predisposed him to become one of the greatest criminals of the period.

Arendt, H, *Eichmann in Jerusalem*, p.287 (Kindle edition), Penguin. London

Arendt on the responsibilities of adults towards children

Education is the point at which we decide whether we love the world enough to assume responsibility for it and by the same token save it from that ruin which, except for renewal, except for the coming of the new and young, would be inevitable. And education, too, is where we decide whether we love our children enough not to expel them from our world and leave them to their own devices, nor to strike from their hands their chance of undertaking something new, something unforeseen by us, but to prepare them in advance for the task of renewing a common world.

Hannah Arendt, *The Crisis in Education*, p. 196, 1961, New York

References

1. Arendt, H, quoted in Benhabib, S, Arendt's *Eichmann in Jerusalem*, p. 75, in (ed. Villa, D), *The Cambridge Companion to Hannah Arendt*, 2000, Cambridge University Press, Cambridge.
2. Quoted in Dolan, F M, *Arendt on philosophy and politics*, p. 262, in (ed. Villa, D), *The Cambridge Companion to Hannah Arendt*.
3. Dolan, op.cit., pp. 264-8; Bernstein, R J, *Arendt on thinking*, pp. 280-2, in (ed. Villa, D), *The Cambridge Companion to Hannah Arendt*.
4. Quoted in Bernstein, op.cit., p. 284.
5. *ibid.*, p. 282.

6. Duarte, E, *The Eclipse of Thinking: An Arendtian Critique of Cooperative Learning'*, in Gordon, M, *Hannah Arendt and Education: Renewing our Common World*, pp. 201-223, 2001, Westview Press, Oxford.
7. Quoted in Wellmer, A, *Arendt on revolution*, in (ed. Villa, D), *The Cambridge Companion to Hannah Arendt*, p. 238.
8. Brunkhorst, H, *Equality and elitism in Arendt*, in (ed. Villa, D), *The Cambridge Companion to Hannah Arendt*, p. 195.
9. Kateb, G, *Political action: its nature and advantages*, in (ed. Villa, D), *The Cambridge Companion to Hannah Arendt*, p. 146; Villa, D, *Introduction: the development of Arendt's political thought, ibid.*, p. 8.
10. Arendt, H, *The Crisis in Education, in Between Past and Future*, p. 178, 1961, Viking, New York.
11. Arendt, H, *The Crisis in Education*, p. 180.
12. Arendt, H, *The Crisis in Culture*, in *Between Past and Future*, p. 204, 1961, Viking, New York.
13. Debray, R, *Éloge des frontières*, 2010, Gallimard, Paris.
14. Levinson, N, *The Paradox of Natality: Teaching in the Midst of Belatedness*, in Gordon, M, *Hannah Arendt and Education: Renewing our Common World*, pp. 11- 36.
15. Gordon, M, *Hannah Arendt on Authority: Conservatism in Education Reconsidered*, pp. 37-65, and Curtis, K, *Multicultural education and Arendtian Conservatism: On Memory, Historical Inquiry, and Our Sense of the Common*, pp. 127-152, in Gordon, M, *Hannah Arendt and Education: Renewing our Common World.*
16. Arendt, H, *Eichmann in Jerusalem*, pp. 229-231 (Kindle edition), Penguin. London.
17. Gilbert, M, *The Righteous*, 2002, Doubleday, London.

Conclusion

What is education for?

HANNAH ARENDT, when reflecting on the nature of thinking, breathed new life into the everyday phrase 'stop and think', drawing attention to what is implied in this simple injunction and its importance in our lives. Literally 'stopping' – standing still and focusing one's thoughts – before acting or not acting, making a decision, or formulating or applying a value judgment, can make the difference between knowing what one is doing and its implications and just reproducing what one has always done, what the small group of people around one is doing, or what the wider society takes for granted.

Pierre Bourdieu, the French sociologist, talked about the way in which fields of activity (*champs*) have their own schema, concepts, language, rules, values and interests.[1] The world of education is such a *champ*. For much of the time, when talking about education and without realising it, one does not 'speak' but 'is spoken for', through the dominant discourse of the *champ* – a *champ* which, in the case of contemporary education, is often swept by ephemeral fads and characterised by jargon, cliché and sentimentalism.[2]

There are two ways in which, in education, one needs continually to 'stop and think' with a view to 'speaking' rather than being 'spoken for': first, in curriculum and pedagogy, so that one can evaluate past practice and proposed innovation; and, second, so that one can react thoughtfully to the hundreds of un-scripted events that occur in the course of any teacher's daily encounters with learners. The decisions one makes in both types of situation depend on one's answer to the question 'what is education for?'

When planning a curriculum it is possible to 'stop and think' at one's leisure about one's answer to this question. When responding to a student's question about the purpose of a particular activity, or reacting to a spontaneous piece of behaviour, however, one does not have this luxury. Unless one is continually reflecting outside these daily situations, one's words and actions are liable to be determined by thought patterns of which one is barely conscious and which take over one's mind and 'speak for' one.

Most national education systems have some kind of vision statement or list of characteristics they are hoping to encourage in young people. Many individual schools have mission statements. I am sceptical about whether enough thought goes into such statements: whether we think profoundly enough about either the meaning of these aims or their practical implications for how we devise our curricula and run our schools.

To think profoundly about the aims of education is also to think profoundly about our values, the kind of society and world we want ourselves to be, and our fundamental ends and purposes as human beings. T S Eliot made this point in his 1932 essay *On Modern Education and the Classics*, describing education as

> a subject which cannot be discussed in a void: our questions raise other questions, social, economic, financial, political. And the bearings are on more ultimate problems even than these: to know what we want in general, we must derive our theory of education from our philosophy of life. The problem turns out to be a religious problem.[3]

Although Eliot was a Christian and an Anglican, he was using 'religious' here in its broadest sense. It was his contention that in post-traditional Western societies we lacked a shared account of who we are, where we came from and where we are going, and that as a result we lacked the fundamental philosophical and religious basis from which to answer the question 'what is education for?'

The chances of returning to this kind of shared account of who we are, even if this were to be desirable, are even more slender now than in the 1930s. That does not mean that we should stop going back to the question 'what is education for?' and trying to answer it in the context of our values and aspirations for individuals and societies.[4] If we do not do so we are likely to end up with education systems distorted by an excessive concern for utilitarian considerations: the alleged needs of 'the knowledge economy' and whatever priorities for social engineering governments have decided to set themselves at any particular time (obesity prevention, water safety awareness, the reduction in teenage pregnancy rates, consumer education, and so on).

It is not that preparation for employment and everyday life is unimportant. It is just that the best way to prepare for adult responsibilities and opportunities is never to lose our focus on the wholeness of the human beings we are educating, encompassing as such a focus does their character, virtues, values, intellect and culture. If there is any single message that emerges from the ten thinkers we have been examining it is this one. The world pictures of these thinkers differ radically and they have different emphases and priorities, but all would have agreed with Montaigne that no education could be deemed successful if, as a result, 'our souls do not move with a better motion' and 'if we do not have a healthier judgment', in other words if we are not both better and wiser.

There is less agreement among our thinkers about what education should include to make us better and wiser. As Aristotle was the first to point out, such matters also vary with the kind of state or society in which one lives. One should not therefore look to these thinkers for ready-made educational solutions but for the characteristics that any set of educational arrangements must have if they are to stand a chance of success. Although impossible to sum up 2500 years of reflection it would not be too reductive to say, in conclusion, that these characteristics must include at least the following.

> The highest aspirations and standards for the kind of person, and his or her intellect, character and virtues, that one's education is aiming to produce. Even Nietzsche would not disagree, although some of his 'virtues', or 'values' as he would have called them, might not be the same as those of other thinkers. Sentimentality – 'one of the great evils that threaten education' according to Dewey – and the misguided praising of qualities and achievements that do not merit praise are not compatible with these aspirations and standards.
>
> A sharp sense of one's fundamental educational priorities, as determined by the hierarchy of criteria one uses for judging oneself and one's fellow human beings, *eg* character, virtue and the quality of one's thinking and judgment come first and 'book learning' (starred As at A level, first class degrees, and being at a school that is top of the league table) second.
>
> Seeing education as a central part in a long chain of cultural transmission, the kind of transmission that, for example, would be necessary to permit the continuation among future generations of educated people of the kind of dialogue that has taken place over the past 2500 years among our ten thinkers and that has been the subject of this book. Rousseau, Nietzsche and Dewey, like many since them, were intermittent backsliders on the importance of transmission in education, temporarily forgetting that they would never have become the radical thinkers they were without first having received or, in Rousseau's case, secured for himself, a deep grounding in the history of Western culture and thought.
>
> A lack of embarrassment about putting ethics at the heart of one's educational aims and practices. This includes promoting the values and virtues necessary for the maintenance and strengthening of those freedoms that have been the West's greatest achievement over the last three hundred years, recognising that to do so will at times face opposition in contemporary societies that can be quick to *feel* (to take offence, demand 'respect') and slow to *think* (to accept that for the sake of one's own freedom one must put up with the freedom of others to say things one does not like).
>
> Accepting that in all true learning the *what* that is being learned is inseparable from the *how*, that is from *the habits of learning*, that are being inculcated. As Michael Oakeshott, drawing on Socrates, put it, the ability to think is learned as a by-product of acquiring information, and learning to think is also learning to recognise and

enjoy the intellectual virtues, which he sees as central to the life of an educated person and which he defines as disinterested curiosity, patience, intellectual honesty, exactness, industry, concentration, doubt, sensibility to small differences, the ability to recognise intellectual elegance, the disposition to submit to refutation, and a love of truth and justice (all of which are to be found in the Platonic dialogues).[5]

Starting with the child, in the sense of maximising one's chances of engaging the child in its education, encouraging children and treating them with the utmost humanity, never under-estimating their potential, never sentimentalising the child, never confining the child to the tyranny of the 'relevant' and the 'here and now' (even Émile was allowed, eventually, to read *Robinson Crusoe* and the writers of classical antiquity), and knowing the child by studying carefully how she or he learns.

Never forgetting that, though starting with the child, one does not end there, *ie* one is driven by a vision of the kind of adult, and the kind of adult society (including the kind of nation state as well as the kind of world order), that education should be helping to create, while at the same time rejecting (with Nietzsche and Arendt) the idea that education is just, or even mainly, about socialisation, *ie* about the creation of 'current men'.

Remembering that life and learning are not just happiness and fun, instilling habits of delayed gratification and learning from one's mistakes, but finding time, nonetheless, with Locke, for a bit of ballroom dancing (or its equivalent).

Ceasing to think that education stops once it ends formally, and understanding that 'lifelong learning', where it continues, is not just a question of career enhancement but of improving oneself intellectually and ethically right up to the day of one's death, even if one no longer believes that one's fate in another world depends on this.

Being innovative where appropriate and willing to consider new ideas – all ten thinkers challenged current orthodoxies in one way or another – without ever falling into the contemporary trap of assuming that innovation is always a good thing and innovativeness the most desirable characteristic of any educational institution or human being. The philosopher Luc Ferry, the most intellectually distinguished of France's recent education ministers – with whom I had an interesting discussion when we both headed our respective national curriculum bodies – sees the harnessing of the creative aspects of global capitalism's 'permanent revolution', and the simultaneous limiting of its destructive aspects, as key challenges facing both society and education.[6]

> Getting out of the habit of thinking that our self-congratulatory modern world is unique in its needs, is the first to have had bright ideas, and has the solutions to all problems, and instead continuing to learn from the thinking and practice of those who came before us.

But the main purpose of our ten thinkers' 'thought fragments' and 'pearls' – which, like divers (in Walter Benjamin's metaphor) we have brought up from the depths of the past – is not mainly the transmission of this relatively obvious, but sometimes overlooked, set of propositions. It is to remind us to 'stop and think' about education, in the full meaning of that phrase, and to do so again and again until such time as we cease to be 'spoken for' and begin to 'speak'.

References

1. Bourdieu, P, *Questions de sociologie*, 1984, Les Éditions de Minuit, Paris.
2. Tate, N, *Intercultural understanding*, p. 52, in Walker, G (ed.), *The Changing Face of International Education*, International Baccalaureate, 2011, Cardiff.
3. *On Modern Education and the Classics*, pp. 161-2, in Eliot, T S, *Essays Ancient and Modern*, 1936, Faber and Faber, London.
4. For an extended discussion of the aims of education in the context of England's national education system, see Tate, N, *What is Education for?*, The Fifth Annual Education Lecture, School of Education, King's College London, 1998, King's College, London; and, in the context of international education, Tate, N, *What is Education for?*, The 2004 Peterson Lecture, International Baccalaureate, 2004, Geneva.
5. Oakeshott, M, *The Voice of Liberal Learning*, ed. Fuller, T, pp. 29, 60-1, 1989, Yale University Press, New Haven and London.
6. Ferry, L, *L'Innovation destructrice*, p. 48 and passim, 2015, Flammarion, Paris.

Further reading

Chapter 1

The unexamined life is not worth living: Plato and Socrates

The Collected Dialogues of Plato, ed. Hamilton, E and Cairns, H, Bollingen Series LXXI, 1961, Princeton University Press, Princeton.

Plato, *The Last Days of Socrates*, trans. Tredennick, H, 1966, Penguin, Harmondsworth

Plato, *The Republic*, trans. Cornford, F M, 1966, OUP, Oxford, or Plato, *The Republic*, trans. Lee, H D P, 1959, Penguin, Harmondsworth.

Benson, H H (ed.), *A Companion to Plato*, 2009, Wiley-Blackwell.

Denham, A E (ed.), *Plato on Art and Beauty*, 2012, Palgrave Macmillan, Basingstoke.

Chapter 2

Education for leisure: Aristotle

Aristotle, *Politics* translated by Barker, E, 1948, OUP, Oxford

Aristotle, *Nicomachean Ethics*, translated by Ross, D, 2009, OUP, Oxford.

Aristotle, *Poetics*. translation and introduction by Kenny, A, 2013, Oxford University Press, Oxford

Barnes, J, *Aristotle*, OUP, Oxford, 1982.

(ed.) Deslauriers, M, and Destrée, P, *The Cambridge Companion to Aristotle's* Politics, 2013, CUP, Cambridge.

Gulley, N, *Aristotle on the Purposes of Literature*, in (ed.) Barnes, J, Schofield, M, and Sorabji, R, *Articles on Aristotle. 4. Psychology and Aesthetics*, 1979, Duckworth, London.

Lord, C.R., *Education and Culture in the Political Thought of Aristotle*, 1982, Cornell University Press, Ithaca and London.

Pieper, J, *Leisure: The Basis of Culture*, with an introduction by T S Eliot, 1965, Collins, London.

Chapter 3

Education for eternity: Thomas Aquinas

St Thomas Aquinas, *Philosophical Texts*, ed. Gilby, T, 1962, London, OUP

Aquinas, *De magistro (On Teaching)*, in *Quaestiones Disputatae de Veritate (Disputed Questions of Truth*. Available online from the Aquinas Translation Project, De Sales University: http://www4.desales.edu/~philtheo/loughlin/ATP/index.html

D'Aquin, Saint Thomas, *De l'enseignement (De Magistro)*, translated into French and introduced by Jolibert, B, 2nd edition, 2003, Klincksieck, Paris

Copleston, F C, *Aquinas*, 1961, Penguin .

Davies, B, *The Thought of Thomas Aquinas*, 1992, Clarendon Press, Oxford.

Davies, B, and Stump, E, *The Oxford Handbook of Aquinas*, 2012, OUP, Oxford.

Knowles, D, *The Evolution of Medieval Thought*, 1962, Longmans, London.

Chapter 4

Donkeys laden with books: Michel de Montaigne

Montaigne, M, *Essays*, trans. Cohen, J M, 1963, Penguin Books, London (includes *On educating children*).

Montaigne, M, *The Essays of Michel de Montaigne*, translated by Screech, M A, 1991, Allen Lane, The Penguin Press, London (and especially *On educating children*, *On schoolmasters' learning*, *On the affection of fathers for their children*, and *On experience*).

Montaigne, M, *L'éducation des enfants. Du pédantisme et De l'institution des enfans*, 1999, arléa, Paris.

Burke, P, *Montaigne*, 1981, OUP, Oxford.

Vieillard-Baron, J-L, *Montaigne et l'éducation humaniste*, in Magnard, P, and Gontier, P (ed.), *Montaigne*, pp. 205-229, 2010, Les Éditions du Cerf, Paris.

Chapter 5

Virtue, wisdom, breeding and learning: John Locke

Locke, J, *Some Thoughts Concerning Education*, ed. Yolton, JW and JS, 1989, Clarendon Press, Oxford.

Locke, J, *Of the Conduct of the Understanding*, in *The Works of John Locke*, volume 2, pp.323-401, 1824, London.

Locke, J, *Some Thoughts Concerning Reading and Study for a Gentleman* (taken from dictation), in *The Works of John Locke*, volume 2, pp.403-12, 1824, London.

Locke, J, *An Essay concerning Human Understanding*, introduction by Phemister, P, 2008, Oxford, OUP.

Axtell, J L, *The Educational Writings of John Locke*, 1968, CUP, Cambridge.

Chappell, V (ed.), *The Cambridge Companion to Locke*, 1994, CUP, Cambridge.

Jeffreys, M V C, *John Locke. Prophet of Common Sense*, 1967, Methuen, London.

Tarcov, N, *Locke's Education for Liberty*, University of Chicago Press, 1984, Chicago.

Chapter 6

The child at the centre: Jean-Jacques Rousseau

Rousseau, J-J, *Émile or on Education (includes Émile and Sophie, or The Solitaries)*, translated by Kelly, C, and Bloom, A, in *The Collected Writings of Rousseau, Volume 13*, 2010, Dartmouth College Press, Lebanon, New Hampshire.

Rousseau, J-J, *Confessions*, 2008, Oxford University Press, Oxford.

Rousseau, J-J, *The Social Contract and Discourses*, 1961, Dent, London.

Bell, M, *Open Secrets. Literature, Education, and Authority from J-J Rousseau to J.M. Coetzee*, 2007, Oxford, OUP.

Dent, N J H, *A Rousseau Dictionary*, the Blackwell Philosopher dictionaries, Blackwell, 1992, Oxford.

Gill, N, *Educational Philosophy in the French Enlightenment. From Nature to Second Nature*, 2010, Ashgate, Farnham.

Reisert, J R, *Jean-Jacques Rousseau. A Friend of Virtue*, 2003, Cornell University Press, New York.

Riley, P (ed.), *The Cambridge Companion to Rousseau*, 2001, Cambridge, Cambridge University Press.

Starobinksi, J, *Jean-Jacques Rousseau. La transparence et l'obstacle*, Gallimard, 1971, Paris.

Chapter 7

Encouraging a cosmopolitan disposition: Immanuel Kant

Kant, I, *Lectures on pedagogy*, *Essays regarding the Philanthropinum*, and *Idea for a universal history with a cosmopolitan aim*, in Kant, I, *Anthropology, History and* Education, 2007, The Cambridge Edition of the Works of Immanuel Kant, CUP, Cambridge.

Kant, I, *Critique of Practical Reason*, 1879, Longmans, London.

Kant, I, *Réflexions sur l'éducation*, introduction by Philonenko, A, 2004, Librairie Philosophique J Vrin, Paris.

Kuehn, M, *Kant. A biography*, 2001, CUP, Cambridge.

Magee, B, *The Great Philosophers* (Dialogue 8 with Geoffrey Warnock on Kant), 2000, OUP, Oxford.

Paton, H, J, *The Moral Law. Kant's Groundwork of the metaphysic of morals*, 1976, Hutchinson, London.

(ed.) Roth, K, and Surprenant, C W, *Kant and Education*, 2012, Routledge, New York and London.

Scruton, R, *Kant*, 1982, OUP, Oxford.

Chapter 8

Education for authenticity: Friedrich Nietzsche

Nietzsche, F, *On the future of our educational institutions*, in *The Complete Works of Friedrich Nietzsche*, Volume 6, trans. Kennedy, J M, 1909, T.N. Foulis, Edinburgh.

Nietzsche, *Untimely Meditations*, trans. Hollingdale, RJ, with an introduction by Stern, J P, 1983, Cambridge University Press, Cambridge.

Nietzsche, F, *Ecce Homo. How One Becomes What One Is*, trans. Hollingdale, R J, 1980, Penguin, London.

Nietzsche, F, *Beyond Good and Evil*, trans. Faber, M, 1998, Oxford University Press, Oxford.

Nietzsche, F, *Human, All Too Human*, 1984, Penguin Books, London.

Nietzsche, *On the Genealogy of Morals*, trans. Smith, D, 1998, Oxford University Press, Oxford.

Nietzsche, F, *The Gay Science*, (ed.) Williams, B, 2001, Cambridge University Press, Cambridge.

Ansell-Pearson, K, *An Introduction to Nietzsche as political thinker*, 1994, Cambridge University Press, Cambridge.

Cooper, D E, *Authenticity and Learning. Nietzsche's educational philosophy*, 1983, Routledge and Kegan Paul, London.

(ed.) Ferry, L, and Renaut, A, *Why we are not Nietzscheans*, 1997, University of Chicago Press, Chicago.

Magnus, B, and Higgins, K M, *The Cambridge Companion to Nietzsche*, 1996, Cambridge University Press, Cambridge.

Mann, T, *Death in Venice*, 1999, Penguin, London.

Onfray, M, *La Sagesse tragique. Du bon usage de Nietzsche*, 2006, Le Livre de Poche, Paris.

(ed.) Richardson, R, and Leiter, B, *Nietzsche*, 2001, Oxford University Press, Oxford.

Safranski, R, *Nietzsche. A Philosophical Biography*, 2003, Granta, London.

Sloterdijk, P, *La compétition des Bonnes Nouvelles. Nietzsche évangeliste,* 2002, Mille et Une Nuits, Paris.

Tanner, M, *Nietzsche: A Very Short Introduction*, 2000, Oxford University Press, Oxford.

Chapter 9

Education for democracy: John Dewey

Dewey, J, *Education Today*, 1941, George Allen and Unwin, London. This includes Dewey's *My Pedagogic Creed*, first issued in 1895.

Dewey, J, *Democracy and Education*, 1916, Macmillan, New York.

Dewey, J, *Experience and Education*, 1963, Collier Books, New York.

Dewey, J, *How We Think,* 1910, D C Heath, New York.